6.50

The English Novel

form and function

THE ENGLISH NOVEL | *form and function*

DOROTHY VAN GHENT

HARPER TORCHBOOKS
Harper & Row, Publishers
New York, Hagerstown, San Francisco, London

TO BEN LEHMAN

who first illuminated for me
the critical approach to
literature as a search for the
principle of form in the
work and implicitly as a
search for form in the self

THE ENGLISH NOVEL: Form and Function
Copyright 1953 by Dorothy Van Ghent
Printed in the United States of America

This book was originally published in
1953 by Rinehart & Company, New
York, and is here reprinted by arrangement. The original edition included a
supplementary section entitled "Problems for Study and Discussion"

First HARPER TORCHBOOK edition published 1961

ISBN: 0-06-131050-6

82 83 84   20 19 18 17 16 15 14

Preface

The present series of studies is designed for the general reader and the student as an accompaniment to a rereading of eighteen classical novels. Aside from *Don Quixote*, the series is confined to English novels, followed in roughly chronological order.

With a number of these novels the reader will have been familiar since childhood. With some of the others, familiarity will have been limited to the title and a certain warped, dusty, elderly look of the back of the book as it stood in the family library. The studies offered here are exercises in curiosity, curiosity to penetrate behind the aspect of familiarity, curiosity to see what these novels will look like when opened up side by side in a perspective of three centuries, and, above all, curiosity to explore each of them in its assumed character as a work of art.

The curiosity is not, I think, of the kind called "idle." Two convictions motivate it. First, that novels have their primary interest in the illumination they cast upon life, not life somewhere else and at another time, but immediately here, immediately now. And second, that novels are able to cast illumination upon life only insofar as they are coherent works of art.

The reason for the chronological order of the series is chiefly that examples of an art are developments of the history of the art, and understanding and just appraisement of the examples ask for experience of the history. Furthermore, a novel does change to our perception when set in a special environment of other novels. In the environment provided here—that of well-known English novels in their historical sequence— each of these familiar books inevitably acquires an aspect of freshness, of newness, just by the special juxtaposition with its neighbors. By sheer arrangement, they illuminate each other—and us.

As for placing *Don Quixote* first in a list otherwise of English novels,

Lionel Trilling has expressed the point of justification when he says, in his essay on "Manners, Morals, and the Novel,"

> In any genre it may happen that the first great example contains the whole potentiality of the genre. It has been said that all philosophy is a footnote to Plato. It can be said that all prose fiction is a variation on the theme of *Don Quixote*.

Particularly in reading English novels of the eighteenth century, one is aware of the model set by Cervantes. But even in much later works, when that model has been superseded by others, and when technique has undergone many changes, one recognizes certain generic concerns that are shared with Cervantes by, for instance, Conrad and James and Joyce, as they were also by Fielding and Sterne and Jane Austen; and the recognition of these concerns enlarges our understanding of the later work and deepens our pleasure in it.

Since the problem of the studies is to understand each novel as a work of art, the matter of techniques in fiction is essential to discussion. I have tried to concentrate the earlier studies on single dominant procedures. The discussion of *Don Quixote*, for example, asks for special attention to the procedures of parody and paradox; that of *The Pilgrim's Progress*, to the uses of symbolism and allegory; that of *Moll Flanders*, to the methods of documentary realism and of irony; that of *Clarissa Harlowe*, to the behavior of myth; that of *Tom Jones*, to the function of plot; that of *Pride and Prejudice*, to the activities of style; and so on. It is hoped that, in this incremental fashion, a shared terminology will be established that will be lucid and consistent for this particular undertaking.

In trying to ascertain and place in focus the pattern of each novel as an aesthetic whole, I have been deeply indebted to the critical work of others. A number of the novels considered here have not received very much attention from analytical criticism; but many of them have had so much expert scholarship brought to them, and so many fine insights turned on them in recent years, that a survey of the present kind can do no more than accept with gratitude and attempt to use those insights for its own limited purpose. Detailed acknowledgment is made in the course of the work wherever the discussion has had its source in the findings or suggestions of others.

The book has a special indebtedness to the students in my courses in the novel given at Kansas University from 1948 to 1951. Their constant determination that the novel needed to justify itself by a relationship with life, with *their lives,* has given the book its chief assurance of orientation toward reality.

I should like to express personal gratitude to Sidney Schiffer and David Fanger for their critical reading of a number of the sections of the book; to Robert Brown for his help in research problems; to Thomas Bledsoe, College Editor of Rinehart's, for his warm good faith, which has exercised itself in palpable, practical ways, as well as for his excellent critical suggestions; and to my son, Roger Van Ghent, for his loyal endurance, his sustaining trust.

D. V. G.

University of Vermont
June, 1953

Contents

Essays in Analysis

Introduction

The subject matter of novels is human relationships in which are shown the directions of men's souls. This is the subject matter also of drama and of the great histories. Let us make a few distinctions among these kinds of writing that have the same subject matter. The distinctions are fairly obvious, but for the sake of common points of reference and common consent it is helpful to get the obvious expressed.

Drama is subject to the conventions of the stage; people are conceived as if they were to be seen and heard in person, under the physical restrictions of tangible space and time. The novel is free of these conventions, although it has others. It can use all sorts of discursive methods that the drama cannot use. But it employs dramatic method most liberally, for it represents human beings *as if* in tangible space and time, that is, "scenically" placed and related. Both the novel and the drama are history in a certain sense: they tell of how people lived or live, their manners, what they held important, how they went about getting what they got, their conflicts, their errors, their heroism. Since some novels look very much like "real" history, like a factual social record, we need to be rather careful in defining the characterizing differences between novels and history.

Like a science, or like mathematics, but unlike history, the novel proceeds by hypothesis. It says, implicitly, "Given such and such conditions, then such and such would take place." The hypothesis on which a novel is built is the abstract aspect of its form. It takes from life the conditions for its hypothesis; that is, it starts from the empirical data that are the "given" data of sentient experience. But it selects and organizes them in a way that suggests a purely creative issue—a series of hypothetical events not "given" at all but cogent as cause and effect from the initial selection.

Being a hypothetical structure, the novel is able to give a leverage to the empirically known and push it into the dimension of the unknown, the possible. Its value lies less in confirming and interpreting the known than in forcing us to the supposition that *something else might be the case*. It is for this reason that the novel is a source of insight.

The fictional hypothesis is peculiar in that it has to carry at every moment the full weight of all its concrete experimental data. For the rate at which bodies fall in a vacuum, it is perfectly irrelevant to science whether the bodies might be feathers or men, ostrich feathers or feathers of a Chinese nightingale, politicians or plumbers. In the equation $x + y = 7$, it is perfectly irrelevant to mathematics whether the figures are written in green ink or blue, on paper or in the sand, or even not written at all. But for fiction the particular body that a thing has is of the very greatest importance to the whole fictional structure. Does it squeak, is it scared, is it brown, is it round, is it chilly, does it think, does it smash? Questions of this kind fiction has to be constantly concerned with in order to have any formal existence at all.

The procedure of the novel is to individualize. As with other art forms, what it has to say that is of collective value is said by inference from individual concrete things. History, on the other hand, proceeds by generalization. It treats people as groups; and when individuals appear they appear as catalysts of large collective actions or as representatives of groups, their significance being that of the group forces, the collection, the sum. This is a difference of convention, and on the conventions of an art depends its special expressiveness.

"After the death of Frederic the Second," Gibbon says,

> Germany was left a monster with a hundred heads. A crowd of princes and prelates disputed the ruins of the empire: the lords of innumerable castles were less prone to obey, than to imitate their superiors; and according to the measure of their strength, their incessant hostilities received the names of conquest or robbery. Such anarchy was the in-evitable consequence of the laws and manners of Europe; and the kingdoms of France and Italy were shivered into fragments by the violence of the same tempest.

Let us place beside this passage, describing a state of anarchy, one from *Vanity Fair*, also describing a state of anarchy. Jos Sedley has just heard the rumor of British defeat at Waterloo.

> Such is the force of habit, that even in the midst of his terror he began mechanically to twiddle with his hair, and arrange the cock of his hat.

Then he looked amazed at the pale face in the glass before him, and especially at his mustachios, which had attained a rich growth . . . They *will* mistake me for a military man, thought he, remembering Isidor's warning as to the massacre with which all the defeated British army was threatened; and staggering back to his bed-chamber, he began wildly pulling the bell which summoned his valet.

Isidor answered that summons. Jos had sunk in a chair—he had torn off his neck-cloths, and turned down his collars, and was sitting with both his hands lifted to his throat.

"*Coupez-moi, Isidor,*" shouted he: "*vite! coupez-moi!*"

Isidor thought for a moment he had gone mad, and that he wished his valet to cut his throat.

"*Les moustaches,*" gasped Jos; "*les moustaches—coupy, rasy, vite!*"

In the passage from Gibbon all is plural and collective. We need to know nothing specific about any prelate or lord or about any individual act of hostility or violence: the sum of all the individual situations is sufficiently communicative. In the passage from Thackeray, all is singular and particular, from particular gesture and thought down to the gasp of the voice and Jos's individually bad French. Communicated by this passage in its context are more than specific images of gestures and sounds, although it is all made up of the specific. In Jos's anarchy of soul is read with horrifying vividness the anarchy of a city, and still more, the anarchy of a culture. And yet the complex general meaning of the scene is dependent wholly upon particularity, or "embodiment," and would disintegrate without such embodiment.

Human experience is organized in patterns that are in movement, patterns that some philosophers call "events"—emphasizing the temporal or moving aspect of them—and that some psychologists call "fields of perception," or *Gestalten*—emphasizing the content of them, as if the content were momentarily static. Inhering in the patterns are sensuous traits (temperature, light, color, texture, sound, and so on); inhering in them also are multitudes of traits of memory, emotion, and thought. We tend to think of events in experience as bodiless, because they slide into each other as stones and trees do not. But held quiet by the mind they are seen to have bodies—to have individual form and function. Fiction tries to isolate the principle of coherence in events, the active principle that holds together all the multitude of particular traits that an event has, and the more extensive principle that makes one event slide into another in human lives. Reflected by the mind, the principle that makes the traits in an event cohere, and the principle that controls the relationship between events, are what we call "ideas."

Philosophy and the sciences use certain abstractive languages for the expression of ideas; and, because of the association of ideas with abstractive language, the reader who turns to the novel from other disciplines may not be willing immediately to recognize the novel's ability to express ideas; for he may feel that the novel's reliance on imagery—imagery of speech sounds and physical groupings and all the other kinds of imagery that make for the novel's necessary "embodiment" of its subject—incapacitates this medium for the expression of valuable ideas. Or he may have the impulse to locate the ideas in a novel only in those passages where the language is that of abstract conceptualism—passages in which, it is possible, the novel's ideas may show at their poorest, or in which the author may even clumsily and blindly falsify the ideas actually inherent in his work. The novel is able to express the most profound ideas, but, because of the nature of this medium, these will lie implicitly in the conjunction of the events that are bodied forth. The ideas in a novel are largely for the reader's inference, his inference of the principles by which the happenings in the book are related to each other.

A novel itself is one complex pattern, or Gestalt, made up of component ones. In it inhere such a vast number of traits, all organized in subordinate systems that function under the governance of a single meaningful structure, that the nearest similitude for a novel is a "world." This is a useful similitude because it reflects the rich multiplicity of the novel's elements and, at the same time, the unity of the novel as a self-defining body. The novel's planetary orbit lies through different minds and different generations of minds, each exerting its special pushes and pulls upon the novel's substance, each interpreting it according to the different spiritual constitution of each. How are we to judge a novel? How are we to evaluate it among other novels? Its strenuous orbit through different minds and generations, each observing it and understanding it with some measure of difference, would seem to deny it any final value status for the reader who approaches it with an awakened critical instinct and a desire for objectively valid judgment.

The sound novel, like a sound world, has to hang together as one thing. It has to have integral structure. Part of our evaluative judgment is based on its ability to hang together *for us.* And like a world, a novel has individual character; it has, peculiar to itself, its own tensions, physiognomy, and atmosphere. Part of our judgment is based on the concreteness, distinctness, and richness of that character. Finally, we judge a novel also by the cogency and illuminative quality of the view of life that it affords, the idea embodied in its cosmology. Our only adequate preparation for judging a novel evaluatively is through the analytical testing of its unity, of its characterizing qualities, and of its meaningfulness—its ability to make us more aware of the meaning of our lives. All these tests test the value of the novel only *for us,* and value for us is all the value that matters. But if the particular novel has been integral and characterful and meaningful for other individuals and other generations as well, however different its appearance to them, the book automatically extends our lives in amplitude and variousness.

ON *Don Quixote*

Perhaps the simplest and yet the most adequate idea which will help us to enter understandingly into this book is the idea of a structure based upon a system of contrasts. The reader is struck first of all with the fertilely humorous contrast between the Knight and his Squire—between the formal, ideal nature of things as they appear to Quixote's mind, and the concrete, down-to-earth nature of things as they appear to Sancho's mind. This contrast offers the germ of the whole drama of adventures; but other contrasts, both minute and on an immense scale, block out the architecture of the book. Between the two volumes of *Don Quixote*—that published in 1605 and that published in 1615—there is a major contrast of narrative design: the 1605 volume contains five individual short novels whose content is apparently dissociated from the main narrative concerning Sancho and Quixote; the 1615 volume contains no digressive interludes of this kind. The settings of the 1605 volume are those of the highway, the inn where strangers meet, lonely landscapes stretching beyond the isolated traveler, craggy mountains, dark night when strange sounds are heard and ominous or lovely visions are conjured up; the settings of the 1615 volume are for the greater part domestic and urban, the populous estate of a grandee where Quixote and Sancho are invited to stay for an extended visit, the town houses of bourgeois gentlemen, city streets, the certainties outlined by sunlight.

Other contrasts are so profuse, from those of the largest and most general kind, down to contrasts between individual motifs (details of action) and even to types of nouns coupled in a single sentence, that we are led to fix on this principle as the governing structural principle of the book. Quixote first comes before the reader as a living person (in the sense in which characters "live" in fiction); but quite suddenly, in the middle of a harrowing adventure, he becomes someone invented by

9

a Moorish author whose manuscripts Cervantes says he has discovered. Thereafter he is a walking hybrid of antitheses: both a man and a literary invention, a living character and an imaginary character, a book-man and a man-book. Among the *novelle* (little novels) of the 1605 volume, one story—Marcela's—is an old-fashioned pastoral concerned with an academic love problem; both setting and problem are idealistic, and the handling is philosophical. Another—Cardenio's story—is a modern story of psychological tenebrosities, the intricate webs formed by the conscience of a solitary individual. Another—Dorotea's history—is a study in the social significance of sex. Still another—the story of the "Curious Impertinent"—is a study in a peculiarly modern performance with which we have become acquainted in the novels of André Gide under the name of the "gratuitous act": a man puts his wife's virtue under trial for no reason at all except the desire to experiment. In these *novelle,* as they follow one after the other, we see contrasts of philosophical handling against psychological handling, problems of the individual moral will contrasted against social problems, inward action contrasted with outward action, solitary aberrations set in contrast with public complacencies and conventions. A number of these stories, related as events that had happened in the past, have their action finished, not in past time, but in the immediate and present time of the main narrative of the adventures of Quixote and Sancho, so that another contrast is set up before the reader's mind, between "story" time and "real" time.

Frequently the contrasts take the form of antithetical parallelisms.[1] At the end of the 1605 volume, Quixote is brought home in a cage with all the indignity of a wild brute; at the end of the 1615 volume, he returns home voluntarily under a contract of honor. There are two descents underground: Quixote descends of his own desire and choice into the cave of Montesinos and has there a consummatory vision, peaceful and beautiful; later Sancho stumbles by accident into a deep pit with his donkey, remains for a while there starved and abandoned, and is finally rescued by a compassionate robber. The idealized pastoral episode of the 1605 volume, in which the heroes dine pleasantly with goatherds and listen to the amorous songs of shepherds, is antithetically paralleled in the 1615 volume by the "pastoral" adventure with the bulls and the

[1] This aspect of the book is discussed by Joaquin Caselduero in his essay "The Composition of *Don Quixote*," in *Cervantes across the Centuries,* edited by Angel Flores and M. J. Benardete (New York: The Dryden Press, Inc., 1947).

swine, an adventure of the most brutal and disillusioning kind. There are similar parallels among other episodes, that are parallel in the sense that the *form* of the adventure is the same in each (the return home, the descent into a cave, and so forth) but antithetical and offering contrast in the sense that one adventure presents us with one kind of reality, one set of values, one order of being, and the other presents us with a different kind of reality, a different set of values, a different order of being.

One readily perceives that, in so complex a world of contrasts, there must be something more at stake than the "right" and the "wrong" of certain ways of thinking and modes of behavior as exemplified by Quixote and Sancho themselves. The contrasts pile up in too great a multitude for any pragmatic moral theory to keep them rigidly systematized; and the contrasted terms do not always form themselves as an occasion for acts of judgment, on the reader's part, between "right" and "wrong" or "true" and "false," but play freely among hundreds of antithetical relationships. Two critical concepts—the related concepts of paradox and parody—will help us to ascertain the function of contrast in *Don Quixote*.

The word "paradox" is formed out of a prefix meaning "beside" or "contrary to" and a root meaning "opinion." It refers to the phenomenon in which one thought, opinion, or interpretation of a situation is set up "beside," and simultaneously with, another and different, even opposing, interpretation. The word "parody" is formed from the same prefix and a root meaning "song" or "poem" and referred originally to a song or poem placed in sequence with ("beside") another song or poem. The common element between the meanings of the two words is the element of a simultaneous appearance of two different things, but it can easily be seen that the meanings would develop dissimilarly, inasmuch as a poem contains a good many more elements than an opinion, so that a "parody" —as this word has come to be applied—might be a vast arabesque of interlinked perceptions, while a "paradox" would continue to refer to a concentrated opposition of two outlooks or views both of which had to be held in the mind at once without a discarding of either one.

We shall speak of paradox first, using for illustration the episode of Quixote's "rescue" of the peasant boy on his first sally. The boy has been tied to a tree and beaten by his master because he demanded honest wages. According to Quixote's interpretation of the situation, the boy's demand is just, the master had treated him unjustly, and a Righter of Wrongs and Liberator of the Oppressed might act here in the rational

11

name of justice. On the other hand, the boy's interpretation of the situation is determined by the physical eventuality far more decidedly than by the justice or injustice of the affair; he receives a much worse beating after he is "rescued" than before; hence, to him, Quixote's justice is an injustice. Clearly, the two outlooks are incommensurable, and yet, as clearly, the reader cannot eliminate either one from his own view of the situation; he cannot eliminate the ideal of human justice as an absurdity, without diminishing his vision of life to the scope of a brute's eye; nor can he eliminate the actualities of human psychology and practice as shown in the relationships of the boy and his master. The situation, then, is "paradoxical," in that one event shows two opposed aspects which are both "real" but which are antithetical to each other.

We should be fairly careful, among the paradoxes of *Don Quixote,* not to engage too freely in speculative "if's" about a hero and a story that are not *this* hero and *this* story—we should be careful, that is, to confine our attention to the book Cervantes has written and not to read it as a book we ourselves might write about a man-of-the-worldly and commonsensical Quixote who avoids such troublesome things as paradox by never allowing a paradoxical situation to arise. It might be suggested, for instance, that Quixote, though right in principle was wrong in his methods, and that "if" he had been sensible enough to make a preliminary investigation of the farmer's whereabouts and then abducted the boy and taken him home for his aunt to adopt, justice would truly have been accomplished, ideal and practice commensurated. Obviously such a hero would have to have another name than Quixote, since the name Quixote stands only for that maladdressed man who makes paradoxes sprout. Adventure after adventure repeats the formula, whose marvelous fertility lies in a simultaneity of contrasted extremes. We would sterilize the book if we should try to wring from it always a moral example or a preference for one kind of action or one view over another. The living reality which the book offers is that of the paradox embodied in action, the ineluctable mixture that is at once ideal and corporeal, spirit and flesh. Is it not in this kind of truth to existence that Sancho and Quixote themselves go forth, as companions?

Parody covers more extensive ground than paradox. It might be thought of as a vast complicated system of paradoxes. This idea of parody, however, would emphasize too strongly the notion of direct oppositions. It is, as a matter of fact, this particular idea of parody that dominates our usual loose use of the word. Loosely, we tend to mean by parody a burlesque imitation of something, showing the weaknesses or falsehood of the object imitated. In this sense, the main feature of parody would be not unlike the main feature of debate, implying that one view of things was a "wrong" view and another the "right" view, just as debate is postulated on the idea that there must be a right side and a wrong side of a question (for example, prohibition should or should not be repealed, the western European countries should or should not receive food or arms support, and so forth). But it is possible for parody to be much more complex than debate. Instead of confronting two opposing views with each other, in order that a decision between them be arrived at, parody is able to intertwine many feelings and attitudes together in such a way that they do not merely grapple with each other antagonistically but act creatively on each other, establishing new syntheses of feeling and stimulating more comprehensive and more subtle perceptions. Parody—except that of the crudest kind—does not ask for preferential judgments and condemnations. It is a technique of *presentation;* it offers a field for the joyful exercise of perception and not a platform for derision.

A parody of romances of knight-errantry provides the germinal suggestion, the propagative idea, as it were, of all the action in *Don Quixote.* We have already become well enough aware of the complexity of the book so that we shall not be tempted to take this statement narrowly to mean—as it has often meant in casual-minded academic discussions of *Don Quixote*—that the book can be pigeonholed as an attempt to laugh the old-fashioned romances of chivalry out of existence. If the book were to be adequately described only in this way, we would probably not be reading it ourselves but would leave it for scholars; for our interest in the reading habits of the seventeenth century and in the fact that some people at that time acquired unrealistic notions from chivalric romances cannot be very intense. The parody of knight-errantry is the governing schematic shape of the action in *Don Quixote,* as a journey into danger is the governing schematic shape of the action in *The Pilgrim's Progress* and in Conrad's novels, and the criminal investigation in some of Dostoevski's novels and in Kafka's *The Trial.* But the technique of parody operates intensively in the detail of *Don Quixote,* as well as providing the framework of the action. To illustrate its operation, let us consider the Knight's vigil at the horse trough, again an incident from his first sally. In the loose and inadequate sense of parody, in which parody resembles debate by offering two sides of a situation or problem, one of which must be "right" and the other "wrong," the vigil at the horse trough tells us that Quixote's world is not what he thinks it is, that "reality" is much rougher and more prosaic than what appears to his idealizing imagination: that the armor is not armor but pasteboard, that the trough is not an altar, that the inn is not a castle, that nothing "sacred" and no "consecration" has taken place but only a psychotic misinterpretation of the use of objects. This would be the meaning of the scene if the parodistic impulse were as simple as the impulse to debate the practical advisability ("truth" in the running sense) of a course of action. What else does the scene contain? Night, moonlight, a deserted innyard, a man pacing up and down alone. Arising conceptually from this poignant incantation of scene are the urgency of devotion, the conviction of mission, the subjective solitude of the individual mind, resonances of ancient stories in which Love and Beauty and Goodness impelled men to action, a sense of the sacredness and loneliness of aspiration, a sense of the sacredness and loneliness of defeat. What else? The great jest, the wonderful release of laughter. The muleteers blunder up out of the night to water their mules at the "altar." Here, as in each of Quixote's and Sancho's adventures, yearning and pathos and jest flower together: emotion and burlesque, tradition and immediacy, felt time and the atemporal time of images, brute fact and conceptual delicacy, the abstract and the concrete, the disciplined and the accidental—all "real" in the intricate mixture of experience, and here designed in a simultaneity and a spiraling intertwining as one act of perception.

In the incidents we have used for illustration, the contrasted terms are each extreme: in the incident of the rescue of the peasant boy, Quixote appears as an extremist of justice, while the actions of the master and the boy offer the other extreme of domination by physical and practical exigency; in the scene of the vigil at the horse trough, Quixote's devotion to the chivalric ideal is of that extreme which transforms objects the most trivial and gross into the sacramental, while the circumstances of the vigil—the ménage in the inn, the arrival of the muleteers—are described in such a way as to emphasize to an extreme the grossly physical and materialistic. In the juxtaposition of the two companions, Quixote and Sancho, we are kept throughout the book in the presence of extremes; for not only do Knight and Squire offer to each other the foil of extremist characters, but each is himself exaggerated beyond the silhouette

of any ordinary man. No one, in life, is so Quixote as Quixote or so
Sancho as Sancho. Yet, strangely enough, it is because they are extremes,
grotesque beyond life, that they strike the imagination so forcibly as being "true to life." In the creation of each of these characters, certain special qualities have been selected out from the fairly amorphous blend of
qualities that make up the ordinary human being, and have been isolated and heightened to extraordinary proportions. The result is a brilliant visibility for these qualities, which are ordinarily so dimmed and
blurred by the swarming commonplaces of existence that we have but a
very vague sense of their presence and of their significance in our lives.
To discover them in *Don Quixote* is to rediscover them in ourselves and
our world, and it is for this reason that we feel the exaggerations and
grotesqueries of the book to be "true to life."

But it is not only by extreme heightening of certain characteristics
that the book allows us this rediscovery. It is by *perspective* that our vision is adjusted. Without being placed in a perspective, any dispropor-
tionately exaggerated form would lack all meaning; it would be grotesque
without significance. Quixote is significant in the company of Sancho;
Sancho, in the company of Quixote; each gives perspective to the other.
Visual perspective is a matter of distinction between foreground and background, allowing for the perception of graded depths between them. We
can expand the meaning of perspective so that it applies to events in
time, to social phenomena, and to psychological and spiritual phenomena.
The crowded streets of Barcelona, in the second volume of *Don Quixote,*
are given the perspective of those lonely plains of La Mancha and the
craggy wilderness of the Sierra Morena in the first volume. The modernism of some of the *novelle,* and the modernism that we feel in Quixote's
own intense subjectivity, is given the perspective of those ancient heroic
ballads and Gothic romances that have stimulated Quixote to action.
Similarly with the enormous multitude of other contrasts that inform
the book. Perspective is achieved by consistent organization of extremes
of difference, so that, from the point of observation of one extreme, the
other term of the contrast is seen significantly. That is, it is given background or it offers background to the other. But since *Don Quixote* is
not a manual of moral *exempla,* since it implies no theoretical principle
or thesis as to what constitutes the "good life," but is, instead, a vision
of life itself, the perspectives that it affords are constantly reversible. In
this respect, the situations in the book are like the figure-ground designs

with which psychologists experiment; depending upon the mechanics of the eye, and upon obscurely fluctuating anticipations in the beholder, the figure becomes the ground and the ground becomes the figure. Thus the total perspective on man's destiny that the book gives us is not a perspective confined to certain limited cultural conditions—as it is, for instance, in the "naturalistic" novel—but a great backward and forward unfolding, from Gothic times to what we can only recognize as the essentially modern, and from the manifold external circumstances of human action to the lonely privacies of spirit.

This depth and reversibility of perspective is achieved again and again, not only in the more obviously violent displacements of narration (as between the various *novelle,* or between the 1605 and 1615 volumes), but also in scenic and even in linguistic detail.[2] When we are told, after the abortive expedition in the enchanted bark, that "Don Quixote and Sancho returned to their beasts and to their state of beasthood," we have a usual play on contrast between a concretion and an abstraction, between the literal beasts (Rosinante and Dapple) and the virtual beasthood of man; while the "beasthood" itself is resonant with double meanings, and can be interpreted in the medieval Christian sense—man is a spirit coupled with a beast, and now, sadly, with the giving up of the supernatural exploit in the bark, the beast prevails—or in a modern naturalistic sense—man *is* beast, and is grossly mistaken if he fancies himself beyond beasthood. We may take the statement one way or the other, as we may take the figure-ground designs of the psychologists one way or the other; clearly, it is "reversible." But what we wish to emphasize here is the depth of perspective in even so slight a statement: the concrete "beast" becomes more significant in the light of the abstract "beasthood," and the Christian and naturalistic, medieval and modern interpretations each more significant in the light of the other.

Let us take as another illustration the scene of the night entrance into Toboso, where Quixote and Sancho go to find Dulcinea. Here the great experiment of the practical test of the soul's truth is made in a tranquil darkness, a darkness naturally symbolic of the subjective loneliness of Quixote's quest, both of its obscurity to outward view and of its serene starlit clarity within. This setting for an act of faith is given what we have called perspective by the homely, immediate foreground sounds

[2] Helmut Hatzfeld analyzes this aspect of Cervantes' style in the essay "The Style of *Don Quixote,*" in *Cervantes across the Centuries,* cited above.

of braying asses, grunting hogs, and mewing cats—that is, by contrast with objective detail grotesquely irrelevant to a spiritual quest. We see the spiritual event from a point of observation in the nonspiritual, and each heightens the significance of the other; or we could reverse our terms here, and say that the homely Tobosan night sounds echo in the perspective of that other night, the creative night of the dedicated soul. Similarly with that palace of Dulcinea's which seems, because of the tensions of Quixote's expectations, to loom so loftily over Toboso: as soon as Sancho speaks, the ghostly structure is riddled with by-lanes and blind alleys, hovels and bawdyhouses, all the commonplaces of a sleeping city; but immediately another displacement of vision occurs, and it rises before us again—only "two hundred paces" away. Both visual and spiritual perspective are phantasmagorically reversible, depending on whether, with Sancho, we see blind alleys and hovels in the foreground, or, with Quixote, see Dulcinea's palace in the foreground. When Quixote rides up to the church and quietly turns from it with the remark, "We are mistaken, Sancho, I find this is a church," his sobriety and rationality before the solid physical evidence offer us a new perspective on the complex life of the spirit; for this man respects what his senses tell him *at the same time* that his inward vision transcends and transforms all the sense evidence of Toboso; and we are persuaded of the transcendency of the vision by virtue, not of Quixote's lack of rationality, but of his rationality. That is, the visionary is placed in the perspective of the rational, the rational in the perspective of the visionary—and both are qualities of the one man. (Perhaps the most striking presentation of this double activity occurs when Quixote tells Sancho that, though no doubt the barber's basin is a barber's basin to Sancho, to Quixote it is Mambrino's helmet, and to another man it may well be something else. In other words, he refuses to falsify either the vision or the sense evidence.)

Finally, in the passage concerning the night entrance into Toboso, we have psychological foregrounds and backgrounds shifting into each other. Sancho has lied as to his having once seen Dulcinea in her palace —this is the foreground fact. But now that he wants to retreat from the chivalrous junket, by confessing his lie, his own known factuality and Quixote's faith in Sancho's factuality turn the lie back on him as a "fact," and to get out of his difficulties he is constrained to enter into Quixote's sphere of idealization and to "enchant" a country wench into Dulcinea. The lie in the psychological foreground is made a background

17

to an imaginative act, a decisive act by which the gross-bellied Sancho commits himself inexorably to Quixote's visionary world—in counter movement to Quixote's own mysterious acceptance of the world of sense and reason. Here again, metaphorically in this psychological realm, we have the reversible perspective of the city of Toboso seen by night, a deep distance linking blind alley and towering palace and transmuting each by the presence of the other.

There are sharp changes, through time, in the ways that a literary work is read. Readers in the eighteenth century, for instance, found in *Don Quixote* a satire on imagination and fancy, and an essay in applause of reason and fact. In the early nineteenth century, the period of Romanticism, the book was read as a celebration of imagination and the ideal, at the expense of prosaic reason and sordid fact. In both the nineteenth century and the twentieth century, *Don Quixote* has been read as a "bitter" and pessimistic book, in which the author sets out to ridicule all faith in ideas and in human ennoblement. In the mid-twentieth century, if we share in a "climate of opinion" common to students in the scientific disciplines, a point of view that is predominantly rationalistic and positivistic, we can again read the book somewhat as eighteenth-century readers read it; or, "conditioned" by certain modern works, we may be inclined to find in it a prophetic projection of the solitude, sterility, and yearning of *The Waste Land,* or of the systematic disenchantment (Cervantes' *desengañado*) and "initiation" of Hemingway's heroes. It would seem that "great books," those in which many generations of readers have been able to find themselves and a clarification of their own worlds, have a very special ambiguity distinguishing them from lesser works. In the case of Cervantes' great novel, this quality seems to lie in the constant reversibility of perspective between deeply distant extremes. To return to the metaphor used in the introduction to this volume, the metaphor of a novel as a "world," we would say that the "world" of *Don Quixote* is marked and characterized by a perspectively organized extremism. This is its structural character, the ground both of its variety and its individuality.

Wishing to place that character decisively in the immediate procedures of the book, we would say that what the reader's attention is directed to is not one aspect (moral or practical) of an action, but the action itself, the adventure itself, as an event with many aspects. It is rather difficult for the rationalizing, moralizing intellect to think in this fashion. We feel the need of singling out some aspect as predominant and as definitive of worth-while values. An eminent critic of Spanish literature, Americo Castro, will help us here. He says that the theme of Spanish literature, and that of *Don Quixote*, "may be summarized as the difficulty of living, when it tries to integrate body, soul, and mind—which is different from giving preference to the latter at the expense of the other two." [3] And he suggests historical backgrounds for this difficult interest in the fact that

> To the Spaniard, ever since the Middle Ages, the supernatural and the natural, the religious and the profane, the spiritual and the physical, the abstract and the concrete, coexisted in one and the same unity of consciousness. There was not the least critical discrimination between actual experience and that which transcends the witness of the senses . . .[4]

George Santayana expresses obliquely the same aspect of Spanish temperament when he says,

> The most miraculous world, if it were real, would subdue the teachable mind to its own habit, and would prove that miracles were—as they are in the Gospels—the most ordinary and most intelligible of events . . . matter [is] the ancient plastic substance of all the gods.[5]

If we look on the adventures of Quixote and Sancho each as total actions, and not designed to emphasize separated aspects of actions, we shall recover what was perhaps the artist's perception, but certainly we shall recover, through insight made body, more of ourselves and of other men —which is to say, more "perspective"—than if we attempt to rigidify *Don Quixote* into a system of preferences. "The scene of so prodigious a spectacle," Americo Castro says,

> is the workshop in which the life of each one is forged, and is not a didactic or logical transcendency superimposed on the process of living. [It is] a question of showing that reality is always an aspect of the experience of the person who is living it.[6]

[3] "Incarnation in *Don Quixote*," in the cited volume, *Cervantes across the Centuries*, p. 147.

[4] *Ibid.*, p. 143.

[5] *Persons and Places* (New York: Charles Scribner's Sons, 1944), pp. 239–240.

[6] Castro, *op. cit.*, p. 144.

19

ON *The Pilgrim's Progress*

The Pilgrim's Progress is designed, in its broad lines, as an allegory. Let us define allegory here as Coleridge defined it, and then let us illustrate the definition in its simplest application. Coleridge says that allegory is the employment of a certain set of characters, actions, and circumstances in such a way that these convey to the mind, under the disguise of sense objects, certain moral qualities or conceptions, and so that all the parts combine to form a consistent whole.[1] The large action of Bunyan's book is that of a pilgrimage, and we see the pilgrim going his way on a solid, earthy road, through mud, through green fields, over rocks; and conveyed under this earthy disguise is the notion of the complicated moral life of man, his occasions of serenity, his occasions of despair, the challenges of his mortal estate. It is an ancient, universal image that Bunyan has used—the image of life as a journey; he has given it a special inflection—the journey is not a mere wayfaring but a "pilgrimage," that is, a journey to a holy place. But our definition says that each of the parts, as well as the whole, conveys a moral idea. To illustrate the allegorical operation of one of the parts, we may use the first image in the book—that of the "man clothed with rags, standing in a certain place, with his face from his own house, a book in his hand, and a great burden upon his back." Isaiah says (64:6): "all our righteousnesses are as filthy rags"; and the Psalmist says (38:4): "For mine iniquities are gone over mine head: as an heavy burden they are too heavy for me." We put an equal sign, as it were, between the man's previous complacent notions of his own goodness and the worthless rags that clothe him, and another equal sign between his guiltiness and his burden. This activity, of the equating of a sense image with a moral concept, we engage in

[1] *Miscellaneous Criticism,* edited by Thomas Middleton Raysor (Cambridge: Harvard University Press, 1936), p. 30.

spontaneously as we read, for Bunyan's imagery is drawn from the commonest human experiences and his moral conceptions are drawn from the common Christian heritage.

However, not everywhere in the book do we find so perfectly natural a relationship between image and concept as we find in the paragraph about the man in rags. We shall be able to see the rich potentialities of the allegorical method more truly if we become early acquainted with its limitations. The following passage—from the episode, in Part II, where Matthew gets the gripes—is a mixture of allegory and realism. The realism is of the kind we associate with genre painting, in which commonplace domestic scenes are represented with homely accuracy of detail. What we wish to notice here is the fact that the concepts Bunyan wishes to convey through his allegory do not relate themselves spontaneously with the realistic sense imagery; the scene itself is projected most clearly for the imagination, but this is all that is successfully projected (and it is charming and it is "enough"); as to the intellectual conceptions of which it is supposed to be the vehicle, Bunyan has to tack them onto it in an additional explanation, and we feel that they are arbitrarily imposed and that we could easily dispense with them. Matthew is "much pained in his bowels," "pulled as it were both ends together." The doctor, Mr. Skill, is sent for, and says that the boy must have eaten unwholesome food, which "lies in his maw undigested." One of the children recalls that Matthew, when they passed an orchard along the way, had plucked some green plums from the trees overhanging the wall. He must take a purge.

> So he [Mr. Skill] made him a purge, but it was too weak; it was said, it was made of the blood of a goat, the ashes of a heifer, and with some of the juice of hyssop, &c. When Mr. Skill had seen that the purge was too weak, he made him one to the purpose; it was made *ex carne et sanguine Christi*. (You know physicians give strange medicines to their patients.) And it was made up into pills, with a promise or two, and a proportionable quantity of salt. Now he was to take them three at a time fasting, in half a quarter of a pint of the tears of repentance. When this potion was prepared, and brought to the boy, he was loath to take it, though torn with the gripes as if he should be pulled in pieces. Come, come, said the physician, you must take it. It goes against my stomach, said the boy. I must have you take it, said his mother. I shall vomit it up again, said the boy. Pray, Sir, said Christiana, to Mr. Skill, how does it taste? It has no ill taste, said the doctor; and with

that she touched one of his pills with the tip of her tongue. Oh, Matthew, said she, this potion is sweeter than honey.

Matthew is prevailed upon to take the medicine, which "put him into a fine heat and breathing sweat, and did quite rid him of his gripes." Allegorically, the green plums that Matthew ate are fruit from the Devil's orchard, "forbidden fruit" representing the willful indulgence of appetite; the ingredients of Mr. Skill's first purge, that was too weak, are those sacrifices which the Law insists be made for sin, but which do not have the power of the Christian sacraments; the second and effective set of pills are the Eucharist—the body and blood of Christ; the child, himself incapable of right decision, is led to the sacrament by the persuasion of his elders; and the "tears of repentance" in which the sacraments must be taken are boiled down to a child's capacity. The arbitrariness of these allegorical equations is highlighted by Matthew's very real stomach-ache, which he could have had from eating real green plums, but which he could scarcely have felt as a result of a consciousness of guilt—unless he were a very modern and neurotic little boy; and by the gross physical effects of the Lord's Supper upon him, putting him into a sweat and causing him to purge—these effects being scarcely appropriate to the taking of the Eucharist, though wholly appropriate to the curing of an indigestion. On the other hand, Bunyan's homely diction in describing the stomach-ache, the typical querulousness of the sick child, the doctor's rough "Come, come, you must take it," and the delicate psychological acumen of the mother when she asks the doctor how the medicine tastes, then tastes it herself first—these details have the directness and animation of life. We have to admit that there is another kind of charm in the very crudity of the allegory here, a charm something like that of a rough medieval woodcut figuring a moral emblem or Biblical parable in the swift, gross traits of common life. But Bunyan's true greatness does not rest on crudity. We shall turn now to another scene, where the allegorical fusion of sense impression and moral concept is complete.

This scene illustrates Bunyan's symbolic use of physical topography —the heights and valleys which Christian and the other pilgrims travel. At the foot of the Hill Difficulty, Christian meets two travelers, Formalist and Hypocrisy, who are going his way.

There were also in the same place two other ways besides that which came straight from the gate; one turned to the left hand, and the other

> to the right, at the bottom of the hill; but the narrow way lay right up
> the hill , . .

Christian refreshes himself with a drink at a cool spring, then bounds
on a run up the hill with a song on his lips. As for the other travelers,

> when they saw that the hill was steep and high, and that there were
> two other ways to go; and supposing also that these two ways might
> meet again, with that up which Christian went, on the other side of the
> hill; therefore they were resolved to go in those ways. Now the name
> of one of those ways was Danger, and the name of the other Destruc-
> tion. So the one took the way which is called Danger, which led him
> into a great wood, and the other took directly up the way to Destruc-
> tion, which led him into a wide field, full of dark mountains, where
> he stumbled and fell, and rose no more.

Bunyan's dream then turns back to Christian, who "fell from running
to going, and from going to clambering upon his hands and knees, because of the steepness of the place." The steep hill itself, the great wood
at one side, the wide field at the other side "full of dark mountains,"
make up a rather crowded terrain, naïvely conceived as by a man who,
never having seen mountainous country, imagines it as did those early
painters who painted their mountains from models made of garden rocks
piled up in ungeological heaps. Nevertheless, we both see it and feel it,
for the imagination does not demand that an actual landscape be photo-
graphed for it with the mechanical accuracy of commercial photography.
What we see and feel is the difficulty of the way, the darkness of the
wood where one man is lost, the terror and despair in that field full of
dark mountains where the other man is lost, the change in Christian's
tempo and in his muscular effort as he is forced to slow down. The
landscape, then, though we can visualize it as something external, to be
seen with the physical eye, is really internal: it is a complex image of various kinds of feeling, of muscular sensations of physical difficulty, and of
fear and the sense of abandonment in the dark. But what moral conception can we point to that the scene allegorically illustrates? It does not
seem to be one that we can rigidly label, although its presence is powerfully felt. It does not, in fact, need a label, for it is simply the moral exertion that we feel in Christian's physical exertion as he takes the straight
way up the hill; without moral exertion, he could not have made the

physical exertion. This sense of the meaning of his action is enforced by the contrast with the other two travelers, who clearly were lacking in moral will in their refusal of the physical difficulty. How naturally and spontaneously the full moral conception, which makes this scene "allegorical," arises out of the concrete foreground image of the rocky, wooded landscape and the travelers choosing their three ways through it! Formalist and Hypocrisy (their names here could just as easily have been Joe and John), in making their choices of the apparently easier ways around the hill, are separated; each now goes alone—and the meaning of their solitude is clear: when choice is unanchored in discipline, the pilgrim is a real wanderer, separate and alone, eventually to be lost in a confused darkness. Christian is also alone, but his aloneness has a different meaning: it is the aloneness of the most strenuous and courageous spirits; and later, when his circumstances become more trying, and both courage and discipline fail him, he will find companions in Faithful and Hopeful. In Part II, we see the weaker spirits, women and children, traveling in company and with the guide Great-heart to show them the way.

Effective allegory has a triple achievement. The moral conceptions on which it rests must be culturally viable, or it will not find adequate metaphors for its meaning in our common experience; its primary appeal to the understanding of the reader must be through our common physical and psychological experience, for this provides it the image traits out of which its metaphors are constructed; and the images that it offers us must have the power of symbols, spontaneously to evoke feelings and emotions that naturally associate themselves with moral attitudes and specifically with those attitudes that make up the conceptual framework of the allegory.

Bunyan uses physical topography—the muddy Slough, the Hill Difficulty, the highway where travelers jog along together gossiping, the deep benighted valleys, the entrancing mountains approached from a distance—in such a way that this road lies on our familiar earth: we are sensible imaginatively of the stickiness and treacherousness of this bog, of the fearfulness of this dark valley, of the freshness and cheerfulness of "this sunshine morning." And if Bunyan were unable to evoke the physical scene, he would be unable to equate it convincingly with the psychological state of the travelers. As it is, the physical scene and atmosphere spontaneously impress us with moral meaning: we know that the scene is not only outside the travelers, but within them also, as their personal spiritual topography. The Slough scarcely needs to be named Despond, nor are we forced arbitrarily to put an equal sign between the name of the Slough and the sin of spiritual torpor and thus by a clumsy intellectual operation to understand its meaning in the story; nor, in the episode of the Slough, do we even need to have named explicitly to us the two pilgrims, Christian and Pliable; for Bunyan has so provided that our own acts of making allegorical equations between physical circumstances and moral conceptions take place undeliberately, with free and yet true feeling. Here are two men who must get to the other side of an apparently impassable bog:

> they wallowed for a time, being grievously bedaubed with the dirt; and Christian, because of the burden that was on his back, began to sink in the mire.

The one traveler, who has no burden, kicks and complains for a few minutes, accusing his companion of getting him into this mess, then climbs out and goes back home.

> Wherefore Christian was left to tumble in the Slough of Despond alone; but still he endeavoured to struggle to that side of the Slough that was still further from his own home .   . but could not get out, because of the burden that was upon his back . . .

At this moment, Help comes. The little episode is related with the greatest economy; a few slight physical traits noted by the verbs "wallowed," "bedaubed," and "tumble," and the simple pictorial concept of a man wearing a burden and struggling to get through a miry place, are sufficient to raise the scene imaginatively before us. And instantly a coil of feelings and judgments spirals in our minds: we know that the man with the burden has been deeply tried in spirit; we know that if he did not have a spirit of a specially complex kind he would not have been subject to such a trial, for he would have been incapable of experiencing it (his friend Faithful, for instance, who is much simpler psychologically, never had to go through the Slough); we know that his companion Pliable was made of poor moral stuff; we easily recognize the mud in which Christian wallows as mud which we too have felt clogging us psychologically, even if only we have felt depressed from wallowing through real mud in bad weather; and we know what is meant by the fact that "Christian was left to tumble in the Slough of Despond alone," for we know that some experiences of struggle are altogether lonely and their content incommunicable. Coleridge said of *The Pilgrim's Progress*, "I read it once as a theologian—and let me assure you, that there is great theological acumen in the work—once with devotional feelings—and once as a poet." [2] Though we may not, at the moment of reading, be able to analyze all the several ways in which we are reading an episode such as that of the Slough of Despond, and though we may lack the training to label our readings as Coleridge did, it is probable that we too read it in several ways at once, and do so spontaneously; for the artistry with which it is designed is of a kind that releases instinct and stored experience in the reader, revealing them to him in the light of a new insight. It is this that we mean when we speak of the "ambiguity" of some of the great literary works: we do not mean by this word that they are equivocal or obscure, but that they are multileveled projections of human experience—and human experience is always itself multileveled.

Before leaving the matter of Bunyan's use of physical topography as a sign of an inward state,[3] let us speak of the two visions of the Delectable Mountains—the one, when Christian sees them from the roof of the house where the sisters arm him; and the other, when Christian and Hopeful see them again after issuing from the prison of Despair. In the first vision,

> he saw a most pleasant mountainous country, beautified with woods, vineyards, fruits of all sorts, flowers also, with springs and fountains, very delectable to behold.

This is all that is said of the mountains in this place. The image remains with us, probably because we have all seen mountains at a distance, verdurous and delicately lighted, and have wished that we might go there. The second vision occurs under very different circumstances. Christian and Hopeful have been through the long and nearly suicidal experience of despair; finally the dungeon door has given way, and with great difficulty they have got through the iron gate; they find themselves safe on the highway. Immediately the Delectable Mountains appear again.

[2] *Ibid.*, p. 406.
[3] This aspect of the book is discussed acutely and at length by André A. Talon, in *John Bunyan, l'homme et l'oeuvre* (Paris: Editions 'Je Sers,' 1948).

. . so they went up to the mountains, to behold the gardens and orchards, the vineyards and fountains of water; where also they drank and washed themselves, and did freely eat of the vineyards. Now there were on the tops of these mountains shepherds feeding their flocks, and they stood by the highway side. The pilgrims therefore went to them, and leaning upon their staves (as is common with weary pilgrims, when they stand to talk with any by the way), they asked, whose Delectable Mountains are these?

The shepherds reply courteously, and give the travelers their directions for the way onward, and "they looked very lovingly upon them, and said, Welcome to the Delectable Mountains." The second scene is fraught with a special charm, a charm founded in psychological truth; for the mountains are now more beautiful than ever because the immediately preceding circumstances have been dark and full of despair. Into the beauty of the mountains, and with that childlike question, "Whose Delectable Mountains are these?" is poured the sense of release from terrible danger. Most clearly here, the outward topography is an objectification of the inward. The physical journey is always what the travelers themselves spiritually make of it.

We turn now to a few of the characters in the story, in order to see the consistency of Bunyan's method as between his description of scene and his description of persons. Let us speak first of some of the minor characters, the false pilgrims. Each betrays what he is by a word, a tone, a turn of syntax. This is Obstinate, speaking always in exclamatory rushes, the man with his mind made up before he has ever begun to think, thumping out short-winded interjections: "What! and leave our friends and our comforts behind us?"—"Tush! away with your book."—"What! more fools still!" And this is Pliable, in a single delightful self-betrayal contrived by a verb: after seeing Obstinate depart, he tells Christian that he has made up his mind to go along on the journey, but instead of saying, "I have decided," he says, "Well, I begin to come to a point." His moral silliness wobbles through the "begin to come," just as we see him later wobbling out of the Slough. As for Mr. Worldly Wiseman, his condescension, his worldly circumspection, his spiritual obtuseness, his amiability hiding actual indifference, are heard in the first words we have from him: "How now, good fellow, whither away after this burdened manner?" To Mr. Worldly Wiseman, the burden is merely a kind of mannerism or eccentricity or foreign custom; he addresses Christian patronizingly as "good fellow," and (in later speeches) uses to him the condescending second person singular pronoun, as if he were addressing a child or a person of low social status. Bunyan's skill in swift characterization is of the very highest; he reproduces, on a person's first entrance into the tale, the precise and inevitable tone of voice, the mood of the verb, the idiom, and the syntactical rhythm which will put the speaker before us in his essential moral life, and which will cast upon the episode the energy and conviction of reality. The essential moral life—but no more. For this is all that Bunyan's design demands. And because he limits himself to this, his people become severally emblematic of several human qualities, each in separation, "personified" as we say. But let us notice that the quality which is personified is not a quality *in the abstract,* but a quality having the concrete texture of living humanity. Bunyan's characters, Coleridge said, are "real persons, who had been nicknamed by their neighbours." Neither Obstinate nor Pliable nor Mr. Worldly Wiseman are truly the abstract personifications of obstinacy, overcompliancy, and worldly cautiousness, but people whom we have often heard speak and will again, people of narrow temperaments in whom a single trait has been comically or cancerously exaggerated. It is only because Bunyan founds his allegory of human qualities in the objective reality of human manners that his allegory "works" at all. Thus, consistently with his treatment of landscape, his treatment of characters is such that they exist objectively as people to the imagination and at the same time are emblematic of moral, "inward" traits.

Foreground characters, such as Christian and Faithful or Hopeful, afford somewhat more complex examples of Bunyan's method. In the first few pages of the book, Christian has no name. He is "the man" or "he." It is only when he has suffered, and taken fear, and entered strenuously upon his difficult pilgrimage, that he emerges from the anonymity of spiritual complacency and obtains a name—Christian. How is he to be made fully known to us now, both as an individual and as a Christian? He talks to certain foolish people, and we see that he is more strong-minded than they; he goes through the Slough of Despond, and we see that he is capable of moral suffering, that he has both physical and moral courage. But this is not all of a man, nor of a Christian. He meets Mr. Worldly Wiseman, and is easily talked into a way of getting rid of his burden "in credit and good fashion," and a way of finding salvation without having to face wearisomeness and painfulness and darkness and—death. Instead of these, he will have "safety, friendship, and content." This Christian has his weakness. Clearly, Mr. Worldly Wiseman is inside Christian himself, a counsel of softness in the soul. While the foolish patter of Obstinate and Pliable could not win him back from the way, a more subtle temptation is able to overcome him. Now he emerges from the pages more recognizably to us, for he has shadows on him, and a man without shadows is not recognizable as a man. Nor to Bunyan, it would seem, is a Christian without shadows typical as a Christian. Therefore he gives him Faithful as a companion, an exceptional man of faith, with no shadows. Faithful has little imagination and a relatively meager sensibility; he carries no burden, he has not gone through the Slough, the lions have not roared at him, his conversion has been sudden and definitive, he voyages without fatigue. Beside the bright firm surface of Faithful, Christian is thrown into relief as a man who has suffered and been afraid and wallowed in mud, a man of complex and difficult temperament, vainglorious at times in his strength, at other times doubtful or despairing.

Later, after the martyrdom at Vanity Fair, Hopeful will take up somewhat the same role as Faithful, and we observe a similar contrast of light and shadow by which Christian is sculptured out for us in the full visible relief of a complex soul. It is Christian who would take the counsel of the Giant Despair and commit suicide; he quite loses his mental balance and deliberately seeks the unconsciousness of hysteria and coma; three several times Hopeful must urge him to have courage. Had Bunyan given Christian no companion of this kind, how would he have been able to sound the full chord of qualities in the strenuous religious mind? Christian would have killed himself, and we would have had only the despairing Christian, the defeated Christian—not the complete Christian. Hopeful—like Mr. Worldly Wiseman—is a projection of the one mind, Christian's mind. Bunyan has split off from the complex main character certain aspects of his temperament that can be personified separately and that can involve Christian in an outward drama which will realize for us, imaginatively, the drama taking place within the alert soul. This is a phase of the allegorical method somewhat different from those we have observed before. It is inaccurate to say of Faithful and Hopeful that they are merely abstract personifications, without vitality and without depth; for they have their concreteness, their vitality and depth, in Christian himself. Allegory of this kind puts a special but a fair demand upon the reader: the reader's own moral imagination must be at work to integrate the separated aspects of the soul into a psychological unity and to perceive the outward drama as inward drama.

The poet Marianne Moore has spoken of poetry as "an imaginary garden with real toads in it." The landscape of *The Pilgrim's Progress* is often a landscape of dream or of nightmare inhabited by our very solid neighbors; and it is often our solid familiar landscape inhabited by creatures of nightmare or dream. Here is a soiled spring muddied by picnickers—we, too, have seen it; and here is St. George's dragon talking like Satan—perhaps we have seen this monster, too, but not by this spring. There are mirage mountains, and now suddenly they come close and we see, as in a primitive painting, minute details of vineyards and fountains and shepherds with their lambs; and here is Madame Bubble, that tall good-looking woman who makes her hard face smile at the end of every sentence, and who has a certain uncontrollable tic—she can't help scrabbling through her purse while she talks. The dream and the solid reality are brought together in a single experience, as a child constantly brings them together; and by this juxtaposition, the dream becomes palpable and the reality becomes mysterious. Bunyan is in touch with ancient sources of feeling, ancient in both childhood and racial lore; he is also in touch with the immediate forms of his own present; around these forms, and through them, he is able to release the atmosphere of the miraculous. It is thus that he makes a new and integral world with its own gravitational law, its own breathing air, its own inhabitants; and it is because he makes a fully independent world that we call him a novelist.

The first lines launch us with great swift strides into that world.

As I walked through the wilderness of this world, I lighted on a certain place where was a Den, and I laid me down in that place to sleep; and, as I slept, I dreamed a dream. I dreamed, and behold I saw a man clothed with rags, standing in a certain place, with his face from his own house, a book in his hand, and a great burden upon his back. I looked, and saw him open the book and read therein; and, as he read, he wept, and trembled; and not being able longer to contain, he brake out with a lamentable cry, saying, "What shall I do?"

It is a world seen in a dream, but the brief past-tense forms of the verbs, with their clear Anglo-Saxon vowels and serried ranks of consonants— "I walked," "I lighted," "I dreamed," "I looked,"—have the energy and hard feel of reality, and hurry us to that cry, "What shall I do?" which must have an immediate answer in drama. Now we are at the center of the dream, carried there by the muscular urgency of the style—and at the center, among these celestial pilgrims with their nude hearts, we no longer remember that it is a dream.

ON *Moll Flanders*

The editorial preface to a popular modern reprint of *Moll Flanders* speaks of the book as "one of the most remarkable examples of true realism in the whole range of fiction." The statement suggests that "true realism" is specifically that kind of realism which *Moll Flanders* exhibits; by implication, other kinds—if there are other kinds—would not be "true." There can be no gainsaying the realism of *Moll Flanders:* Defoe's book describes minutely the local scene, London; it refers circumstantially to contemporary customs (although not to those of the mid-seventeenth century in which Moll supposedly had her career, but to those of the early eighteenth century when Defoe was writing); it employs "documents" (Moll's "memorandums," quoted letters, hospital bills, etc.) in order to increase the illusion of verifiable fact; and, in general, it aims at "objective," "reportorial," "photographic" representation, as if from the standpoint of an artless observer. In other words, the whole book is oriented toward what we call "facts"—specifically toward those "facts" which are events and objects that have spatial-temporal determination. But it is unfortunate that factual orientation in the novel should have come to determine the definition of realism in the novel; for "realism" inevitably implies a doctrine of the "real"; and it implies, when it is used to describe the factually oriented novel, that spatial-temporal facts are the only "real," and therefore that the factually oriented novel is closer to "reality"—a more trustworthy representation of reality—than any other kind of novel. What is suggested by the statement quoted at the beginning of this essay is not an evaluation of *Moll Flanders* as literature, but a certain popular philosophical conviction of the exclusive "reality" of material facts, a conviction that the so-defined "realistic" novel seems to flatter and support; and what is blurred over by the statement is the *hypothetical* structure of even the most "documentary" or "circumstantial" kind of fiction, a hypothetical structure that it shares generically with all fiction.

The hypothesis on which *Moll Flanders* is based might be phrased in this way: given a human creature "conditioned" to react only to material facts, then the world where that person lived might cogently assume the shape that Moll's world assumes—a shape astonishingly without spiritual dimension. In a parallel fashion one might phrase the hypothesis on which *The Pilgrim's Progress* is based: given a person for whom relationship with God was the only "reality," then, in his world, material facts would show as misleading appearances, and the shape taken by his adventures would be altogether spiritually dimensioned. If the world of the particular novel is to create itself fully for us, we must waive for the moment our own *a priori* convictions as to whether material fact or relationship with God is the prime reality; we must approach the fictional hypothesis with as much respect for its conditions and as much attention to its logic as we would give to a scientific or mathematical hypothesis. Defoe's "realism" must be looked upon as a consistent use of certain devices for the creation of a special kind of world, just as Bunyan's allegorical method is a consistent use of certain devices (some of them "realistic" in the same sense as Defoe's) for the creation of a special kind of world. Eventually, the trained and sensitized reader finds that novels called "realistic" are as symbolic as Bunyan's allegory.

The questions we must ask of *Moll Flanders* are those we ask of any other novel: what are its elements? how are they made to cohere in a unity? how are its special technical devices (in this case, those of "realism") appropriate to the making of this particular world? We notice, for instance, that Moll's world contains many *things*—tangible things such as watches and wigs and yardage goods and necklaces and dresses and barrels and bales and bottles and trunks. We may make some judgment as to the kind of world presented in a novel simply on the basis of the frequency with which an author uses certain substantives and images, to the exclusion of others. In *Moll,* there is relatively great frequency in the use of words naming that kind of object which constitutes material wealth. This singularity of *Moll Flanders* becomes striking when we try to remember how many dresses Christiana had for her long journey, and whether Mr. Worldly Wiseman wore a wig or carried a watch.

But let us make a further distinction: these tangible, material objects with which Moll is so deeply concerned are not at all vivid in texture. When Moll tells us that she put on a "good pearl necklace," we do not know whether the pearls were large or small or graded or uniform in size, or whether the necklace hung low on her bosom or was wound around her throat three times, nor do we know if the pearls were real or artificial; the word "good" here indicates simply that the pearls looked costly to a sophisticated eye, and were of a kind that a woman of substantial social position might wear; the "good pearl necklace" is mentioned not in a way that will make a sense image for us, but only in a way that will suggest the market value of the necklace and (through the market value) its value as an indicator of social prestige. Similarly, when she tells us that she gave her son a fine gold watch, we have no sense image of the watch; we do not know its size or design or delicacy or heft; we know only that it is a watch which would bring a good price. Therefore, in saying that the world of *Moll Flanders* is made up to a large extent of *things,* we do not mean that it is a world rich in physical, sensuous textures—in images for the eye or for the tactile sense or for the tongue or the ear or for the sense of temperature or the sense of pressure. It is extraordinarily barren of such images. And yet sense images are certainly "real" even in a world exclusively composed of "facts"; they are the constant means by which we are made aware of facts (the scientific observer himself is dependent upon their evidence). Clearly, then, an intense selectivity has limited the facts of Moll Flanders' world to a certain few kinds of facts, and has ignored great masses of other facts that we think of as making up the plenum of factual reality. Such selectivity warns us that this realistic novel is not actually an "objective," "reportorial," "photographic" representation of reality; its selectivity is that of the work of art, whose purpose is not that of an "objective" report.

What is important in Moll's world of things is the counting, measuring, pricing, weighing, and evaluating of the things in terms of the wealth they represent and the social status they imply for the possessor. What is unimportant (and we learn as much by what is unimportant as by what is important) is sensuous life, the concrete experience of things as they have individual texture. The unimportance of sensuous life in Moll's world is fairly astonishing inasmuch as Moll herself is a lusty, full-bodied, lively-sensed creature. Our instrument or medium of knowledge about Moll's world is Moll. The medium is a sensual medium (what woman, weak in sensuality, would remark, as Moll does: "I never was in bed with my husband, but I wished myself in the arms of his brother . . . in short, I committed adultery and incest with him every day in my desires . . ." or would have given us the scenes in the inns at Glouces-

35

ter and Bath?); but communicated through this medium is an assemblage of objects entirely desensualized, inaccessible to sense, abstract—abstract because represented only by name and by market value on the commercial and social markets. We may speak of this contradiction as an irony, and we shall wish to use the word "irony" here as indicating one characteristic *mode of relationship between elements in a novelistic structure.* Irony can imply many kinds of discrepancy, contrast, contradiction; paradox is a form of irony; there is irony in a statement that appears to say one thing and actually signifies another; and there is irony in a life situation or in a story situation that contrasts with or contradicts what might be expected from certain of the circumstances. We are always aware of Moll's sensuality, even though it often lies subterraneously or at a subverbal level in the novel; a great many of her adventures are sexual; but the life of the flesh is faded completely by the glare of the life of the pocketbook; and the incipience of sensuality, its always latent presence, contrasts ironically with the meagerness and abstractness of a sensibility which frantically converts all sense experience into cash value.

We shall continue to speak of ironies in *Moll Flanders,* and as we shall be speaking of them as aspects of the book's internal structure, let us formulate what we mean by the structural function of irony. We shall do so most easily by analogy. A round arch is made up of a number of wedge-shaped blocks, and each of these blocks is pulled earthward in obedience to gravity, but each also exerts a sideways push against its neighbor because of its wedge shape and the weight of other blocks around and over it. If there were only the one pull, freely earthward, the blocks would fall and there would be no arch; but because of the counterforce, acting in the sideways direction, the structure of the arch is defined and preserved. The contrasting significances of an ironic statement or of an ironic situation may be compared with the counteracting stresses that hold the arch up and hold it together—that give it its structure. In *Moll Flanders,* a complex system of ironies or counterstresses holds the book together as a coherent and significant work of art. We may speak of the ironies, then, as "structural." In the example that we have cited, Moll's latent sensuality acts as a counterstress to her devotion to financial abstractions, and the cross-pulls of these two tendencies define Moll and her world meaningfully for us.

To illustrate further, let us follow some of her characteristic mental processes. Here is one chief inflection of her psychology—the reader will

36

find it repeated again and again as he listens to her tale. It appears in her account of her first marriage, her marriage to the younger brother of her seducer. Five years she has been married to him, she has had two children by him, she has known a long and important period (important because she is still very young) of domesticity and marital tenderness and mother-hood. How does she tell us of these matters?

> It concerns the story in hand very little to enter into the further particulars . . . only to observe that I had two children by him, and that at the end of the five years he died. He had been really a very good husband to me, and we lived very agreeably together; but as he had not received much from them [the parents], and had in the little time he lived acquired no great matters, so my circumstances were not great, nor was I much mended by the match. Indeed, I had preserved the elder brother's bonds to me to pay me £500, which he offered me for my consent to marry his brother; and this, with what I had saved of the money he formerly gave me, and about as much more by my husband, left me a widow with about £1200 in my pocket.

We know in some degree from this context, and with added conviction from other similar contexts, what Moll means by a "very good husband" and by saying that they lived "very agreeably": the man had enough money to keep Moll from want, he spent money freely enough to maintain her in comfort and in that kind of social respectability which the spending of money guarantees—therefore he was "good" and their life was "agreeable." Any other characterization of this husband or of their marital life we should not be able to guess at; for Moll, simply by her exclusion of any other kind of perception from her story, stringently limits our own imagination of character; and we must judge that Moll has no other perception of character. The phrases "received much," "acquired no great matters," "my circumstances were not great," and "mended by the match," all focus together on one kind of referent: money. And when we find similar phrases in other contexts, we shall expect that "much" and "matters" and "circumstances" and "great" and "mended" (though these words might have immensely different meanings in other books) will have the same common referent again. As Moll uses them, they are very abstract words, colorless little words, words as limited in meaning as a mathematical sign. By their frequency they compose a picture of Moll's mentality and sensibility, so exclusively focused, so narrow and intense, that if (conceivably) we were offered the same description of symptoms in a clinical case history, we should say that it was a picture of a madwoman. But Moll's is not a case history; it is a hypothesis of personality development in an acquisitive world; and in this world Moll is by no means a clinical subject—she is "well adjusted."

What five years of her young womanhood, marriage, domesticity, and motherhood mean to Moll are certain finances, certain bonds amounting to so much, a certain quantity of cash in her pocket. Of her children by this husband, she says,

> My two children were, indeed, taken happily off my hands by my husband's father and mother, and that was all they got by Mrs. Betty.

The statement informs us, with powerful obliquity, that the way to be happy through children is to have them taken off one's hands; it informs us also that children may be useful in settling family debts. With the greatest placidity and aplomb on Moll's part, the children are neatly converted into a shrewd price by which she gets out of a bad bargain with clean skirts. Schematically, what has been happening here is the conversion of all subjective, emotional, and moral experience—implicit in the fact of Moll's five years of marriage and motherhood—into pocket and bank money, into the materially measurable. It is a shocking formula, shocking in its simplicity and abruptness and entireness. It confronts us again with the irony, or system of ironies, that is structural to the book. A great mass of responses that might be expected from the circumstances (marriage, death, birth) is not what is presented; what is presented of that pyramid of human experience, as its only symbol and significance, is a cash sign. And yet another irony is involved: that is the paradox of Moll's superb "sanity," witnessed by her perfect "adjustment" to her world, and her violent abnormality as a representative of the species called human. A person is sane who is socially adapted in his time and his place, in tune with his culture, furnished with the mental and moral means to meet contingencies (to "mend" his circumstances, in Moll's phrase, when they need mending), accepting the values that his society accepts, and collaborating in their preservation. By these tokens, Moll is eminently sane. She is a collector of quantities of things and of cash, for in the world in which she lives, the having of things and of cash is necessary for survival; it is an expression of the will to live. She has one thing to sell, in order to obtain them, and that is her sex. When this commodity fails her, she simply takes the things and the cash—steals them. In either case, she shows her sanity, her "adjustment" to her world, her ability to meet all contingencies. In this sense she is "normal," exhibiting in her activities and attitudes the social norm of her world; in terms of the full emotional variety of what we think of as the "human," she is monstrously abnormal. Her abnormality is her exclusive abstractiveness as a counter of cash; her subjective life is sunken nearly to a zero.

What will Moll do when she is under severe emotional stress; that is, when there is nothing in her situation that she can abstract into numbers, measurements, cash value, and when whatever is left for her perception to work on is the internal or subjective life of feeling and emotion? At the crisis of her career, she is taken for thieving, put into Newgate prison; and Newgate is hell. We have only Moll's own words for this experience, and how are Moll's words—dictated by a perceptive apparatus adapted exclusively for enumerating and calculating—to describe hell for us? Hell, Milton's Satan said, is a place within the self; that is, it is a subjective place, a place defined by horror and suffering and deep distress of spirit. In all her other circumstances, Moll has never failed to describe and define with the utmost precision such experience as she is capable of. But the hell of Newgate is "impossible to describe." The impossible description of this dead end of human suffering she fills up with negatives, words denying any possibility of description, for she has only negatives and blank counters for the subjective.

> . . . indeed, nothing could be filled with more horror . . . nothing was more odious to me than the company that was there . . . indeed no colours can represent that place to the life.

To get over these impossibilities, the hell of Newgate is expressed by generalized reference to noises and smells (Newgate is most painful because it is not "respectable"; there are loud noises and bad smells here as there are in the slums), and by abstract stereotypes of fiendishness.

> . . . the hellish noise, the roaring, swearing, and clamour, the stench and nastiness, and all the dreadful afflicting things that I saw there . . . ; I thought of nothing night or day, but of gibbets and

halters, evil spirits and devils; it is not to be expressed how I was harassed . . .

With the intervention of the minister, Moll says she is "perfectly changed," she becomes "another body." But since her perceptions are limited to their familiar categories of number and quantity, suitable for inventory-ing gold watches and bonds and purse change, but scarcely suitable for the description of grief or guilt or purity, the heaven of her repentance is as ineffable as the hell of Newgate. "The word eternity," she says,

represented itself with all its incomprehensible additions, and I had such extended notions of it that I know not how to express them. Among the rest, how absurd did every pleasant thing look!—I mean, that we had counted before—when I reflected that these sordid trifles were the things for which we forfeited eternal felicity.

But immediately, after these weightless matters, these incomprehensible additions and extended notions, Moll and her husband are back at the reckoning, the formulary conversion of death and birth, heaven and hell, into cash.

Our first business was to compare our stock. He was very honest to me, and told me his stock was pretty good . . . I gave him an account of my stock as faithfully . . . My stock which I had with me was £246 some odd shillings; so that we had £354 between us . . .

With her heart lifted up in gratitude to Providence, Moll plans an ir-reproachable life, for an irreproachable life is now truly possible: Chris-tian virtue and "stock" have become metaphysically identified, an eternal equation in the mysterious plan of things. From now on, God punches the buttons of this cash-register world, and it is virtue that lies in the till. Most grotesque of ironies: the "sordid trifles," the "pleasant things" that now look so "absurd" to Moll, the things for which she now refuses to forfeit her "eternal felicity," come to her henceforth in greater quanti-ties than ever before, precisely as the sign of grace and redemption, the temporal guarantee of her eternal felicity.

In speaking of the structure of *Moll Flanders* in terms of a hierarchy of ironies—a system of stresses and counterstresses (to return to our figure of the arch) that "hold the book together" in significant unity—we are faced with the need, sooner or later, of making some tentative distinction between what the author might have intended ironically and what actually functions ironically in the book. This question, of the author's deliberate intention, arises particularly in connection with irony; for we think of an author as knowing what he is doing better than another person might know what he is doing, and if he is being elaborately ironic, then—one would assume—he must "intend" at least some of the irony. Irony is "double-talk." But if the author is "sincere" and intends no double-talk, would it not be more consistent usage, on our part, to say that the book is "sincere" in the same sense that the author is sincere, that it contains no double-talk, no ironies?

Let us illustrate this difficulty as it suggests itself in the specifically moralizing portions of *Moll Flanders*. Moll robs a child, comes near to murdering the infant, and moralizes the adventure thus:

> . . . as I did the poor child no harm, I only thought I had given the parents a just reproof for their negligence, in leaving the poor lamb to come home by itself, and it would teach them to take more care another time . . .

She rolls a drunk, after a night spent whoring, comes home to count and weigh her loot, and accompanies her highly satisfactory calculations with moving reflections on the sins which fathers visit upon their children by drunkenness and wenching; she is even inspired to quote Solomon on the foul disease. These reflections are followed by a complacent account of how the adventure, into which she had led the gentleman, had brought him to reform his ways, restored him to the bosom of a loving wife, and secured the happiness of an innocent family. It is to these moralizing thoughts of Moll's that Defoe is undoubtedly referring the reader, in his Author's Preface, when he advises us to make "virtuous and religious uses" of the story. He even mentions, in his Preface, the incident of the robbery of the little girl, and the moral message he associates with this incident is precisely that given it by Moll herself—parents who deck their children in finery and allow them to go to dancing school alone are given a "good memento" of what may ensue; and, generally, the moral that he would have us find in Moll's accounts of her criminal practices is that which Moll (now a reformed soul and "honest" woman at the time of writing her memoirs) is herself always anxious to inculcate. But what, objectively, is the relationship of Moll's moralizing thoughts to her adventures? Her adventures are criminal, but she herself is not a criminal type; she is not a woman of the underworld, but a woman of the bourgeois world; her aspirations are thoroughly middle-class—she wants, above all, economic security and middle-class respectability. She thinks middle-class thoughts; her morality is middle-class morality—platitudinous, stereotypic, a morality suited to the human species in its peculiar aspect as cash-calculator, and a morality, therefore, most particularly suitable to the prostitute.

Criminal in action, Moll will have to moralize crime as a social good: and so she does. Her robbery of a child will have prevented many future crimes of this kind; her depredations upon one drunk will have preserved the happiness of many families: all the readers of *Moll Flanders* will have received her benefactions. Moll's moralizing thoughts are the harmonies of the cash-register world in which she lives, for the cash register, like the celestial spheres, has its harmonies too, as the buttons are punched, the mechanism throbs, and the till rolls out. But these harmonies are so divergent from the harmonies of what we know, from our own observations and from the history of ethical ideas, as the spiritually and morally sensitive life, that their meaning in the total context of the book offers itself as ironic meaning: the morality that is preached by Moll is a burlesque of morality.

But if Defoe "intended" Moll's little moral sermons as the message of his book (and he does, in his Author's Preface, so guarantee them for us as his own persuasions), how can they be said to be ironic? We are left with two possibilities. Either *Moll Flanders* is a collection of scandal-sheet anecdotes naïvely patched together with the platitudes that form the morality of an impoverished soul (Defoe's), a "sincere" soul but a confused and degraded one; or *Moll Flanders* is a great novel, coherent in structure, unified and given its shape and significance by a complex system of ironies. The most irreducible fact about the book is that we read it—and reread it—with gusto and marvel. We could not do this if it were the former of our alternatives. That it may be the latter is justified by the analysis it yields itself to, as an ironic structure, and most of all justified by our pleasure in it. Shall we, then, waive the question of Defoe's "intention" and "sincerity"? Speculations as to these apparently can add nothing to the book nor can they take anything from it; the book remains what it is. And we do not have appropriate instruments for analysis of

Defoe's intention and sincerity, in the deepest meaning of intention and sincerity. We might guess that a great book could not be written by an impoverished soul, and that imponderable traits of moral sensitivity and prophetic intuition might lie in an author and realize themselves in his book without his recognition of them: these would be guesses. Not guess, but inescapable assurance from the quality of the book, is Defoe's understanding of his creature, Moll, whatever else he might not have recognized or understood in the work that was going on under his own hand as the product of his observant eye and his faculty for clean selection and coherent arrangement. In understanding his creature without the slightest divarication from her movements and her thoughts, he gave to Moll the immense and seminal reality of an Earth Mother, progenetrix of the wasteland, sower of our harvests of technological skills, bombs, gadgets, and the platitudes and stereotypes and absurdities of a morality suitable to a wasteland world.

ON *Clarissa Harlowe*

Clarissa is the antithesis of Moll Flanders, as heroine. In the earliest episode of importance in *Clarissa Harlowe*—the attempt of the Harlowe family to force the girl into marriage with "rich Solmes"—we see her in revolt against that materialism to which Moll "adjusted" so nicely and with which she so tirelessly collaborated. The central action of Clarissa's story is a rape, an experience which might have assumed a position of minor importance among Moll's adventures in adultery, bigamy, and incest—conceivably an incident that Moll might even have forgotten to make a "memorandum" of. But Clarissa is sent to her grave by it, and not only does it cause her death, but upon it are made to hinge the sanctions of family life, the structure of society, and the power relationships between the orders of the divine and the diabolic. The chief idiosyncrasy of Moll Flanders' world is the tendency to externalize life, to convert all experience into measurable material quantities and cash; the chief idiosyncrasy of Clarissa's is exactly the reverse: it is the tendency to convert the external forms of life—social customs, physical action, material quantities—into subjective quality and spiritual value. This, at least, describes a striking difference between the two heroines and the two books at the literal level; though we must hesitate, at this point, to decide how deep the difference in values lies.

With materials whose tendency is so strongly subjective, the form of this novel will be one that allows a careful sifting of motives and a sensitive representation of emotions. The technical problem with which we are confronted here is that of the "point of view" (or "focus of narration"), a problem which may be phrased thus: given a certain kind of subject matter, how can it be brought into focus for the reader? From what "angle," what point of observation, can the drama best be seen? From the author's own? or from that of the chief character in the novel?

or from that of one of the minor characters? or from the points of view of several characters? or from some presumably automatic and mechanical point of view (like that of a camera)? Both of Richardson's protagonists must, for the full evolution of the tragedy, die in its throes, without that calm distance and settled state of health required for the writing of memoirs. Furthermore, the dramatic impact of the material lies in the vital immediacy, not of only one person's motives and emotions, but of those of at least two persons—Clarissa and Lovelace. If either of the protagonists had been allowed to tell the tale from his own point of view alone, neither would have been able to penetrate into the subjective life of the other. Richardson could not, therefore, solve the problem of point of view as Defoe did, by using the "seeing eye" of a single character. Nor could he use the point of view of the "omniscient author," as did Cervantes, which implies a removed standpoint, disinvolvement on the part of the observer, and a godlike sweep of vision and knowledge of the meaning of events. The reader must be as implicated as Clarissa herself, or as Lovelace, in false hopes, disappointments, expectations, torments, with as little foreknowledge of the way out; he must, moreover, be able to follow the drama from day to day, as it takes place within the minds of both protagonists. Thus the event must be recorded as if at the moment of its taking place; it must be recorded from a subjective point of view; and —additional problem—a certain amount of information must also be allowed to come to the reader concerning a number of other people's attitudes and activities. Richardson used the vehicle of a series of letters, written by major and minor characters, and representing a variety of points of view, all subjective.

The epistolary form of the book slows down the pace of the story almost intolerably, for we are dependent for information upon the mechanics of the postal system and the finger-and-elbow mechanics of the pen wielders. Certain significances attach to this slowness of pace. Before the reader can find out "what has happened" at any one point in the action, he must wait until a half dozen people have had time to write letters, receive answers, and reply; for no one in the story himself ever knows precisely and objectively "what has happened," inasmuch as "what happens" lies not in the objective event but in a multitude of subjective reactions. It is only by the mixed evidence of a number of letters that the "action"—being of a subjective character—can receive clarification. A psychological node, or system of interconnections and cross references,

46

dense, complex, and life-resembling, is thus contrived from the operations of a group of minds on a single event, each mind offering its own fractional information or insight as to what the event is and signifies. Illumination is suspended until each of the fragments falls into place in the slowly accreted group, and meanwhile the action is kept under the pressure of doubt, hope, indecision, misconception, and fatality.

The central event of the novel, over which the interminable series of letters hovers so cherishingly, is, considered in the abstract, a singularly thin and unrewarding piece of action—the deflowering of a young lady —and one which scarcely seems to deserve the universal uproar which it provokes in the book. There is very little subplot. The rape is in the offing, it is at hand, it is here, it is over, Clarissa sickens and dies, and that is all. Against this simplicity of event, one thinks of Moll Flanders' "threescore years of continuous variety." And yet *Moll,* with its long roll of statutory crimes and broken taboos, offers a flat fictional landscape, uniform, unaccented, horizontal (though fascinating in its own quality as are some flat physical topographies, such as the southwestern deserts or the Florida Everglades); whereas *Clarissa* is a dramatically vertical world of fabulous heights and rank profundities, with God the Father at the top, and, at the bottom, the lurid gleam and the foul stench of hell. The epistolary form of the novel provides us with a partial explanation for the fact that Richardson has been able to create so dramatic a world with so simple a theme. This slow and hovering form endows the physiological event—the rape—with profound attraction and significance by holding it up slantwise to view in a murk of shadows, turning it mysteriously, allowing it to emerge slightly, withdrawing it, allowing it to emerge again, and so on. It is as tantalizing and evasive as a trout. Only at long length are we permitted to get it into clear focus, while, in the meantime, we have been steadily bombarded, page after page, with an imagery deriving from various submerged but exceedingly powerful impulses and attitudes.

We have spoken of images and symbols to some extent in our previous studies. With *Clarissa,* these become of primary concern. An image, in its technical psychological sense, is a mental representation of a sense impression, visual, tactile, aural, gustatory, olfactory, thermal, or kinesthetic. In life, the image is frequently bound up with the actual sensation; but in speaking of imagery in a poem or a novel, we should be carefully aware that what we are referring to is the mental representa-

47

tion alone, quite divorced from sensation. Furthermore, an image is rarely single; a whole setting, or a moment of drama in which several characters participate, may form "an image," but it will be an image of a very complex kind, actually a construct of images acting as a unity. Again, a relatively simple image, like that of a porcelain teacup, or a green silk purse, or a parasol with the sun shining through it, though we may speak of it as "vivid," does not necessarily derive its vividness from imagined sensory impressions associated with such a teacup, purse, or parasol. It may be "vivid" as an image while the sensory impressions associated with it are extremely thin and vague. Its "vividness" will be a function of the context in which it finds itself, the way it is spoken of by the author, associations of attitude with the object that may not be sensory associations at all. There are many optical images of this kind in *Clarissa:* for instance, Clarissa in white clothes, kneeling in prayer, seen through a keyhole. What makes this image sharp and vivid are associations of purity and piety with whiteness and with prayer (most particularly in the dramatic context of Clarissa's captivity in a sordid house by a man of foul intentions); also the keyhole frame sharpens the image for us, as if we were looking at her through a telescope, for it focuses the eye on the single figure, cutting off any surrounding area, at the same time that it puts her at a distance like a person in a picture, removing her from any approach except the optical approach (this removal contributes, of course, to the "vividness" of our sense of her purity and piety).

By reiteration and accumulation, and by other always specific contextual conditions, an image may act as a symbol. That is, it may automatically begin to stand for a complex structure of feelings and values that are of great significance in the total structure of the book. We have seen this happen in *Moll Flanders.* So insistently does *Moll* bombard us with gold watches, gold necklaces, gold rings plain or fancy, gold guineas, that when the Bath gentleman opens the drawer full of gold guineas and asks Moll to scoop up a handful, we are—even perhaps without framing the thought deliberately—under the strong impression of a symbolic action, an action that focuses the predilections and values of everyone in the *Moll Flanders* world. Let us consider the evolution of a symbol in *Clarissa Harlowe:* that of the "Clarissa-symbol" itself. In the early scene when Clarissa is brought down into the parlor for a family conference, we are given a picture of the girl as she sees herself in the mirror beside her chair—pale, debilitated, and distraught, with heaving bosom, and most interesting and attractive. Cumulatively, many similar images reinforce this picture of attractive, desirable womanhood: Clarissa wilting like a broken lily on its stalk, Clarissa resting her lovely pale head on the motherly breast of Mrs. Lovick, Clarissa lifting her eyes in gratitude to heaven for a simple bowl of gruel or glass of water, Clarissa on her knees in prayer in miraculously dirt-resistant white garments, or Clarissa in torn clothes and with streaming eyes, prostrated at the feet of her demon-lover. The womanly quality which Richardson has made attractive in these images is that of an erotically tinged debility which offers, masochistically, a ripe temptation to violence. Thus the image of Clarissa achieves, under construction in the context, the status of a symbol, a focus of feelings and attitudes, rich, dense, and deep, however strange and even perverse.

In understanding the Clarissa-symbol, we should add to its associations the effect of the optical framing. Naturally, given the point of view that Richardson has adopted, we must always see Clarissa through someone else's eyes or else as she sees herself in a mirror. This would seem merely an exigency of the letter form of the book; but when we consider, along with this natural optical tactic, the fact that special devices (such as mirror or keyhole) are so often employed to emphasize the *seeing* of Clarissa by someone, and usually under conditions where she must be unconscious of being looked at, we begin to feel that the optical tactic must be "working" in a somewhat complex strategic way. The most extreme case in point is, of course, the episode of the rape itself, when the door of the room is left open and "female figures flit" across it, watching. One effect of this strategy is to make of the reader a Peeping Tom, to make him share in the dubious delights of voyeurism. Also, as strategy, it is consistent with that of the letter vehicle: as the letters "tell all" and the letter writer exposes all, turning himself inside out to his confidant, so the handling of the images offers all—not particularly to be experienced (in imagination) at first hand—but to be *seen*. Paradoxically enough, though the material of the novel is so largely subjective, "inner," yet a definitive quality of the *Clarissa* world is its publicity: no one is alone, can ever be alone, in *Clarissa*, not even in the most private performances of prayer, sex, and death. *Clarissa* is not a world of the individual soul, but, in the most extensive sense, a social world, a public world. We shall

49

perhaps see, in a later consideration of this novel as myth, how the publicity tactics of *Clarissa* are technically coherent with its mythical significance, its significance as a projection of a social dream.

An immense number of the Clarissa-images occur in an erotic context; but Clarissa's whiteness, her narrow range of stances and gestures (she kneels, she prostrates herself, she tears her neck ruffles and exposes her bosom, she wields a key or penknife or scissors), and the distancing and framing of the image for the eye, exclude a large number of associations that might operate in an erotic context—as color modulations, tactile impressions, nature sounds, and so forth. In other words, the erotic situations that are dramatized are excessively simple and abstract, limited to suggestions of bodily violence or violence done to clothes (stabbing or tearing) and the converse, suggestions of violence suffered (weeping, fainting, dying). Clarissa herself is offered as the ideal woman in her purity and debility—and these qualities, too, are extraordinarily limited abstractions from the complex of qualities that might be conceived as making up complete womanhood; at the same time, pure and debile as she is, paradoxically she offers an ideal of the sexual woman (in the world of this book), the physically desirable woman. She is a kind of love goddess, a Venus. She is not the Venus of the Renaissance, with an erotic apparatus of Mayflowers, delicately tinted veils, sinuous tresses, zephyrs, lutes, and cupids, suggesting many enjoyments for the senses, suggesting also the aesthetic act of contemplation.[1] She is much more abstract than that. She is the love goddess of the Puritan middle class of the English eighteenth century, of the bourgeois family, and of mercantile society. She is pure (to be paraded for the sight as an expensive chattel—or, in later generations, to show herself voluntarily as "career girl"), and yet to be violated (for in a society that has desexualized its professed mores, sex is a violation), but still to be seen while she is being violated (for sex insists on perpetuating its attractions, but they must be enjoyed by proxy, as in the movies, or *sub rosa*). The lover to whom she deploys her attractions is the lover as narcissist, as voyeur, as sadist—all abstractionists. Her mythical features still appear to us—for it would be a mistake to think that the Clarissa-myth does not still have deep social and psycho-

[1] In one of his erotic fantasies, Lovelace visualizes Clarissa in a situation bearing some pictorial resemblance to that of the Renaissance Venus with her bevy of cupids, but the difference is significant. He sees her "with a twin Lovelace at each charming breast . . . full of wishes for the sake of the pretty varlets, and for her own sake that I would deign to legitimate; that I would condescend to put on the nuptial fetters."

logical roots—in her two chief aspects: they appear on the covers of *Vogue* magazine, in the woman who is a wraith of clothes, debile and expensive, irrelevant to sense-life or affectional life, to be seen only; and they appear on the covers of *True Confessions* and *True Detective Stories,* in the many-breasted woman with torn dishabille and rolling eyeballs, a dagger pointing at her, a Venus as abstract as the *Vogue* Venus in her appeal to the eye and the idea alone, but differing in that she is to be vicariously ripped and murdered. Clarissa is a powerful symbol because she is both.

Similarly, an image of "the man" begins its evolution into a symbol when Clarissa has her private interview with "odious Solmes." She speaks of his splay feet, his posture "asquat" (like a toad), and his "ugly weight" that presses against her hoop. Perhaps no single word with emotional resonance occurs more frequently in this novel than the word "man." Solmes's own function in contributing to the symbol of "the man" is rather quickly over with; all he has to do, as suitor, is to be repellent; his real status is similar to that of the Harlowe males with whom he is hand-in-glove in action—that is, he is economic man, desexualized man. "The man" proper, as this symbol is deployed, is the man as lover, as the sexual threat. Clarissa screams, when she sees Lovelace in the garden, "A man!" "Ah, this man, my dear!" she exclaims to Miss Howe. "The man, my dear, looked quite ugly!" she tells her friend, after a predatory approach on Lovelace's part. She speaks of his "savage kiss" reddening her hand. Miss Howe confirms her notions of men: they are a "vile race of reptiles." Somewhere Joseph Conrad speaks of "the fascination of the abomination," a phrase which applies nicely to the image of "the man" in *Clarissa;* for as the image grows by reiteration and variation into a symbol, attractive elements are fused with the repellent elements, so that the abominable toadlike reptilian "man" becomes demonically fascinating: a creature obsessed with the desire to violate virginal, high-minded, helpless womanhood, and so single-tracked in his passion to destroy this divinity that he, too, assumes divine stature: he is the evil divinity, the devil himself. It is no wonder that even Miss Howe, after being present at a party where Lovelace has fluttered the dovecotes, confesses to Clarissa that she has begun to see him in her dreams.

The modern reader may fail to see at once in Lovelace the Satan, the archfiend, which many generations of readers have found in this character. Magnificently projected as Lovelace is, we may be inclined to see him as a study in psychopathology, or as a portrait of an egotist, or as a portrait (as one critic has said) of an "overgrown schoolboy." All these he may be, but, to read *Clarissa* in its fulness of implication, we should also be aware of the mythical resonances of the character. There can be no doubt that Richardson and the contemporary audience saw him as an embodiment of "splendid sin,"

> of the pride of life (as reproved by medieval theologians), of irresistible and pernicious fascination, the eighteenth century Lucifer, in fact, a worthy antagonist to his paragon of virtue, Clarissa.[2]

Lovelace himself, as he thinks of Clarissa as "divine," certainly considers himself to be one of the damned. In a dream he sees her angelic white-clad figure rising in a company of angels to the abode of the Seraphim, while an abyss opens at his feet and he falls headlong into it. Nor is this notion of the mythological significance of Lovelace, in relation to Clarissa, confined to Lovelace's own idea of himself, or to Richardson's intention, or to what older generations of readers may have found in the book. André Gide puts the matter succinctly when he says that "in the pages of *Clarissa,* heaven is continually being offered cheap to hell."

We have, in the preceding paragraphs, frequently spoken of *Clarissa Harlowe* as myth, and it is through the conception of this novel as myth that we are able to explain more fully to ourselves the strange fact that, though the book reflects an essentially perverse psychology, it is nevertheless a great and powerful piece of fiction. But let us first of all divest ourselves of the idea that myth is something "untrue." A myth cannot be "proved" logically or by the observation of physical fact. Whatever "truth" a myth may hold is not susceptible of this kind of proof. Myth is a dramatic vision of life, and we never cease making myths, accepting myths, believing in myths; even in our own positivistic age, we see life dramatically through the myths offered us by Hollywood, by the commercial advertisements, by the detective story, by local politics, by international diplomacy, or by the physicists. Myth appears in a novel when the action and the particular set of manners represented in the book are organized in a total symbolic construct of such a kind that it not only reflects the aspirations and ideals, the attitudes and customs, of a large social group, but also seems to give to these attitudes and customs the sanction

[2] Brian W. Downs, *Richardson* (London: Routledge & Kegan Paul, Ltd., 1938), p. 116.

of some "higher authority," perhaps the authority of ancient tradition, perhaps supernatural authority, perhaps the authority of some vaguely defined power-and-knowledge concept such as "law" or "government" or "science" or even "society" itself. Finally, this total symbolic construct is, in myth, projected dramatically. We shall need, for greater clarity, to differentiate myth from allegory, as allegory was defined in the essay on *The Pilgrim's Progress*. Allegory, too, is an organized symbolism; but the differentia of allegory is the fact that its elements are, in gross, to be read off in point-to-point equations into an abstract, discursive, intellectual system. Myth does not offer an intellectual system. What it offers is the dramatization of powers that are assumed to have universal authority over the actions of men. The dominion of allegory (as a total system) is the intellect; the dominion of myth is the irrational.

We shall speak of *the* myth of *Clarissa Harlowe,* but we must be prepared to see it in several different aspects, or as several different sets of mythological ideas which have been mingled and fused by Richardson and given coherence in the large, simple dramatic shape of the story, but which can be singled out as sub-systems for examination. An analogy may help us here. It is as if the *Clarissa*-myth, as a whole, were a universe described by a number of different planetary orbits; the different sets of "mythological ideas" are the different orbits, but these orbits have interrelationships in the larger system of the *Clarissa*-universe, and the whole is held together by complex magnetic correspondences. The analogy helps us to visualize both the strong internal unity of the major system and the distinct existence of the subsystems. For convenience, then, we shall be speaking as if of a number of different myths ("the Puritan myth" in *Clarissa,* for instance, or "the myth of class"), but we should continue to think of them as not actually independent or self subsistent, but as operating only by virtue of the magnetic laws binding them in the unit of the whole.

Certain of these we have already touched on, but we must see them now in fuller articulation and in their correspondences with others. The most evident, and one which had Richardson's own conscious deliberation behind it, is the Puritan religious myth, which was alive in Richardson's culture and which he used to give edificatory significance to his materials. His aim, as he expressed it, was to teach the "highest and most important doctrines of Christianity," and his success in this project is witnessed by the comment of a contemporary Dutch Mennonite divine, who said that if *Clarissa* had formed one of the canonical books of the Bible, it would have furnished proof positive of divine inspiration. The Puritan myth, as it is inflected in *Clarissa,* is a daemonic view of life. Deity and the evil spirit are deeply concerned in the affairs of men. Through charm of body and other lures—wit, worldly graces, worldly power, mobility, uninhibited freedom—and with the most cunning deceit, the evil spirit tempts the woman as he tempted Eve. The ultimate obsession of the devil is, of course, sex, for in the Puritan mythology sex is the culmination of all evil, the unmasked face of fear: Like the Satan who tempted Job, this Lucifer is not interested in small fry. Job was "the greatest of all the men of the east," there was "none like him in the earth," he was "a perfect and an upright man." Similarly, Clarissa is a paragon of virtue, a "divinity of a woman," which is the reason why she holds any interest for the prince of evil spirits. She is virtuous in many ways, she is charitable "to the industrious poor," she disciplines herself to deserve 144 merit marks for virtue every week, and if she omits to earn one of them she has to add it onto the next week's budget. But above all she is chaste. As the devil's evil obsession is sex, so the woman's virtuous obsession is her chastity; but it must be observed that chastity is here a physical attribute (quite as it is in *Moll Flanders*), that innocence of spirit is not distinguished from bodily intactness, that the two are identified as one. Therefore, when the devil has succeeded in befouling the woman's body, he will have obtained a victory over her soul—save for the intervention of the Deity. The woman's will for purity makes her subject to an inspiration of Divine Grace. As Job was selected from among all men for the severest trial of faith, so Clarissa has been selected from among all women for unique travail as preparation for sainthood. Potent as the devil is, the universe is well loaded against him, and when the crisis is over, Providence begins distributing rewards and punishments with remarkable accuracy to everyone in the book, thoroughly satisfying poetic justice. Lovelace is, as Richardson puts it, "condignly punished"; the infamous Sinclair dies in incredible torments of a vile disease; Miss Howe, Mr. Hickman, Belford, the worthy Norton, are all made "signally happy"; the Harlowes themselves are so deeply afflicted in conscience that they take the backstairs the rest of their lives to avoid passing the martyred Clarissa's room; James becomes involved in insupportable financial difficulties; Arabella's husband is unfaithful to her and her wedded life horrid; even the servants are paid off with minute attention to their respective deserts. As for Clarissa, she has received the crown of all joys: her bridegroom is Christ. We may observe that, far from being the tragedy which Richardson, as a literary man with some knowledge of the traditional structure of tragedy, worked hard to make it (Clarissa's "tragic flaw," for instance, is designed with high deliberation), the novel is really a comedy—a "divine comedy"—if we use as the generic distinction between comedy and tragedy the happy and the unhappy ending. It has a "happy ending," the good are rewarded, the evil are punished; and it has this ending by virtue of the Puritan world view whose powerful outlines dominate the novel.

We turn now to another mythological aspect of *Clarissa,* and if, for the sake of clarity, we must pin labels on each of these, we shall call this one a myth of social caste or class. We have said that Lovelace, who has the place of the devil in the Puritan myth, offers the lures of wit, worldly graces and power, mobility, uninhibited freedom; but these are qualities and privileges of aristocracy, and Lovelace himself is a member of the aristocratic class and heir to a title. By contrast, the woman he woos is the daughter of middle-class parents. The Harlowes are London tradesmen, representatives of the prosperous bourgeoisie that has been supreme in society and politics since the consolidations of the seventeenth century. It is a class not distinguished by the social refinements and gallantries or by the intellectual graces, a class that has acquired power through hard work, cash calculation, and sobriety, a class therefore by definition unable to afford aristocratic freedoms such as impulsiveness, enthusiasm, idleness, extravagance, debauchery (as these freedoms are conceived in Richardson's middle-class fantasy on the aristocratic theme).[3] Just as Lovelace, the aristocrat, is drawn larger than life, both as to his vices and his charm, so also the Harlowes are drawn larger than life: not only Clarissa—who is the epitome of that virtue of virginity which, besides a fortune, is the best trade commodity of the middle-class woman, determining her price bracket—but the others as well, the mother and the uncles, and particularly Mr. Harlowe and the son James, with their concentration on hard cash and the consequent brutalization of their feelings. Clarissa herself is powerfully attracted to Lovelace. Possible marriage with him is kept constantly in the foreground of the novel; in-

[3] The discussion of this aspect of the book owes much to the essay "From Pamela to Clarissa," by William M. Sale, Jr., in *The Age of Johnson* (New Haven: Yale University Press, 1949).

deed, even after the crisis, when she has excluded that possibility, it is still kept in the foreground by the other characters, by Miss Howe, for instance, who sees the marriage as a sensible way to settle the hullabaloo and make everybody happy yet. Marriage with Lovelace would be a symbolic act, uniting middle class and aristocracy, bringing the middle class within those delightful open ranges of freedom that are the aristocratic privilege, and endowing it with the refined talents and the graces that it lacks. Clearly, in reading *Clarissa* in this way, we are reading the whole action as "larger than life," larger than a private family's adventures. We are reading it as a symbolic construct reflecting the ideals of a whole culture—that is, we are reading it as myth. A modern commentator has said that Richardson realized

> for his generation the emotions engendered by the conditions of life that defined his generation's hopes and that set limitations upon the fulfillment of those hopes. Before his novels appeared, however, eighteenth century Englishmen were sufficiently aware of the fact that their vital social problem was the interpenetration of the emergent middle class and the surviving aristocracy. His contemporaries had read authors who sought to educate the middle class in the manners and decorum of the disappearing aristocracy; they had been amused by authors who pointed up the gaucherie of the new man and woman, the new peer.[4]

Richardson's particular dramatization of this social condition was the exposure of his middle-class heroine to seduction by a nobleman. The significance of the act lies, on the one hand, in the fact that—up to a point—the heroine does seek union with the aristocrat who threatens her integrity, and, on the other hand, in the fact that the marriage does not, after all, take place. If *Clarissa* may be read as a "parable on the antithesis of the aristocratic and middle-class codes," the parable contrives to demonstrate finally the superiority of the latter.[5] The aristocracy is put in its place (Lovelace, we presume, goes to hell) and Clarissa, on her way to heaven, bestows blessings that assuredly have magical virtue (like the blessings bestowed by Isaac and by Jacob) on her mother and father, her sister, her brother, her uncles, Miss Howe, Mrs. Norton, the nurse, the servants. That is, by her death, symbolically she makes great

[4] *Ibid.*, p. 129.
[5] Downs, *op. cit.*, p. 182.

her class, gives supernatural sanction to its code, donates to it her mana, making of it an embodiment of the order of the universe.

Noticeably, the religious myth and the myth of class overlap in a good many places, for, whether by historical accident or inevitability, Puritanism became the moral code and the religious faith of the commercially prosperous middle class. Noticeably also, however, there are places where these two mythological aspects of the book seem to contradict each other. Lovelace's part in the religious myth is to represent evil; he is to be hated; above all, he is to be feared. But in the class myth he has an ambivalent status; he exerts powerful attraction; nevertheless, as the drama evolves, he is seen to be too vicious after all. Fear of what the aristocracy stands for (or what it stands for in Richardson's fantasy) overcomes the attraction of what it stands for. What has been indulged by this myth is the middle-class wish to be aristocratic, to be elegant and idle and uninhibited; for, like dreams, myths indulge the hopes and passions and impulses of men. But, also like dreams, they are subject to a "censor." The indulgence may be sidled up to, but it must not be carried too far. In actual dreams, the "censor" in the psyche acts by disguising the wish either under forms that can be morally approved, or under forms apparently so fantastic and incoherent that they seem morally irrelevant. In myths, on the other hand, where whole dramas are acted out with narrative coherence, the "censor" may offer a dramatic resolution which negates the indulged wish by substituting some other attraction—as, in *Clarissa*, the wish to be aristocratic is negated by a counterwish, the wish to embody in the middle class itself the universal order, both divine and social. The latter wish offers no moral difficulties; one has merely to look upon oneself and one's class as the highest product of the human race, the epitome of what God intended man to be; and, implicitly, what Richardson tells his readers is that the middle class, to see an image of what is socially and morally desirable, need not look beyond itself, but will find that image in what it already is. This is comforting doctrine, most particularly since the myth has already underhandedly indulged the desire for aristocratic pleasures.

Myth has its power and fertility not in singleness of meaning (like allegory) but in multiplicity of meaning—meaning that changes historically with social changes, and that changes at any one glance with the center one chooses to see in it. We shall have to add another center and another contour to the *Clarissa*-myth: namely, a dramatic vision of family

57

life and its sanctions. If *Clarissa* were a "novel of manners" alone, we should find in it a description of how a family lived and sinned and suffered in the eighteenth century, all possibly psychologically fascinating and perhaps with some universal significance. But, being myth, its vision of family life is raised to intimacy with the supernatural. The Harlowes acquire their "bigness" from other equators and other ecliptics than those that would circumscribe family life in a novel of manners. For Richardson, the family was a microcosm of society. Families were, he said, "so many miniatures" of the community of the world. But the family was not only a miniature of the world; it was an expression of divine order. In a later book, *Sir Charles Grandison* (the hero of which is Lovelace's opposite and thus a moral therapy for readers too attracted to the aristocratic rake), Sir Charles expresses himself on the concerns of Deity: "Does He not," he asks, "interest Himself, if I may so express myself, in the performance of filial duty? May it not be justly said, that to obey your parents is to serve God?" The particular family relationship that is eminent in *Clarissa* is that of female child to male parent, and it is brought dramatically to bear on the affair of marriage. We may learn something enlightening about this relationship from eighteenth-century conduct books. A parent "can no more force a Child to marry against her Consent, than a Child is permitted to act contrary to the Parent." [6] This is a situation comparable to a modern highway situation in Florida, where a sign at a railroad crossing decrees that neither vehicle, car or train, can go ahead until the other one has started. Another conduct book (one which the printer Richardson himself probably printed) offers the possibility of reciprocal modulation and of decision of act. "There is one instance," this writer says,

> wherein obedience to parents is of more importance to children than any other in life, and yet where they too often fail to pay it; and that is in the article of marriage: for, as long as children continue a part of their parent's family . . . they are absolutely in their parent's power, and have no more right to dispose of themselves than they have to dispose of the parents' fortune, or inheritance, or any of their goods . . .

[6] This and the two following passages from conduct books are quoted by Alan D. McKillop, in *Samuel Richardson* (Chapel Hill: University of North Carolina Press, 1936), p. 135.

And then he takes up the parents' responsibility.

> Prudent parents well know, that such accomplishments as either arise
> from, or tend to establish true worth, can alone render any pair happy
> in an union that must last for life. This, I say, all prudent parents
> very well know; and therefore are best fitted to make a right choice for
> their children; but still with this caution, that they do not offer vio-
> lence to their inclinations, by forcing them to marry against their will.
> For the rest, it were infinitely better, that perverse children should
> actually die in the disappointment of their inclinations, than that they
> should make both themselves and their parents for ever miserable, by
> an unfortunate and undutiful marriage.

The critical and helplessly ambiguous situation with which Clarissa is
faced is, as one critic has said, a "crisis that affects not merely the future
of any imaginary individual but the social position of the eighteenth century unmarried woman." [7]

"To obey your parents is to serve God." But Clarissa, dangerously
for this code, is economically independent. She could, practically speaking, do whatever her impulse led her to do. She could seek satisfaction
anywhere that she chose. And she does "go off with a man." Richardson
said, in correspondence, "Going off with a Man, is the thing I wanted
most to make inexcusable." The "man," as we have seen, is an outlaw,
a pariah, a threat, a social terror. But for this particular reading of
Clarissa as a myth of family life, he is—in a word—the lover. Clarissa's
"going off with" him is a symbolical alliance of daughter with lover
against family, an alliance with the outlaw and criminal who represents
enjoyments (in this context, enjoyments of love) which the financially
consolidated bourgeois family cannot tolerate inasmuch as enjoyment
of love would mean failure of sobriety, which is the moral pillar of
family unity and financial security. The book begins with this rebellion.
Actually, however, as the story progresses, it is not the daughter's rebellion that is thematically paramount, but the daughter's obedience; for
her father's curse is far more effective emotionally upon her than the
attraction of the lover, or than her desire to escape the sterile and brutal
cash alliance with the suitor approved by the family. Furthermore, the
father's curse is dramatically correlated with and confirmed by Lovelace's
own viciousness; the lover who would take the daughter out of the family

[7] F. C. Green, *Minuet* (London: J. M. Dent & Sons, Ltd., 1935), p. 403.

is exposed as the worst of all evildoers. From this point of view, the lover is indirectly a kind of moral employee of the father: he is the living scourge exercised by the father upon the rebellious daughter. The paramount motif is, then, not rebellion and escape, but acquiescence in parental values and return. Clarissa is the family's consoling symbol of the right-minded daughter. She has a great act to perform: her financial independence is not societally right; she voluntarily gives it up. And she returns to the parental nest. For Clarissa does make a symbolic return "to her Father's house" (her last, punning, highly disingenuous letter to Lovelace tells him that she will meet him there). "Her Father's house" is, in this context, heaven, and here the Puritan myth and the myth of family life coincide. Mr. Harlowe is proxy for God, and Clarissa's return to her Father's house is a supernatural equivalent of the necessary "return" of all daughters to the parental authority. The values that are given final sanction here are the typical values of the right-thinking bourgeois family: the father's authority is supreme; the daughter must not wed for satisfaction of personal impulse, but, if she weds, must do so for the further consolidation and enrichment of the clan; the lover is condemned; there must, in a word, be no love, except insofar as love can serve the family economy.

Clarissa's whiteness, her debility, and her death are correlatives of the sterilization of instinct and the impotence that are suggested as the desirable qualities of family and social life. As we have said previously, Clarissa's death does not provide a tragic ending for the story, but a "happy ending," inasmuch as her death is equated with supernatural joys and rewards. The scene in the death room is an astonishing one. The room is crowded with people, all pressing around the dying woman to obtain her blessing. The mourning is as public as possible; every sigh, every groan, every tear is recorded. One is given to understand that nothing could be a greater social good than Clarissa's death, nothing could be more enjoyable than to watch her in her death throes (she performs them charmingly), nothing a greater privilege than to be present at this festival of death and to weep and sniffle in the common orgy. An instructive grace note to the scene is Mrs. Judith Norton's observation that to have her own eyes closed in death by her young friend Clarissa was a "pleasure" which she had often "promised" herself—a pleasure now, alas, not to be obtained. This macabre satisfaction crowns the value system of *Clarissa*, triumphantly capping a code of Puritanism in morals, parental authoritarianism in the family, and the cash nexus as the only binding tie for society at large—a cult, in short, of death.

Clarissa returns "to her Father's house" as the perfect daughter, the model of all daughters. The novel offers the symbolic formula for such perfection: Clarissa is the sexless daughter, the dead daughter. In reading *Clarissa* finally as a sexual myth, we are reading it as a construct of irrationals similar to a dream (although, in the case of myth, the myth-maker is "dreaming" not only his own dream, but society's dream as well), and, irrationally, the sexless daughter manages to have the most violent of sexual experiences. It has been said of Clarissa that, by setting such a price upon herself, she "represents that extreme of puritanism which desires to be raped. Like Lovelace's her sexuality is really violent, insatiable in its wish for destruction." [8] In a sense, she keeps her cake while eating it—a proverbial paradox that expresses aptly what happens in dreams, where the forbidden wish is indulged under a disguise of nonindulgence. The mythical potency of *Clarissa*, in this respect, is witnessed by the fascination held for generations of readers by the motif of the carnal assault on a virgin. Novel after novel repeated this motif, obviously feeding an immense appetite of the reading public for more of the same. The assault is sometimes frustrated, sometimes carried through (*Clarissa*, of course, allows both: Lovelace accomplishes his vile ends, but the lady, being drugged, is in a sense not there; moreover, her death and sainthood negate the whole affair). Abduction by a handsome nobleman, captivity in a house of ill fame, and the use of drugs on the virtuous heroine, are devices almost obligatory in these books.[9] Richard Chase, writing on the nature of myth, has suggested that "myth is the repository of repressed wishes" and that

> part of the magic power of myth stems from its ability to furnish "recognition scenes," in which we have the thrilling experience of coming face to face with a disinherited part of ourselves.[10]

[8] V. S. Pritchett, *The Living Novel* (New York: Reynal & Hitchcock, 1947), p. 28.

[9] Cf. Mrs. Davys' *The Accomplish'd Rake* (1756), Jane Marishall's *History of Miss Clarinda Cathcart* (3d ed. 1767), Mrs. Sarah Scott's *Cornelia* (1750), Mrs. Woodfin's *Sally Sable* (before 1764), Diderot's *La Réligeuse* (1760). In the romances of Mrs. Radcliffe, as Mario Praz has pointed out, the motif of captivity manages to exploit the same set of sado-masochistic attractions.

[10] *Quest for Myth* (Baton Rouge: Louisiana State University Press, 1949), p. 101.

The modern reader may be disinclined to find, in the captivity-and-assault sequences in *Clarissa,* "recognition scenes" of this kind, and indeed the device used by Lovelace appears extraordinarily crude; but the reader's disinclination may merely reflect the fact that Hollywood has elaborated subtler stratagems of wish fulfillment, under a more refined censorship. Lovelace's own frenzied fantasy was undoubtedly prophetic when he saw himself in the dock on trial for his life, and all the sympathies of the audience with the handsome criminal: "Even the judges, and the whole crowded bench will acquit us in their hearts! and every single man wish he had been me."

As for Clarissa's own perverted sexuality, we read it in the profusion of sexual images that, paradoxically, at the level of professed narrative intention are meant to illustrate her resistance to Lovelace and her protection of her virginity—for surely we must find ambiguous those contexts which illustrate the virtue of chastity and the wickedness of sex by an imagery making defloration attractive and exciting; but more especially we find her sexual violence in the constant identification of sex and death, phallic images and images of assassination. The identification of love and death is one of the oldest puns and one of the oldest of myth motifs; it is found in the great love stories—in the stories of Tristan and Iseult, Phaedra and Hippolytus, Dido and Aeneas, Antony and Cleopatra (it is found also quite literally in the life histories of salmon, ephemerids, and some spiders, a fact which is perhaps of significance in deepening our appreciation of the literary instinct in this matter). The sexual myth in *Clarissa* is founded in the love-death identification, and acquires power from that ancient and universal perception; but as *Clarissa* formulates the love myth, it becomes perverse, inasmuch as "love" here is conceived so strangely and exclusively as physical violation, an act of stabbing or ripping, with no implication of any aspect of sexual passion except a passion to murder and be murdered. Indeed, it is impossible to think of either Clarissa's or Lovelace's attitudes as involving any sensuality; for the word "sensual" pertains to gratification of the senses, and we find it difficult to discover those senses which might be gratified by stabbing. Their passion symbolizes gratification, not of sensual life, but of a submerged portion of the emotional life whose tendency actually opposes gratification of the senses—the death wish, the desire for destruction. And it is here that the mythical representation of sexual relationships in *Clarissa* coincides with and deeply reinforces the mythical representation of social values and the values of family life. From each point of view, the book is a paean to death. Richardson is the great poet of the adolescence of our own acquisitive, aggressive culture—a culture that has elaborated the cognate political myth of a world divided between two powers, one "good," one "bad," each engrossed in the devising of magical weapons for the destruction of the other, each "censoring" the grand death wish with a diplomacy designed to bring about a marriage in all profit and decency.

Dr. Samuel Johnson said of Richardson's heroines that they all had "a kind of obliquity in their moral vision," and, commenting particularly upon the casuistry which he found in Clarissa, he complained, "You may observe there is always something which she prefers to truth." Clarissa's character has been read by certain critics as a study in the divided mind. We must certainly acquiesce in a reading of her story as a psychological study; but our own reading of the novel as myth finds the psychological study to be but one level in a multileveled construct whose depth and richness derive from vast social dreams in which the individual character, however interesting from the point of view of character study, is at the same time more than an individual character—is a fabulous creature of epic stature, clothed with the ideals of a culture and of a race. In this reading, Clarissa's moral "obliquity," her "divided mind," are a function of mysterious indulgences in the forbidden, through which a Puritan-capitalistic culture found its systematic inhibitions gratefully removed, while, at the same time, it had in Lovelace a whipping boy for the same indulgences. But through Clarissa also the systematic inhibitions of this culture must receive their supernatural sanction, their "higher authority"; for the race does demand "higher authority" for its mores, simply in order to face itself with equanimity and to perpetuate itself proudly. Having so much dependent on her, so many and such complex duties to perform for her readers, Clarissa may well appear as a moral casuist and a divided mind.

ON *Tom Jones*

In order to place *Clarissa* in such a light that it may be viewed all round about, in its complexity, we have had to try to lever it up out of unconscious darknesses where it has much of its nourishment and its vitality. With so vast a book, so deeply rooted in subliminal matter, the process of levering it into critical daylight is a struggle; even after we get it out where we can see it, strange, only half-transparent growths still attach to it, like the rubbery growths of the sea bottom. *Tom Jones,* by Richardson's great contemporary Fielding, is all out in mental sunlight. The product of a generously intelligent, tough and yet elegant art, it too is a complex book, but its complexities are within the immediate view of the reason. Structurally, it is characterized, like *Don Quixote,* by a systematic organization of contrasts, a playing off of one attitude and one way of life against another attitude and another way of life, with a constant detail of contrast in the character relationships, scene relationships, and even verbal relationships; for with this novel, for the first time in English fiction, the full and direct artistic impact of *Don Quixote* is felt (as distinguished from the general direction which Cervantes set for the modern novel). And like Cervantes, Fielding uses the "point of view" of the omniscient author; his world is too populous and too extensive in its spatial design for the survey of any one character within the book; and the author's own humorous irony is itself one of the materials of the novel, providing, in the "head-chapters," one more contrast in the total aesthetic system—the contrast of plane between the author and his book, between criticism and creation, between intelligence focused *on* the human situation he has created and the intelligence of the characters *within* the created situation.

We have been using the term "structure" to mean the arrangement and interrelation of all the elements in a book, as dominated by the gen-

65

eral character of the whole. It is a term that is sometimes used to mean "structure of action" alone, that is, the plot. But, certainly at least with *Clarissa,* we have seen that the total architecture of a novel involves a great deal more than plot, and we have to have some word for that architecture. The word "structure" will do, and we shall distinguish structure, then, from the narrative arrangement of episodes, the plot, plot being but one element among the many that constitute a structure. *Tom Jones* has a far more elaborate plot than any we have yet encountered in these studies, elaborate not only in the sense that the book contains an immense number of episodes, but also in the sense that all these episodes are knit, as intimate cause and effect, into a large single action obeying a single impulse from start to finish. One of our objectives in analyzing the book will be to understand why intricate plot should have such importance, as an element of structure, in this particular novel—or, in other words, to understand what significance, what meaningful character, is given to the *Tom Jones* world by its intricacy of action.

The plot movement follows the curve characteristic of comedy plots, taking the protagonist from low fortune to high fortune. Tom comes on the scene as a bastard; his very earliest activities enforce "the universal opinion . . . that he was certainly born to be hanged"; and his reputation and his hopes are progressively blackened until he reaches his nadir in London, "kept" by Lady Bellaston (a circumstance perhaps more reprehensible to a modern reader's eyes than to eighteenth-century eyes), then accused of murder and thrown in jail, and finally—as if anything still could be added in the way of blackening—presumptively guilty of incest with his mother. But the nadir of his fortune also marks its "reversal" or crisis, and with the concurrent exposure of Blifil's malicious machinations and of Tom's true goodness, his fortune sails to the zenith of romantic happiness; he is proved to be of high birth, he marries the girl of his choice, and he inherits wealth. This is the general plot curve, the concave curve of comic drama (as against the convex curve taken by tragic drama—a metaphor of plot design that has its origin in the medieval emblem of the wheel of Fortune, on whose spokes people were represented as clinging in various stages of shabby or resplendent clothing, while the wheel turned round, carrying them from doubtful beginnings to pleasant endings, or from promising beginnings to unpleasant endings).

Tom goes under and up Fortune's wheel from "low" to "high," and in this shape of his career lies one salient set of contrasts as boldly definitive of the design of the action as the "high" beginning and the "low" end of Oedipus in the Sophoclean tragedy. But in order that the action may evolve in its curve, the wicked Blifil is needed—Tom's "opposite," chief cause of his sorrows, and affording the chief character contrast in the book. For while the curve of tragedy is spun, like the spider's thread, from within the tragic protagonist, produced out of his own passions and frailties, the curve of comedy is spun socially and gregariously, as the common product of men in society. The tragic curve leads to the hero's "self-discovery," the comic curve sprouts a various ornament of "self-exposures" on the part of many men. Also in connection with this characteristic difference between tragic action and comic action, we may notice that while the tragic hero "changes" (that is, comes eventually to a new and revolutionary realization of what he is and what he has done), the characters of comedy are laid under no artistic obligation to "change," since the reason for their artistic existence is that they may be exposed, in their "true" natures, to the eyes of other men—to society. The point is rather important for a reader of Fielding, for the development of the modern novel has accustomed us to look for "change" in characters and to feel that the profundity and importance of a book is somehow connected with such change; and we may therefore be inclined to feel that Fielding's conception of his material is comparatively "shallow," however witty and engrossing. It is well for us, then, to bear in mind the generic characteristics of the comic mode, and the fact that the characters in comedy may remain relatively static while the broad social panorama of comedy need not for that reason be lacking in seriousness and depth of significance. We are confronted in *Tom Jones* with a picture of social interaction among souls already formed, already stamped with operative character, and out of this gregarious action the conflict between hero and villain is propelled to a resolution in which the rogue who appeared to be a good man is exposed in his true nature as rogue, and the good man who appeared to be a rogue is revealed in his true good nature, with many similar exposures of other people along the way.

We can thus indicate, in some degree, the aesthetic necessity of elaborate plot in Fielding's novel: the episodes must cumulate functionally toward a final, representative revelation of character; but, because the significance of this revelation is for all men in the given society, the episodes must illustrate subtle varieties of character and interaction, at the same time representing the complexities of human nature and contributing toward the final revelation which will be, although narrowed down to hero and villain, symbolic of all those complexities. The book must, therefore, have both variety of episode and "unity of action." But we must now describe the plot as it signifies a "theme" or "meaning." In *Tom Jones,* life is conceived specifically as a conflict between natural, instinctive feeling, and those appearances with which people disguise, deny, or inhibit natural feeling—intellectual theories, rigid moral dogmas, economic conveniences, doctrines of *chic* or of social "respectability." This is the broad thematic contrast in *Tom Jones.* Form and feeling ("form" as mere outward appearance, formalism, or dogma, and "feeling" as the inner reality) engage in constant eruptive combat, and the battlefield is strewn with a debris of ripped masks, while exposed human nature—shocked to find itself uncovered and naked—runs on shivering shanks and with bloody pate, like the villagers fleeing from Molly Seagrim in the famous churchyard battle.

But let us stop to weigh rather carefully what Fielding means by that "human nature" which he says is his subject matter, and which we see again and again exposed during that conflict we have described above. Its meaning is not univocal. Broadly it refers to that mixture of animal instinct and human intellection which is assumed to obtain in every personality. But, in many of the incidents in the book, its meaning tips to one side: it tends to lean heavily toward "animal instinct," simply for the reason that the animal and instinctive part of man is (in the *Tom Jones* world) so frequently disguised or denied by the adoption of some formal appearance. Instinctive drives must therefore be emphasized as an important constituent of "human nature." Again, the curious, sometimes beneficial, sometimes damaging uses of intelligence are "human nature." We see "human nature" in the wicked Bilfil's calculative shrewdness, in Black George's rationalization for keeping Tom's money, in the absurd intellectual formulas elaborated by Thwackum and Square. But we see it also in Allworthy's high-minded ethics, and in Tom's own idealism. In Blifil himself, "nature" seems to be congenitally and helplessly bad, and we may be led to speculate on his inheritance from a tenderly hypocritical mother and a brutally hypocritical father; and then, in Tom, "nature" seems to be, on the whole, congenitally good, though he had the same mother as Blifil and a father on whom we cannot speculate at all, as he is not described. Let us sum up these meanings of "human nature" so far:

human nature is a balanced mixture of instinctive drives and feelings and intellectual predilections; it is (dependent on the emphasis given by the specific incident) instinctive feeling alone; it is the human tendency to pervert instinct by intellection; it may be altogether bad (as in Blifil); it may be altogether good (as in Allworthy). Obviously we must expect trickiness in this term, and not be too quick to pin it down to any one meaning. But let us cite another and most important meaning that it has, an ideal meaning which the book strives to give to "human nature." Ideally, "human nature" is what is seen in the best specimens of the human species—a nature to which all should aspire. Under this ideal, it is assumed that the best specimens of the species exhibit a homogeneous configuration of instinct and intelligence—not a suppression of instinct by intellect, nor a suppression of intellect by instinct, but a happy collaboration of the two in the full and integrated man. In this sense, "human nature" is "good." This adjustment Squire Allworthy exhibits from the beginning: but because Fielding has given so many meanings to "human nature" in his book, we may feel that Allworthy is too crystallized a specimen, not really representative of all the possibilities of "human nature"; hence the hero, Tom, offers himself more aptly as a representative of "human nature" inasmuch as he has to learn, with difficulty, the appropriate balance in the process of the action, rather than having it given to him in crystallized form at the beginning. Tom yields formidably and frequently to instinct, and in so doing he exhibits the "naturalness" and therefore the "rightness" of instinct as a constituent of the personality, thus correcting the overemphasis on formal appearances which we see in other characters; but at the same time, in these incidents, he shows a remarkable absence of that useful social sense which we call discretion, a lack of which is damaging certainly to himself and a cause of confusion for others. On the other hand, Tom is no fool: he is an admirer of Handel, he philosophizes with dignity in discourse with the Old Man of the Hill—nor could his proposal to Sophia, at the end of the book, be couched in more civilized, more exquisite language. On the whole, "human nature" in Tom, in all its intricacies and difficulties and mistakes, is a splendid thing; and (and this is its real significance) it is fine and splendid because it is undisguised, it is all out in the sunlight of the social air, the air of common intelligence, readily to be understood, without mask, unpretentious. To schematize over-simply the contrasting aspect of "human nature," let us say that "nature" is not fine and splendid, but indecent and embarrassing when a man, either through inherited disposition or through acquired predilection, adopts a mask for appearance's sake, hugs it too closely and too long, and allows it to warp instinct. Then—when we are allowed to look under the mask—"nature" shows itself perverted. It is the incongruity between what a man might "naturally" be (that is, if he did not deform himself by some kind of over-emphasis) and what he makes of himself by adopting a formulary appearance or mask, that gives "human nature" its variety and funniness and treacherousness. The indecency of "nature" when it has been going around in a mask, and the mask is suddenly ripped off, is illustrated grossly by the exposure of the philosopher Square, squatting "among other female utensils" when the curtain in Molly's bedroom accidentally falls. Square's mask of deistic theory has corrupted his instinctive nature into the narrow channel of lust. Uncorrupted by the cult of appearances, "human nature" is nature committed to the intelligence, opened before the intelligence of all men, and therefore "good" in itself—in a world conceived as fundamentally intelligible and tending in all its phenomena toward the general highest good of total intelligibility.

Let us glance now at the disposition of the separate books of the novel, and the contribution of each to the action. In this discussion, we shall confine ourselves to a very rapid glance at the whole, and then turn back to the first book, and to the first scene of the first book, for a more detailed examination. This method has its handicaps, for it would seem to imply that the first book is more important than the others, more worthy of inspection, which is obviously not at all the case. But a close examination of one book, and then of one scene, has the virtue of showing, in very small scope, those contrasts and tensions which govern the whole novel, and of indicating the precision of Fielding's art in the detail as well as in the whole.

In Book I, Tom is found in Allworthy's bed, Jenny Jones is accused of being Tom's mother and is got out of the way for the time being, and Bridget Allworthy marries Captain Blifil. In Book II, Partridge is fixed upon as Tom's father and is, like Jenny, removed from the picture, and Captain Blifil dies. In Book III, Tom's character comes under attack;

> . . . he had been already convicted of three robberies, viz., of robbing an orchard, of stealing a duck out of a farmer's yard, and of picking Master Blifil's pocket of a ball . . .

and concurrently young Blifil's malignity begins to receive attention, while Black George and his family are inauspiciously introduced. In Book IV, the romance begins between Tom and Sophia. Let us stop here for a moment, to see what has been accomplished and how it has been accomplished. The group composed of Squire Allworthy, Bridget Allworthy, and Captain Blifil has been described with a few swiftly drawn traits, and by the end of Book II, Captain Blifil has been disposed of, leaving on the scene his chief contribution—his son, Tom's half-brother and mortal antagonist; while the group composed of Jenny Jones and Partridge has contributed its special complication to the action—the red herring drawn across the trail of Tom's birth—and has been removed, not to appear again until needed for the ultimate complications. By Book III, the stage has been cleared for the confrontation of young hero and young villain, and here, swiftly and with precision, the chief character contrast is sketched; while the apparently incidental appearance of Black George and his family lays the shadow of that critical blackening of Tom's reputation which will drive him from home. Book IV offers the romance complication, a double complication in itself: Black George's daughter is scooped up from Book III, to cast darkness on Tom's sexual morality, and Tom and Sophia are involved in an emotional affair that is socially impossible because of Tom's birth.

It should be of value to the critical reader to follow these spreading complications, with their multiple intricate knottings, through in this fashion from book to book, until the final unraveling—not simply in order to be able to state "what happens," which is a rudimentary critical project, but to trace out the unity of design as the many incidents contribute to that unity. We shall indicate here, as one suggestion of unifying design, only the pursuit motif from Book VI on: Tom is turned out of doors, and Sophia follows him; she catches up with him in the inn at Upton, and for ample and adequate reasons the pursuit then reverses its character, and from Upton it is Tom who pursues Sophia; meanwhile, Squire Western has set out in pursuit of his daughter; and finally Squire Allworthy and Blifil must go to London in pursuit of the Westerns. The scenes at Upton occur at the center of the story (Books IX and X, in a volume of eighteen books), and it is here that we again pick up Partridge and Jenny Jones, Tom's reputed father and mother, both of them implicated in the initial circumstances of the action and both of them necessary for the final complications and the reversal. It is at Upton also that the set of London characters first begins to appear, with Mrs. Fitzpatrick and her husband as its representatives (again under the aspect of pursuit: Fitzpatrick is after his wife), involving both Sophia and Tom in their London destinies. From the central scenes at Upton Inn, the novel pivots around itself. There have been six books of country life, in the center are six books of life on the highways, and the final six books are concerned with life in London—on a smaller and more local scale, much in the manner of Cervantes' multiple contrasts of perspective; and it is at Upton Inn, in the mathematical mid-point of the story, that country and city come together.[1] The initial pursuit motif, beginning at the end of Book VI, finishes its arabesque at the end of Book XII, again with nice mathematical balance, when Tom reaches London and is enabled to meet Sophia. Now it will be Blifil who is in pursuit of Sophia, so that eventually everyone will wind up in London for the denouement. As to the coincidences by means of which Fielding manages to gather so many pursuing and pursued people together, in the proper places and at the proper times for intricate involvement and complicated intrigue, one may say that "it is, after all, a small world": sooner or later, when people pursue each other with assiduity, they are bound to meet. The pursuit motif is, then, not only a provision for comic situation, but, as the immediate dynamics of action, is integral to the plot development.

Fielding was a writer for the theater before he was a novelist, and one of the reader's strongest impressions is that of dramatic handling of scene and act (the chapters may be thought of as "scenes," a single book as an "act"): the sharp silhouetting of characters and their grouping in such a manner as to avoid any confusions even in so populous a drama; the bright lighting of the individual episode; the swift pacing of scenes so that they flash past for the eye and ear at the same time that they maintain a clear system of witty contrast; and above all, the strict *conceptualizing* of the function of each scene, in relation to the larger unit of the "act" (or book) and to the over-all unit of the drama (the novel), as well as the *objectifying* of the individual scene as a subject in itself, a subject clear and significant in its own right.[2] We are using the word "scene" here purely in its dramatic sense: as the smallest full-formed division of an action, during which there is no change of place and no lapse in con-

[1] Aurelien Digeon makes this analysis of the action in his *The Novels of Fielding* (New York: E. P. Dutton & Co., Inc., 1925), pp. 172–175.

[2] V. S. Pritchett emphasizes these aspects in his chapter on Fielding in *The Living Novel* (New York: Reynal & Hitchcock, 1947).

tinuity of time. In Book I, there are three definite shifts of scene (and time and place), correlated with three definite groups of characters, and Fielding prefaces each shift with a brief, sharp delineation of the new character, or characters, who are to contribute a new direction to the action. The first scene is that of the finding of Tom in Mr. Allworthy's bed, and so that we may have the fullest ironic understanding of the scene, we are first given (in the language of the table of contents) "a short description of Squire Allworthy, and a fuller account of Miss Bridget Allworthy," while Mrs. Deborah Wilkins quite adequately introduces herself during the action. The place of action is shifted now to the parish, upon which Mrs. Deborah descends as investigator of morals; and again we are given "a short account of Jenny Jones," before the scene gets under way. We move, then, back to Squire Allworthy's house, with the scene between the Squire and Jenny, after which Jenny is dispatched out of the book for the time being. Now the new group, composed of the Blifils, is introduced into the original group—the Squire and his sister—with, again, "a short sketch of the characters of the two brothers," before the action itself is released, the curtain goes up. This is the method of the theater. As V. S. Pritchett has said, in the theater

> there is an idea before there is a scene; and one of the fascinating things in *Tom Jones* is the use of the summary method to set the scene, explain the types of character, cover the preparatory ground quickly by a few oblique moralizings and antics so that all the realism is reserved for the main action.[3]

But let us notice the precise relationships of a few scenes in this first book. Mr. Allworthy's compassionate and honest-hearted reaction to the discovery of the foundling is set in almost instant contrast with Mrs. Deborah's furious descent upon the village and upon the supposed erring mother, in all Mrs. Deborah's theoretical righteousness; while we who are *rereading* the novel (and in rereading, as we must in a study of this kind, we are first actually *reading*) have meanwhile, even in so short a sequence, been slyly made aware of the multiple ironic significance of this contrast: of the genuinely compassionate and feelingful character of Allworthy's humanity, for though the babe (as we know, but as he does not know) is his own nephew, his compassion is directed toward the child

[3] *Ibid.*, p. 21.

as a foundling—that is, any child, any helplessness; while Mrs. Deborah, who would have cast out the child but has been reoriented by her servility (an economic convenience), takes the opportunity for an explosion of vicious passion upon the supposed mother; while the real mother, Miss Bridget, is protected by her position, her deceit, and her exploitation of the humanity of Jenny herself, so that she is able self-righteously to condemn the sexual indulgences of the lower classes, and at the same time preserve (under moral forms and "appearances") the fruit of her own indulgence. Now, immediately, this seething complex of human motive and passion is capped, ironically, by Squire Allworthy's simple, well-meaning sermon on chastity, directed at poor Jenny; and in the next chapter we are moved outside the door, to the keyhole, where Miss Bridget and Mrs. Deborah are listening, ears glued, each picking up from the well-meant sermon her own corrupt nourishment—Mrs. Deborah taking the vicarious satisfaction of sexual innuendo, and the direct satisfaction of another woman's downfall, and Miss Bridget the satisfaction of her own concealment and of an opportunity to exhibit the virtue of charity toward a woman whom she has herself placed under social condemnation. Thus from scene to scene, and in the interplay of scenes, contrast is effected, character is exposed, masks slip, wholly under the impetus of social interaction—or, in aesthetic terms, "plot"; and we see the Squire, in whom "nature" (here as spontaneous human feeling) has been committed fully and openly to the whole personality and made socially intelligible, contrasted with the two women in whom "nature" (again as instinctive feeling, but particularly as biological drive) has been suffocated under the mask of appearance and therefore dwarfed and distorted. The reader's appreciation of the elaborate and yet strictly controlled interrelationships of scene with scene, as each sets up with the other a contrast of human motivation, will be extended by his own objective analysis of such interrelationships in other books of *Tom Jones*.

We return now to the first scene, and to the internal contrasts within the scene itself and their function in realizing the subject matter of the novel ("human nature"), in defining the theme (the contest between instinctive feeling and formulary appearances), and in illustrating the theme in style. This scene takes place in Chapter III of Book I, where the babe is discovered. Mr. Allworthy, we are told, has just returned from London where he has been gone on business for a full quarter of a year (the notation of "a full quarter of a year" is innocent enough on first reading, full

of implication for the plot and for Miss Bridget's conduct on second reading); it is late in the evening, and he has retired much fatigued to his
chamber, where despite his fatigue, he "spends some minutes on his knees";
then

> he was preparing to step into bed, when, upon opening the clothes,
> to his great surprise he beheld an infant, wrapt up in some coarse
> linen, in a sweet and profound sleep, between his sheets. He stood
> some time lost in astonishment at this sight; but, as good-nature had
> always the ascendant in his mind, he soon began to be touched with
> sentiments of compassion for the little wretch before him. He then
> rang his bell, and ordered an elderly woman-servant to rise immedi-
> ately, and come to him; and in the mean time was so eager in con-
> templating the beauty of innocence, appearing in those lively colours
> with which infancy and sleep always display it, that his thoughts were
> too much engaged to reflect that he was in his shirt when the matron
> came in. She had, indeed, given her master sufficient time to dress him-
> self; for out of respect to him, and regard to decency, she had spent
> many minutes in adjusting her hair at the looking-glass, notwithstand-
> ing all the hurry in which she had been summoned by the servant, and
> though her master, for aught she knew, lay expiring in an apoplexy,
> or in some other fit.
>
> It will not be wondered at that a creature who had so strict a
> regard to decency in her own person should be shocked at the least
> deviation from it in another. She therefore no sooner opened the door,
> and saw her master standing by the bedside in his shirt, with a candle
> in his hand, than she started back in a most terrible fright, and might
> perhaps have swooned away, had he not now recollected his being un-
> dressed, and put an end to her terrors by desiring her to stay without
> the door till he had thrown some clothes over his back, and was be-
> come incapable of shocking the pure eyes of Mrs. Deborah Wilkins,
> who, though in the fifty-second year of her age, vowed she had never
> beheld a man without his coat.

The obvious contrast here is in character, as brought out by the reactions
of two people to an unusual event. Mr. Allworthy, though tired, is immediately touched by humane feeling toward an innocent creature (let
us note, in relation to Fielding's stated subject—"human *nature*"—that
it is Mr. Allworthy's "good-*nature*" which is ascendant at this moment),
and his spontaneous feeling makes him so forgetful of social forms and
appearances that he neglects to cover his nightshirt when Mrs. Deborah

comes to the door. Mrs. Deborah, on the other hand, called at an extraordinary hour of the night and therefore aware that the need must be great—perhaps her master is expiring in an apoplexy—has, out of respect to him, given him *sufficient time to dress himself* (usually done when one is expiring in an apoplexy), and also, in her regard to decency, has spent some minutes adjusting her hair at the looking glass. The ironic contrast of character is carried, by a few sly words (such as "good-nature" and "respect to him" and "regard to decency"), beyond the individuals and made into an extensive contrast between generous, uncalculating feeling and calculation of appearances and consequences. The second paragraph caps this original contrast with the shock Mrs. Deborah suffers from seeing the squire in his nightshirt; she is so shocked by his *appearance* (which his feeling has made him forget) that she would have swooned away, no matter what might be the "nature" of the circumstances which had caused him so to neglect appearances, if he had not immediately had the good *nature* to clothe himself in order to alleviate her fright. For Mrs. Deborah "vowed," we are told, "she had never beheld a man without his coat," and in the innocent word "vowed" lies another sly play upon nature and appearance, for one may "vow" much in keeping up appearances. More ironically explicit, her "pure eyes" are "pure" as far as appearances go— "pure," for instance, as she adjusts her hair before the looking glass—but with a dubious purity inasmuch as she cannot see the innocent helplessness and human difficulty of the circumstances in front of her.

Let us remain a moment longer with this scene, to see if "nature" defines itself more fully in the context. Mr. Allworthy's "good-nature had always the ascendant *in his mind*." His good nature, then,—his "sentiments of compassion," as the next phrase qualifies it—is neither raw, untrained feeling, nor is it mental calculation divorced from feeling, but it is feeling as a quality of *mind*. It is civilized feeling, social feeling, intelligent feeling, and it takes total possession of the Squire, making him forgetful of forms and appearances; in other words, there is nothing either covert or to be "exposed" about the Squire, since feeling has been committed to the mind and to the total personality, open to view. Against this intelligential feeling is set an abstruse mental calculation on Mrs. Deborah's part (would we be going too far if we suggested that the fact that her master was a wealthy widower had anything to do with Mrs. Deborah's performances before the mirror?); and though the calculation takes place in Mrs. Deborah's mind, we know that it is *unintelligent* (in the world of this book, though possibly not in the world of *Moll Flanders*), for it makes her engage in a stupid reversal of values, makes her—because of her stupidity of feeling—a comic object, an object of laughter. Later in the novel we see many examples of the same calculative shrewdness and the same stupidity of feeling (the Blifil brothers, Thwackum and Square, young Blifil, Mrs. Western, Lady Bellaston, and a host of others), and always such shrewdness is made to appear, not intelligent, but unintelligent, because it is not informed with natural feeling, and because it succeeds in corrupting natural feeling. At the opposite end of the spectrum is Tom himself, all feeling and little calculative shrewdness whatever. Tom's "mind," indeed, does not seem to operate very frequently at all. And yet, as his career progresses, we become aware that—in this particular world of values—natural feeling is itself *intelligent;* for Tom, after all, does the "right" things, in the long run the "intelligent" things, in acting from his heart and his instincts, as compared with the stupidity of the shrewd and calculative persons.

With these correlations between intelligence and feeling, we may return once more to the scene of the finding of the babe in Mr. Allworthy's bed, to discover in the drawing of the picture a style which contrives to make of the subject, "nature," a conceptual subject (just as the dramatic handling of plot has been constantly under the governance of concept or idea), a comprehensible "idea of human nature," a subject intelligible to the mind. And here, for the sake of emphasis and historical comparison, we may suggest the difference between Fielding's outlook or *Weltanschauung* and the modern world view underlying prevalent philosophies of despair: Fielding looks upon humankind and all its proclivities as offering an ideal of intelligent order; whereas two world wars and the prospect of a third, universally disintegrating, offer to the modern view a notion of humankind as governed by irrational motives, self destructive, incognizant of what civilized order might mean. Our own "nature," as representing humanity, we see as incalculable, shadowy, dark, capable of inexplicable explosions. Fielding's "nature" offers itself not as submerged and incalculable profundities, but as wholly accessible to the intelligence, and his style reflects this attitude. The foundling is described thus:

> . . . he [Squire Allworthy] beheld an infant, wrapt up in some coarse linen, in a sweet and profound sleep, between his sheets. . . . He then

> rang his bell . . . and in the mean time was so eager in contemplating the beauty of innocence, appearing in those lively colours with which infancy and sleep always display it, that his thoughts were too much engaged . . .

The description is generalized. This is any sleeping infant. The generalized image of the child immediately equates with a conception of the meaning of infancy in general—"the beauty of innocence"; while the qualifying phrase—"appearing in those lively colours with which infancy and sleep *always* display it"—again accents the general, the inclusive, the universal, the timeless aspect of infancy, an aspect yielding itself entirely to conceptualization (as if sleeping infancy would always inspire these reflections and impulses in men, even in a concentration camp). In other words, what is illustrated in the style of even so incidental a passage is the thorough *intelligibility* of "nature," its yielding of itself to a concept supposed to have universal and timeless applicableness. What can be recomposed wholly as idea has the implied status of objectivity and universality; for all civilized men can, assumedly, share an idea, as they cannot share their shadowy, indeterminate subjective feelings as individuals. "Nature," as conceived in *Tom Jones* and as illustrated in the character of the hero, is that "nature" which all men presumably share, and the mark of its universality is its intelligibility. Those characters in the book in whom "nature" has been perverted by the distortion of "appearance" are in the long run social outcasts, or die bad deaths, or are made to suffer a violent shaking-up in order to bring their "nature" out into the open where it can enter into the intelligible universal order.

In *Clarissa Harlowe,* the "plot" appears under the aspect of fatality, as a movement from one point on a circle, around the circle and back to its beginning: from Clarissa's passion for purity, through its exaltation as a passion for death, down to the closing of the circle where purity and death become one. Not fatality but Fortune rules events in *Tom Jones*—that Chance which throws up event and counterevent in inexhaustible variety. Tom himself is a foundling, a child of chance. In the end, because he is blessed with good nature, he is blessed with good fortune as well. Mr. Allworthy, we are told, "might well be called the favorite of both Nature and Fortune": from Nature "he derived an agreeable person, a sound constitution, a sane understanding, and a benevolent heart," and from Fortune "the inheritance of one of the largest estates in the county." Good nature "had always the *ascendant* in his mind": a metaphor derived from astrology, the science of the influence of the stars over man's life and fortune. The reader might be interested in tracing other metaphors of this kind in Fielding's diction, and in relating them to his view of human life. By chance or fortune, acting occultly, the curtain falls down in Molly's room, exposing the philosopher Square. An obsolete meaning of the word "square" is that of "rule" or "principle." Significant in Square's situation in this incident is Fortune's or accident's treacherous play with "squared" (straight-edged) principles, philosopher's rules, dogmatic formulas; for nothing that the philosopher Square might say, to "square" his position, would alter the ignominy of his exposure. Fortune, capricious as it is, has some occult, deeply hidden association with Nature (in Fielding); therefore, in the long run, good nature does infallibly lead to good fortune, bad nature to bad fortune.

The signature of Fortune's favor is wealth. Tom's blessings, at the end of the book, are not dissociable from the fact that he is Allworthy's heir: this is the center and fulcrum of all the rest of his good fortune. In *Moll Flanders,* the signature of the favor of Providence was also wealth, but the wealth had to be grubbed for with insect-like persistence and concentration; to obtain wealth, even with the help of Providence, one had to work for it and keep one's mind on it. In *Clarissa Harlowe,* again, wealth was to be worked for and schemed for: the Harlowe males work as hard and concentratedly, after their fashion, to acquire Solmes's wealth and the title it will buy for them, as Moll does for her gold watches, her bales, cargoes, and plantations. But in *Tom Jones,* wealth is not got by work or calculation or accumulation or careful investment. Blifil, who works shrewdly to obtain it, fails of his ends; Tom, who never thinks of it, is richly endowed with it. The benefits of money are as candidly faced by Fielding as they are by Defoe, or as they will later be by Jane Austen: people need money in order to live pleasantly, and though to be good and to be in love and loved are fine things, the truly harmonious and full life is possible only when one is both good and rich. Fielding is a man of the same century as Defoe and Richardson, the same society and culture (in the anthropological sense of "culture"), but his outlook toward the getting of wealth is radically different. V. S. Pritchett has described one eighteenth-century attitude in this matter: "Fortune," he says,

> the speculator's goddess—not money—pours out its plenty from the
> South Sea bubbles and the slave trade in the eighteenth century. Sacks
> of gold descend from heaven by fantastic parachute, and are stored in
> the gloating caves, and trade is still spacious and piratical.[4]

Obviously these statements have not much applicability to the attitudes of
Defoe or Richardson, but they do cast some light on Fielding's. Also,
we find in Fielding the more traditional, aristocratic attitude toward
wealth: one simply has wealth—say, in landed properties, like Squire
Allworthy—and how one got it is Fortune's business, a mysterious dona-
tion of free gifts to the worthy. But what we are fundamentally interested
in here is the coherence of this attitude with other elements in the book:
that is, the aesthetic coherence and integrity of the whole. We have considered the plot under the aspect of the surprise plays of Fortune, occultly working out its game with Nature, and it is clear that Tom's un-
sought blessing of financial good fortune in the end is consistent with,
all-of-a-piece with, the other activities of Fortune that are exhibited in
the action.

There is a certain distortion involved in the attempt to represent a
book by a visual figure, but sometimes a visual figure, with all its limitations, helps us to grasp a book's structure. We have spoken of *Clarissa*
as making the simple figure of a circle, a figure of fatality. We may think
of *Tom Jones* as a complex architectural figure, a Palladian palace perhaps: immensely variegated, as Fortune throws out its surprising encounters; elegant and suavely intelligent in its details (many of Fielding's sentences are little complex "plots" in themselves, where the reader
must follow a suspended subject through a functional ornament of complications—qualifying dependent clauses and prepositional phrases and
eloquent pauses—to the dramatic predication or denouement); but simply,
spaciously, generously, firmly grounded in Nature, and domed with an
ample magnitude where Fortune shows herself as beneficent artisan. The
structure is all out in the light of intelligibility; air circulates around and
over it and through it. Since Fielding's time, the world has found itself
not quite so intelligible. Though intelligence has been analytically applied to the physical nature of things in our time much more thoroughly
than eighteenth-century scientific techniques allowed, our world is tun-
neled by darkness and invisibility, darknesses of infantile traumata in the

[4] *Ibid.*, p. 110.

human mind, neurotic incalculabilities in personal and social action, fission in the atom, explosion in the heavens. We may feel, then, that there was much—in the way of doubt and darkness—to which Fielding was insensitive. Nevertheless, our respect is commanded by the integrity and radiance of the building that he did build.

ON *Tristram Shandy*

In Sterne's deceptively frivolous, deceptively ingenuous novel *Tristram Shandy*, a new type of structure makes its appearance, a type that is of singular importance for the development of the modern novel. This is a structure modeled on the operative character of consciousness as such. Sterne conceives the behavior of consciousness in terms not of logical continuities but of the spontaneous association of ideas. The word "structure" implies controlled form and a unity, and it would seem that mere association of one thing with another could issue in nothing but haphazard multiplicity. Sterne's interest, however, is that of a novelist and not that of a theoretical psychologist. That is, his concern is to create a world. The world that he creates has the form of a mind. It may perhaps help us to grasp the notion of a structure of this sort if we think of the mind in the figure of one of Leibnitz's monads, those elemental units of energy that have "mirrors but no windows": the mirroring capacity of the unit makes of it a microcosm of the universe, in that all things are reflected in it; and yet, because it lacks "windows," it is a discrete world in itself, formally defined only by internal relationships; while the reflections in its "mirrors" have a free energetic interplay unique for this monad —this mind—differentiating it from all others at the same time that it is representative of all others.

The novelty of the method employed in *Tristram Shandy* becomes striking as we review the other novels we have read in terms of the importance of action or plot as an organizing factor in each, and as we consider the relative unimportance of plot in *Tristram Shandy*. *Don Quixote* and *The Pilgrim's Progress* trace the episodes in a hero's quest or mission; the hero goes somewhere to do something or find something, and the manifest concrete substance of these books lies in the actions he engages in along the way. Similarly, *Moll Flanders* is plotted upon a series of episodic actions, the whole held together formally as Moll's biography. With *Clarissa Harlowe* and *Tom Jones,* action takes on a more unitary —as distinguished from episodic—character: the action of the one book (at least as conceived by Richardson) is that of tragic drama, the action of the other that of comic drama, and obviously both books are unthinkable except with reference to plot complication, reversal, and denouement. What is the "action" of *Tristram Shandy?*

Presumably, like that of *Moll Flanders,* it is episodic and biographical: *The Life and Opinions of Tristram Shandy, Gent.* is the full title. But Tristram is not born until a third of the way through the book; not christened until fifty pages later; the story is more than half over when we are told that he has reached the age of five (scarcely yet the age for "opinions"); is two-thirds finished by the time he is put into breeches; suddenly he appears as a gentleman on his travels in France; and the novel ends with an episode that concerns not Tristram but Uncle Toby. Those sporadic flickers of narrative in which Tristram is seen in chronological circumstance as the hero-in-action (if the hero *can* be thought of as "acting" while he is being born, christened, circumcised, etc.) evidently do not serve 'the same purposes of narrative that we have observed elsewhere; they are, rather, if they are anything, an intentional mockery of "action." Chronological and plot continuity are, then, not definitively organizational to *Tristram Shandy.* The fact appears extraordinary when we stop for a moment to consider how naturally, habitually, almost stubbornly we tend to think of all experience as somehow automatically dished up to us, like a molded pudding, in the form of chronology; and how this tendency to see experience as actions related to each other undisturbedly by the stages of the clock and the calendar leads us to expect of fiction that it will provide a similar unidirectional action, or series of episodes, taking place chronologically. *Tristram Shandy* pays lip service to this expectation—at least by allowing Tristram to be born before he is christened, to be put into breeches before he goes traveling in France —but so mockingly as to make us aware that Sterne is engaged in deliberate demolition of chronological sequences and (inasmuch as our notions of "time" and "action" are inextricably related) deliberate destruction of the common notion of "action."

But this is the negative aspect only, and if this were all there were to Sterne's concern with the relationship of time and human experience, then the squiggly lines he draws in Chapter XL of Book VI, to show the haphazard progress of his novel, could represent just that: its haphazard-ness, its lack of form. But it is anything but haphazard or formless. Obey-ing formal laws of its own, it is as skillfully and delicately constructed as *Tom Jones*. Having ruled out plot chronology as a model of the way ex-perience presents itself, Sterne offers another model: that of the opera-tions of consciousness, where time is exploded, where any time-past may be time-present, or several times-past be concurrently present at once, and where clock-time appears only intermittently as a felt factor. As Cervantes' *Don Quixote* offers fiction as many models as it can use, so it offers this one also. In the episode of Quixote's descent into the cave of Montesinos, the time of dream and of poetry, the ancient heroic time of Montesinos and Durandarte, the modern time of coinage and "new dimity petticoats," and the actual hours of the descent and of the Knight's sleep, merge as one time.

But what is to give unity to this model, if we cannot plot the hero's adventures on clock and calendar in order to know when they be-gin and when they are ended, and if we do not, after all, have a hero to "act" in the ordinary sense—no time, no hero, no action? The unity of any novel may be described on several different levels; we may speak of the unifying function of theme, or of plot, or of symbolism, or of other ele-ments that appear to have superior importance. The total structural unity of a work does not yield itself to a simple description, but only to a quite lengthy analysis of the complex interrelationships of all major elements. At the most conspicuous level, the unity of *Tristram Shandy* is the unity of Tristram's—the narrator's—consciousness.[1] This is a representative kind of unity, psychologically true to the way in which experience appears to all of us to have its most rudimentary unity; for though clock-time may seem to cut experience into units, these are arbitrary units that melt into each other unrecognizably in the individual's self-feeling; and though we may assume that a shared experience has a certain definite, common form and description for those who share it, yet we know that, as the experi-ence is absorbed into and transformed by the individual consciousness, it is something very different for different people, and that its form and "oneness" or unity are felt most concretely only as the experience is stamped by the character of the individual consciousness.

[1] This point of view with regard to the unity of the work is developed by Benjamin H. Lehman in his essay on Sterne, "Of Time, Personality and the Author," in *Studies in Comedy* (Berkeley: University of California Press, 1940).

Sterne's project in *Tristram Shandy* was not to have a parallel, in the work of a major novelist, until Proust wrote *Remembrance of Things Past.* Though each of these books, so far separated in time and in local culture, carries the highly singular and special flavor of its historical circumstances and of the original genius of its author, they have a strong kinship in subject and plan and quality. Each makes of the narrator's consciousness its subject matter; the artistry of each lies in the "objectifying" of this "subjective" material in its own right and for its own sake, so that the "subjective" becomes an object to be manipulated and designed and given aesthetic form according to laws inherent in it; and each creates an Alice-in-Wonderland world that is unique and inimitable because the individual consciousness is itself unique and inimitable. We do not think of Proust's work as the story of Swann, or the story of Charlus or of Albertine or even of Marcel, or as the history of a transmogrification of social classes and manners in the late nineteenth century, although it is these and other stories and histories as well. Nor do we think of *Tristram Shandy* as a series of character sketches of Uncle Toby and Walter Shandy and Corporal Trim and the Widow Wadman, or as a mosaic of sentimental and slapstick anecdotes, some gracefully pathetic, some uproarious, and all peppered with off-color puns and *doubles-entendres,* the indulgences of a neurotic clergyman—although it is these and still other things. We think of *Tristram Shandy,* as we do of Proust's *Remembrance of Things Past,* as a mind in which the local world has been steeped and dissolved and fantastically re-formed, so that it issues brand new. Still more definitive of the potentialities of Sterne's method, as these have been realized in a great modern work, is James Joyce's *Finnegans Wake,* where the hero's dream swallows and recomposes all time in its belly of mirrors, and where the possibilities lying in Sterne's creative play with linguistic associations—his use of language as a dynamic system in itself, a magic system for the "raising" of new perceptions as a magician's formulas "raise" spirits—are enormously developed. Joyce himself points out the parallel. In the second paragraph of *Finnegans Wake,* "Sir Tristram, violer d'amores," arrives from over the sea "to wielderfight his penisolate war" in "Laurens County," and we know—among these puns —that we are not in wholly unfamiliar territory.

Sterne's project, like Proust's, was to analyze and represent in his novel the creative process; and that Sterne should be the first practitioner of what is called the technique of the "stream of consciousness" in fictional writing is consonant with the kind of subject he set himself. Our fictional center of gravity is not a happening or confluence of happenings nor a character or concourse of characters under emotional or moral or social aspects of interest; it consists rather in the endlessly fertile rhythms of a consciousness, as those rhythms explore the comic ironies of a quest for order among the humdrum freaks of birth and paternity and place and time and language. In reading *Tristram Shandy,* we are never allowed to forget that the activity of creation, as an activity of forming perceptions and maneuvering them into an expressive order, *is itself the subject;* the technique does not allow us to forget it—for let alone the harum-scarum tricks with printer's ink, the narrator plunges at us in apostrophes, flirts his addresses at us with "Dear Sir" or "Dear Madam," explodes into the middle of a disquisition or a scene in defiance of time, space, and logic. Uncle Toby, pursuing the theory of projectiles in the pages of half a dozen military authors, becomes involved among parabolas, parameters, semiparameters, conic sections, and angles of incidence, and Tristram suddenly cries out,

> O my uncle;—fly—fly, fly from it as from a serpent . . . Alas! 'twill exasperate thy symptoms,—check thy perspirations—evaporate thy spirits—waste thy animal strength,—dry up thy radical moisture, bring thee into a costive habit of body,—impair thy health,—and hasten all the infirmities of thy old age.—O my uncle! my uncle Toby.

Toby's investigations were conducted some years before Tristram was born. It is as if Tristram were sitting in a moving-picture theater, watching on a most candid and intimate screen the performance of his progenitors. He is struck suddenly with admiration or consternation, stands up, waves his arms, applauds, boos, wrings his hands, sheds tears, sits down and tickles the lady next to him.

We have said that the unity of *Tristram Shandy* is the unity of the narrator's consciousness; but—without the discipline afforded by chronology, or an objective "narrative line," or a moral thesis of some sort—what is the principle of selection by which the contents of that consciousness present themselves? Sterne himself puts the question, in Chapter XXIII, Book III, and as he states it, it is the problem of every novelist. In setting up a certain body of human experience novelistically, what should come first? what last? what should follow or precede what? Should not everything appear at once and in fusion, inasmuch as this is the way the author's consciousness grasps it in its fullest truth? But the novel itself is an artifact subjected to time law; words follow words and pages follow pages in temporal sequence, necessarily imposing temporal sequence upon the material; everything cannot be said at once, although this disability may seem to injure the wholeness and instantaneousness of the material as the author grasps it. Trim announces to Toby that Dr. Slop is in the kitchen making a bridge. " 'Tis very obliging in him," Toby says, mistaking the bridge (meant for Tristram's nose) for a drawbridge. The author must elucidate Toby's error; but when? Right now, at the moment Toby makes the remark? But the goings-on upstairs in Mrs. Shandy's bedchamber are of the greatest consequence now. Later, then, among the anecdotes of Toby's amours with Widow Wadman? Or in the middle of Toby's campaigns on the bowling green? All of these circumstances press upon the author at once, and are, in the atemporal time of consciousness, contemporaneous. By what principle of selection is he to subject them to the time demands of the novel?

> O ye powers! [Sterne cries] . . . which enable mortal man to tell a story worth the hearing—that kindly shew him, where he is to begin it —and where he is to end it—what he is to put into it—and what he is to leave out— . . .
>
> I beg and beseech you . . . that wherever in any part of your dominions it so falls out, that three several roads meet in one point, as they have done just here—that at least you set up a guide-post in the centre of them, in mere charity, to direct an uncertain devil which of the three he is to take.

Sterne's uncertainty is not really uncertainty at all. His cry of authorial distress is one of the many false scents he lays down humoristically in order to give to his work the appearance of artlessness and primitive spontaneity. At the same time it points up the paradox of all novel writing, the paradox of which Sterne is very much aware: the antagonism between the time sequences which the novel imposes, and the instantaneous wholeness of the image of complex human experience which the novel attempts to present. Sterne has his guidepost in the philosopher John Locke, and it is according to Locke's theory of the human understanding that he finds his way down all the several roads that are continuously meeting in one point in *Tristram Shandy,* or, conversely, we might say that it is with the guidance of Locke that he contrives continually to get

his roads crossed. To the French Academician, M. Suard, he said in conversation that "those who knew the philosopher (Locke) well enough to
recognize his presence and his influence would find them or sense them on
every page, in every line." Locke had attempted to explain the genesis
of ideas from sensation. Simple sensations produce simple ideas of those
sensations; associated sensations produce associated ideas of sensations, a
process which becomes immensely complicated with the accretion of other
associations of this kind. Besides the capacity of the mind to form ideas
from sensations, it has the capacity of reflection. By reflection upon ideas
acquired from sensation, it is able to juggle these into new positions and
relationships, forming what we call "abstract ideas." Thus the whole body
of logical and inferential "knowledge" is built up, through association,
from the simple primary base of sensation. There are two aspects of this
theory which are of chief importance in Sterne. The one is the Sensational
aspect, the other the Associative.[2] From the notion of sensation as the
prime source of knowledge and as the primitive character of experience,
arises that doctrine of "sensibility" or "sentimentality" which Sterne made
famous: the doctrine that value lies in *feeling* as such. With this we shall
concern ourselves later. But at this point let us see how the associative aspect of Locke's theory appears structurally in *Tristram Shandy*.

Tristram starts out on the first page with a disquisition on the need
of parents to mind what they are about when they are in the act of begetting. Why? Because their associated sensations at that moment have a
determining effect upon the nature and destiny of Homunculus. (Note the
manner in which, from the beginning, Sterne's imagination *concretizes*
an abstraction, here an abstraction of eugenical theory: the "humours
and dispositions which were then uppermost" in father and mother suf-
fuse, somewhat like a glandular tincture, the "animal spirits" passed on
to the son; and the metaphor hinted by "animal spirits" becomes instantly
a picture of unharnessed horses—"Away they go cluttering like hey-go
mad." This concreteness of imagination is one of the secrets of Sterne's
surprises and of the Alice-in-Wonderland character of his world, for it
is with a shock of astonished and delighted recognition that we suddenly
see the pedantic abstraction taken literally and transformed into physi-
ology, complete with hooves, feathers, or haberdashery.) What went wrong
with Tristram's begetting was that Mrs. Shandy, accustomed to associate

[2] These observations are based on Herbert Read's discussion of Sterne in *The Sense
of Glory* (New York: Harcourt, Brace & Company, Inc., 1930).

the winding of the clock with the marital act (like Pavlov's dogs and the dinner bell), missed the association appropriate at the moment, and in speaking of it to Mr. Shandy distracted his attention and prepared for poor Homunculus nine long months of disordered nerves and melancholy dreams (a pre-Freudian comment on the assumed bliss of this period). Mrs. Shandy's remark about the clock leads then, by association of ideas, to a portrait of Uncle Toby, typically "wiping away a tear"; for it was to Uncle Toby that Tristram owed the information as to the circumstances of his begetting. Again, by association with conception, origin, *the egg*, we are led, in Chapter IV, into a discussion of Horace's dictum on the technique of beginning a literary work: "as Horace says, *ab Ovo*"— which Horace did not say but which nevertheless serves as an apology for Sterne's own technique; thence to an explanation of Mrs. Shandy's unfortunate association between the winding of the clock and the marital act—"Which strange combination of ideas," says Sterne,

> the sagacious Locke, who certainly understood the nature of these things better than most men, affirms to have produced more wry actions than all other sources of prejudice whatsoever.

The explanation leads to a determination of the date of Tristram's geniture and the manner of his birth, which involves a digression into the history of the midwife, which in turn involves a digression into the history of the parson Yorick, who was responsible for establishing the midwife in her vocation; and the history of Yorick necessitates first a description of his horse (before we can get back to the midwife), but the parson's horse recalls Rosinante, and that steed, that belonged to a famous gentleman with a hobby, sets Sterne off on the subject of hobbyhorses in general, which leads to . . . (When are we going to learn the circumstances of Tristram's birth?) Sterne's comment on "the sagacious Locke," who understood the "strange combination of ideas" to which men's brains are liable, indicates the method here. It is precisely in the *strangeness* of the combinations or associations that Sterne finds the contour of his subject, the logic of its grotesquerie and the logic of its gaiety. At the same time, he is in perfect control of the "combinations," as we are slyly reminded again and again; for we *do* come back to the midwife.

Nor, in terms of total structure, is Mrs. Shandy's remark about the clock, in the first chapter, quite as irresponsible as it would seem. In this odd world, where the methodical Mr. Shandy winds up the house clock, together with "some other little family concernments," on the first Sunday night of every month, time is of the utmost importance and the utmost unimportance.[3] Let us illustrate. In Chapter IX of Book IV, Toby and Mr. Shandy are conversing as they walk down the stairs, and from Chapter IX to Chapter XIV we are kept, presumably, in the chronological span that covers their descent from the top to the bottom of the staircase. Chapter IX starts out,

> What a chapter of chances, said my father, turning himself about upon the first landing, as he and my uncle Toby were going downstairs—

and there follows a page of conversation between the two. With the beginning of Chapter X, Sterne reminds us that we are still on the staircase and have not got to the bottom yet.

> Is it not a shame to make two chapters of what passed in going down one pair of stairs? for we are got no farther yet than to the first landing, and there are fifteen more steps down to the bottom; and for aught I know, as my father and my uncle Toby are in a talking humour, there may be as many chapters as steps: . . .

a remark which obviously calls for the insertion here of his "chapter upon chapters" (which he has promised us, along with his chapter on noses, his chapter on knots, and his chapter on whiskers). Hence, by Chapter XI, we are not yet to the bottom of the staircase.

> We shall bring all things to rights, said my father, setting his foot upon the first step from the landing.—

With Chapter XII, Susannah appears below.

> —And how does your mistress? cried my father, taking the same step over again from the landing, and calling to Susannah, whom he saw passing by the foot of the stairs with a huge pin-cushion in her hand— how does your mistress? As well, said Susannah, tripping by, but without looking up, as can be expected.—What a fool am I! said my father, drawing his leg back again—let things be as they will, brother Toby, 'tis ever the precise answer—And how is the child, pray?—No answer.

[3] Sterne's treatment of time, as discussed here, is central to the essay by B. H. Lehman, cited above.

>   And where is Dr. Slop? added my father, raising his voice aloud, and
> looking over the ballusters—Susannah was out of hearing.
>   Of all the riddles of a married life, said my father, crossing the
> landing in order to set his back against the wall, whilst he propounded
> it to my uncle Toby—of all the puzzling riddles . . .

In Chapter XIII, Sterne desperately appeals to the critic to step in and
get Uncle Toby and Mr. Shandy off the stairs for him. Obviously, what
has been presented to us in this bit of fantasy is the incongruity between
the clock-time which it will take to get the two conversationalists down
the stairs, and the atemporal time—the "timeless time"—of the imagination, where the words of Toby and Mr. Shandy echo in their plenitude,
where their stances and gestures are traced in precise images (as a leg is
lifted or a foot withdrawn from the step), and where also the resonances
of related subjects (such as chance and chapters and critics) intertwine
freely with the conversation of Toby and Walter; and we are made
aware of the paradox of which Sterne is so actively aware, and which he
uses as a selective principle and as a structural control: the paradox of
man's existence both in time and out of time—his existence in the time
of the clock, and his existence in the apparent timelessness of consciousness (what has been called, by philosophers, "duration," to distinguish it
from clock-marked time).
      But the time fantasy still piles up, in Chapter XIII, in odder con-
tours. We are reminded, by Walter's interchange with Susannah, that this
is the day of Tristram's birth; and the autobiographer Tristram is also
suddenly reminded of the passage of time.

> I am this month one whole year older than I was this time twelve-
> month; and having got, as you perceive, almost into the middle of
> my fourth volume—and no farther than to my first day's life—'tis
> demonstrative that I have three hundred and sixty-four days more
> life to write just now, than when I first set out; so that instead of ad-
> vancing, as a common writer, in my work with what I have been doing
> at it—on the contrary, I am just thrown so many volumes back . . .
> at this rate I should just live 364 times faster than I should write—

—a piece of mathematical calculation which the reader will follow as he
is able. Again, what the fantasy suggests is the paradoxical temporal and
yet atemporal status of consciousness, whose experience is at once past ex-

perience, as marked by the passage of time, and present experience, inasmuch as it is present within the mind. These considerations of time may seem abstract as set down here, but we are simplifying Sterne's performance so that we may see it structurally and schematically. Actually, what his acute time sense provides is never the dullness and ponderousness of abstraction, but the utmost concreteness of visualization—a concreteness which we have seen in the descent of Toby and Mr. Shandy down the stairs. Mr. Shandy turns himself about upon the first landing; he sets his foot upon the first step from the landing; he takes the same step over again; he draws his leg back; he looks over the balusters at Susannah; he crosses the landing to set his back against the wall. These are Sterne's typical time markings, showing the procession of stance and gesture, but they are also the delicately observed details of the dramatic picture, which bring it alive and concrete before our eyes, and which make of the characters of *Tristram Shandy* creatures who, once known, remain unfadingly, joyously vivid to our imagination.

It is because of Sterne's acute awareness of time passage and of the conundrums of the time sense, that he is also so acutely aware of the concrete moment; or, conversely, we could say that it is because of his awareness of the preciousness of the concrete moment, that he is so acutely aware of time, which destroys the moment. In the eighth chapter of the final book, he engages in an apostrophe.

> Time wastes too fast: every letter I trace tells me with what rapidity Life follows my pen; the days and hours of it, more precious, my dear Jenny! than the rubies about thy neck, are flying over our heads like light clouds of a windy day, never to return more—everything presses on—whilst thou art twisting that lock,—see! it grows grey; and every time I kiss thy hand to bid adieu, and every absence which follows it, are preludes to that eternal separation which we are shortly to make.—

Which calls for a new "chapter" of a single line—"Now, for what the world thinks of that ejaculation—I would not give a groat." The philosopher, with his head full of time, is never allowed to sail off into abstraction; he keeps his eye on Jenny twisting her lock. For it is not in abstract speculation about time, but precisely in Jenny's gesture as she twists her lock, that the time sense finds profoundest significance; or in Trim's gesture as he drops his hat on the kitchen floor to illustrate to Obadiah and Susannah the catastrophe of mortal passage into oblivion.

Let us stay with Trim's hat for a moment, for it will illustrate for us another and equally important structural irony in *Tristram Shandy*.

> —"Are we not here now;" continued the corporal, "and are we not"—(dropping his hat plump upon the ground—and pausing, before he pronounced the word)—"gone! in a moment?" The descent of the hat was as if a heavy lump of clay had been kneaded into the crown of it.—Nothing could have expressed the sentiment of mortality, of which it was the type and fore-runner, like it,—his hand seemed to vanish from under it,—it fell dead,—the corporal's eye fixed upon it, as upon a corpse,—and Susannah burst into a flood of tears.
>
> Now—ten thousand, and ten thousand times ten thousand (for matter and motion are infinite) are the ways by which a hat may be dropped upon the ground, without any effect.—Had he flung it, or thrown it, or cast it, or skimmed it, or squirted it, or let it slip or fall in any possible direction under heaven, . . . the effect upon the heart had been lost.
>
> Ye who govern this mighty world and its mighty concerns with the engines of eloquence . . . meditate—meditate, I beseech you, upon Trim's hat.

What, of course, gives the scene that incongruity in which humor lies, is the use of Trim's gesture with his hat as a symbol of mortality: that is, the equating of the trivial with the serious, the unimportant with the important. Coleridge, speculating on the "one humorific point common to all that can be called humorous," found that common point to lie in

> a certain reference to the general and the universal, by which the finite great is brought into identity with the little, or the little with the finite great, so as to make both nothing in comparison with the infinite. The little is made great, and the great little, in order to destroy both; because all is equal in contrast with the infinite.[4]

It is indeed Sterne to whom Coleridge immediately refers for illustration of the point. Trim's gesture with his hat is one among innumerable instances in the book. It is the "finite little" brought into identity with the

---

[4] *Miscellaneous Criticism* (Cambridge: Harvard University Press, 1936), p. 444. Herbert Read, in his discussion of Sterne in *The Sense of Glory*, analyzes Sterne's humor in these terms.

"finite great" (and the references to tens of thousands and the "mighty world" domesticate the "finite great" in the Shandy kitchen and in the even smaller quarters under the crown of Trim's hat), making of both "nothing in comparison with the infinite."

If we are accustomed to think of "humor" as the type of the comic strip, we may feel that Coleridge's definition of humor, and its application to *Tristram Shandy,* are much too serious—too "deep"—to have relevance to the funny. How can we laugh, if our minds are supposed to be oriented to the "finite great" and the "infinite"? It has been said, very wisely, that "comedy is a serious matter"; and though we are not speaking of "comedy" here (for we have reserved this term for dramatic writing of the order of *Tom Jones,* which is constructed on traditional principles of comic drama), but of "humor," we may say that humor, too, is a serious matter. Nor would it be improbable that, in analyzing the source of humor in the best comic strips, the observer would find that Coleridge's definition was applicable. (Needless to say, we do not laugh when we are analytically intent on understanding *why* we laugh. The laughter has come first.) It is a definition of humor that is fertile also for an understanding of certain neglected aspects of modern writers, such as Dostoevski and Kafka, who, though deeply "serious" writers, are at the same time great humorists; and our understanding of the "seriousness" of Sterne's humor can prepare us for a larger understanding of those authors nearer our time, who are concerned seriously with the problems of our time, but who are sensitive also to the sources of laughter.

Let us take one more passage to illustrate our meaning. We have said that we would need to consider rather more carefully that influential aspect of Locke's theory of the understanding which is its Sensationalism —its grounding of knowledge in sensation—and of Sterne's indebtedness to Locke for his doctrine of "sensibility" or "sentimentality," which measures the value of experience in terms of its feeling-fulness, the experience that is full of feeling ("sensation," "sensibility," "sentiment") being the valuable experience. We shall not take one of the famous "sentimental" passages—such as that concerning Uncle Toby and the fly, or the death of Le Fever. Tristram's encounter with Maria (Chapter XXIV, Book IX) will do. What we shall look for here is the equating of "great" and trivial, which resonates in humor because of the strange balance contrived between these incommensurables. Tristram is on his way to Moulins, and hears a flute player on the road.

—They were the sweetest notes I ever heard; and I instantly let down the fore-glass to hear them more distinctly—'Tis Maria; said the postillion, observing I was listening—Poor Maria, continued he (leaning his body on one side to let me see her, for he was in a line betwixt us), is sitting upon a bank playing her vespers upon her pipe, with her little goat beside her.

The young fellow utter'd this with an accent and a look so perfectly in tune to a feeling heart, that I instantly made a vow, I would give him a four-and-twenty sous piece, when I got to Moulins—

—And who is poor Maria? said I.

The love and piety of all the villages around us; said the postillion —it is but three years ago, that the sun did not shine upon so fair, so quick-witted and amiable a maid; and better fate did Maria deserve, than to have her Banns forbid, by the intrigues of the curate of the parish who published them—

He was going on, when Maria, who had made a short pause, put the pipe to her mouth, and began the air again—they were the same notes;—yet were ten times sweeter: It is the evening service to the Virgin, said the young man—but who has taught her to play it—or how she came by her pipe, no one knows; we think that heaven has assisted her in both; for ever since she has been unsettled in her mind, it seems her only consolation—she has never once had the pipe out of her hand, but plays that service upon it almost night and day . . .

We had got up by this time almost to the bank where Maria was sitting: she was in a thin white jacket, with her hair, all but two tresses, drawn up into a silk-net, with a few olive leaves twisted a little fantastically on one side—she was beautiful; and if ever I felt the full force of an honest heart-ache, it was the moment I saw her—

This is the adumbration of a pathetic, a "sentimental" story, in the manner of Cervantes' pastorals (and Sterne apostrophizes Cervantes at the beginning of the chapter). What comes under the denomination of the "finite great" in it is the pathos, the communicated feeling or sensation of pity (the postillion speaks "in tune to a feeling heart," and Tristram feels "the full force of an honest heart-ache") over Maria's love tragedy and madness, and the inference of Heaven's interest in her sad career. But the sketch ends suddenly on a different note. Under the spell of Maria's melancholy cadences, Tristram has leaped out of the coach and seated himself beside her on the bank, between Maria and her goat.

> Maria look'd wistfully for some time at me, and then at her goat—
> and then at me—and then at her goat again, and so on, alternately—
> —Well, Maria, said I softly—What resemblance do you find?

The typical goatishness here, and the "sportive pattern of alternation" [5] (with Maria looking at Tristram, then at the goat, then at Tristram—a pattern which is one of the distinguishing traits of Sterne's style) illustrate that term of the humorous equation which is the "finite little," the trivial, the whimsical, and which, capping off the full-blowing cumulus of Maria's pathos, asks finite judgment to suspend its intoxicated action for a moment in a healthy smile at its own potency for exaggeration, hysteria, and error. Sterne wrote to a hesitant admirer, who had objected to his detailed treatment of Dr. Slop's fall in the mud,

> I will reconsider Slops fall & my too Minute Account of it—but in general I am persuaded that the happiness of the Cervantic humour arises from this very thing—of describing silly and trifling Events, with the Circumstantial Pomp of great Ones—perhaps this is Overloaded— & I can soon ease it.

Happily, he did not "ease it," but left Dr. Slop in full benefit of his original tumble, "unwiped, unappointed, unannealed." Sterne's insight into the nature of the humorous situation, as expressed in the letter, is simply the immediate technical version of Coleridge's later and more philosophical analysis of humor that we have cited; for to identify the "finite great" with the "finite little" becomes, in the actual handling of situation, a description of "silly and trifling Events, with the Circumstantial Pomp of Great Ones"—or the converse of this, as in the story of Toby and the fly, where the trifling event is treated with the grand diction and gesture and the palpitating feeling of pompous circumstance. Sterne has been taken to task, many times over, for his indulgence in pruriency, his slips into indecency, his tendency—as in the story of Maria—to lapse into goatishness and spoil a softly solemn, tear-jerking story. That he was perfectly capable of writing the tear-jerker is evident, nor was anyone more aware of this than Sterne. Frequently, one feels, he must have been tempted to outsentimentalize the sentimentalists, knowing the delicacy of his hand

[5] The phrase is that of Ernest Nevin Dilworth, in *The Unsentimental Journey of Laurence Sterne* (New York: King's Crown Press, 1948).

97

at the pathetic (as in the story of Le Fever's death). But his genius was the humorous genius, and he remained faithful to it. What have been considered his indecent lapses must be taken as an essential element in the whole Sterne, one term of a structural irony, and a provision for keeping the sentimental and the emotional and the pathetic in the same human world with the obscene and the trivial and the absurd. His reference, in the letter quoted above, to the "Cervantic humour" reminds us that the high-minded knight, Quixote, could not continue on his travels without his low companion, Sancho.

ON *Pride and Prejudice*

It is the frequent response of readers who are making their first acquaintance with Jane Austen that her subject matter is itself so limited —limited to the manners of a small section of English country gentry who apparently never have been worried about death or sex, hunger or war, guilt or God—that it can offer no contiguity with modern interests. This is a very real difficulty in an approach to an Austen novel, and we should not obscure it; for by taking it initially into consideration, we can begin to come closer to the actual toughness and subtlety of the Austen quality. The greatest novels have been great in range as well as in technical invention; they have explored human experience a good deal more widely and deeply than Jane Austen was able to explore it. It is wronging an Austen novel to expect of it what it makes no pretense to rival—the spiritual profundity of the very greatest novels. But if we expect artistic mastery of limited materials, we shall not be disappointed.

The exclusions and limitations are deliberate; they do not necessarily represent limitations of Jane Austen's personal experience. Though she led the life of a maiden gentlewoman, it was not actually a sheltered life —not sheltered, that is, from the apparition of a number of the harsher human difficulties. She was a member of a large family whose activities ramified in many directions, in a period when a cousin could be guillotined, when an aunt and uncle could be jailed for a year on a shopkeeper's petty falsification, and when the pregnancies and childbed mortalities of relatives and friends were kept up at a barnyard rate. Her letters show in her the ironical mentality and the eighteenth-century gusto that are the reverse of the puritanism and naïveté that might be associated with the maidenly life. What she excludes from her fictional material does not, then, reflect a personal obliviousness, but, rather, a critically developed knowledge of the character of her gift and a restriction of its exercise to the kind of subject matter which she could shape into most significance. When we begin to look upon these limitations, not as having the negative function of showing how much of human life Jane Austen left out, but as having, rather, the positive function of defining the form and meaning of the book, we begin also to understand that kind of value that can lie in artistic mastery over a restricted range. This "two inches of ivory" (the metaphor which she herself used to describe her work), though it may resemble the handle of a lady's fan when looked on scantly, is in substance an elephant's tusk; it is a savagely probing instrument as well as a masterpiece of refinement.

Time and space are small in *Pride and Prejudice*. Time is a few months completely on the surface of the present, with no abysses of past or future, no room for mystery; there is time only for a sufficiently complicated business of getting wived and husbanded and of adapting oneself to civilization and civilization to oneself. Space can be covered in a few hours of coach ride between London and a country village or estate; but this space is a *physical* setting only in the most generalized sense; it is space as defined by a modern positivistic philosopher—"a place for an argument." The concern is rational and social. What is relevant is the way minds operate in certain social circumstances, and the physical particular has only a derived and subordinate relevance, as it serves to stimulate attitudes between persons. Even the social circumstances are severely restricted: they are the circumstances of marriageable young women coming five to a leisure-class family with reduced funds and prospects. What can be done with this time and space and these circumstances? What Jane Austen does is to dissect—with what one critic has called "regulated hatred" [1]—the monster in the skin of the civilized animal, the irrational acting in the costumes and on the stage of the rational; and to illuminate the difficult and delicate reconciliation of the sensitively developed individual with the terms of his social existence.

"It is a truth universally acknowledged, that a single man in possession of a good fortune must be in want of a wife." This is the first sentence of the book. What we read in it is its opposite—a single woman must be in want of a man with a good fortune—and at once we are inducted into the Austen language, the ironical Austen attack, and the energy, peculiar to an Austen novel, that arises from the compression between a barbaric

[1] D. W. Harding, "Regulated Hatred: An Aspect of the Work of Jane Austen," *Scrutiny*, March, 1940.

subsurface marital warfare and a surface of polite manners and civilized conventions. Marriage—that adult initiatory rite that is centrally important in most societies whether barbarous or advanced—is the uppermost concern. As motivation for the story, it is as primitively powerful an urgency as is sex in a novel by D. H. Lawrence. The tale is that of a man hunt, with the female the pursuer and the male a shy and elusive prey. The desperation of the hunt is the desperation of economic survival: girls in a family like that of the Bennets must succeed in running down solvent young men in order to survive. But the marriage motivation is complicated by other needs of a civilized community: the man hunters must observe the most refined behavior and sentiments. The female is a "lady" and the male is a "gentleman"; they must "fall in love." Not only must civilized appearances be preserved before the eyes of the community, but it is even necessary to preserve dignity and fineness of feeling in one's own eyes.

The second sentence outlines the area in which the aforementioned "truth universally acknowledged" is to be investigated—a small settled community, febrile with social and economic rivalry.

> However little known the feelings or views of such a man may be on his first entering a neighborhood, this truth is so well fixed in the minds of the surrounding families, that he is considered as the rightful property of some one or other of their daughters.

Here a high valuation of property is so dominant a culture trait that the word "property" becomes a metaphor for the young man himself; and the phrasing of the sentence, with typical Austen obliquity, adds a further sly emphasis to this trait when it uses an idiom associated with the possession of wealth—"well fixed"—as a qualifier of the standing of "truth." We are told that the young man may have "feelings or views" of his own (it becomes evident, later, that even daughters are capable of a similar willful subjectivity); and we are warned of the embarrassment such "feelings or views" will cause, whether to the individual or to the community, when we read of those "surrounding families" in whom "truth" is "so well fixed"—portentous pressure! And now we are given a light preliminary draft of the esteemed state of marriage, in the little drama of conflicting perceptions and wills that the first chapter presents between the imbecilic Mrs. Bennet and her indifferent, sarcastic husband. "The experience of three and twenty years had been insufficient to make his wife understand his character." The marriage problem is set broadly before us in this uneasy parental background, where an ill-mated couple must come to terms on the finding of mates for their five daughters. A social call must be made, in any case, on the single gentleman of good fortune who has settled in the neighborhood. With the return of the call, and with the daughters set up for view—some of whom are "handsome," some "good-natured"—no doubt he will buy, that is to say, "fall in love" (with such love, perhaps, as we have seen between Mr. and Mrs. Bennet themselves).

In this first chapter, the fundamental literary unit of the single word—"fortune," "property," "possession," "establishment," "business"— has consistently been setting up the impulsion of economic interest against those non-utilitarian interests implied by the words "feelings" and "love." [2] The implications of the word "marriage" itself are ambivalent; for as these implications are controlled in the book, "marriage" does not mean an act of ungoverned passion (not even in Lydia's and Wickham's rash elopement does it mean this: for Wickham has his eye on a settlement by blackmail, and Lydia's infatuation is rather more with a uniform than with a man); marriage means a complex engagement between the marrying couple and society—that is, it means not only "feelings" but "property" as well. In marrying, the individual marries society as well as his mate, and "property" provides the necessary articles of this other marriage. With marriage, so defined, as the given locus of action, the clash and reconciliation of utility interests with interests that are nonutilitarian will provide a subtle drama of manners; for whatever spiritual creativity may lie in the individual personality, that creativity will be able to operate only within publicly acceptable modes of deportment. These modes of deportment, however public and traditional, must be made to convey the secret life of the individual spirit, much as a lens conveys a vision of otherwise invisible constellations. Language itself is the lens in this case—the linguistic habits of social man.

Below language we do not descend, except by inference, for, in this definitively social world, language is the index of behavior, the special machine which social man has made to register his attitudes and to organize his dealings with others. We have spoken of Jane Austen's exclu-

---

[2] This point of view is developed by Mark Schorer in the essay "Fiction and the 'Analogical Matrix,'" in *Critiques and Essays on Modern Fiction,* edited by John W. Aldridge (New York: The Ronald Press Company, 1952), pp. 83–98.

sion of the physical particular. One might expect that in her treatment of
the central problem of marriage she could not avoid some physical particularity—some consciousness of the part played by the flesh and the
fleshly passions in marriage. Curiously and quite wonderfully, out of her
restricted concern for the rational and social definition of the human performance there does arise a strong implication of the physical. Can one
leave this novel without an acute sense of physical characterizations—
even of the smells of cosmetic tinctures and obesity in Mrs. Bennet's
boudoir, or of the grampus-like erotic wallowings of the monstrous Mr.
Collins? Nothing could be stranger to an Austen novel than such repre-
sentations of the physical. And yet, from her cool, unencumbered understanding of the linguistic exhibitions of the parlor human, she gives us,
by the subtlest of implication, the human down to its "naturals," down to
where it is human only by grace of the fact that it talks English and has
a set of gestures arbitrarily corresponding to rationality.

Among the "daughters" and the "young men of fortune" there are a
few sensitive individuals, civilized in spirit as well as in manner. For these
few, "feeling" must either succumb to the paralysis of utility or else must
develop special delicacy and strength. The final adjustment with society,
with "property" and "establishment," must be made in any case, for in
this book the individual is unthinkable without the social environment,
and in the Austen world that environment has been given once and forever—it is unchangeable and it contains the only possibilities for individual development. For the protagonists, the marriage rite will signify
an "ordeal" in that traditional sense of a moral testing which is the serious
meaning of initiation in any of the important ceremonies of life. What will
be tested will be their integrity of "feeling" under the crudely threatening
social pressures. The moral life, then, will be equated with delicacy and integrity of feeling, and its capacity for growth under adverse conditions. In
the person of the chief protagonist, Elizabeth, it really will be equated with
intelligence. In this conception of the moral life, Jane Austen shows herself
the closest kin to Henry James in the tradition of the English novel; for
by James, also, the moral life was located in emotional intelligence, and
he too limited himself to observation of its workings in the narrow area
of a sophisticated civilization.

The final note of the civilized in *Pride and Prejudice* is, as we have
said, reconciliation. The protagonists do not "find themselves" by leaving society, divorcing themselves from its predilections and obsessions.

In the union of Darcy and Elizabeth, Jane and Bingley, the obsessive social formula of marriage-to-property is found again, but now as the happy reward of initiates who have travailed and passed their "ordeal." The incongruities between savage impulsions and the civilized conventions in which they are buried, between utility and morality, are reconciled in the symbolic act of a marriage which society itself—bent on useful marriages—has paradoxically done everything to prevent. Rightly, the next to the last word in the book is the word "uniting."

We have so far attempted to indicate both the restrictive discipline which Jane Austen accepted from her material and the moral life which she found in it. The significance of a given body of material is a function of the form which the artist gives to the material. Significance is, then, not actually "found" by the artist in his subject matter, as if it were already and obviously present there for anyone to see, but is created by him in the act of giving form to the material (it was in this sense that poets were once called trouvères, or "finders"). The form of the action of *Pride and Prejudice* is a set of "diverging and converging lines" [3] mathematically balanced in their movements, a form whose diagrammatic neatness might be suggested in such a design as that given below, which shows the relationship of correspondence-with-variation between the Darcy-Elizabeth plot and the Jane-Bingley subplot, the complication of the former and the simplicity of the latter, the successive movements toward splitting apart and toward coming together, and the final resolution of movement in "recognition" and reconciliation between conflicting claims, as the total action composes itself in the shape of the lozenge (see the chart opposite).

But significant form, as we have noted in previous studies, is a far more complex structure of relationships than those merely of plot. An Austen novel offers a particularly luminous illustration of the function of style in determining the major form. Our diagram of the plot movements of *Pride and Prejudice* will serve as visualization of a pattern of antithetical balances found also in the verbal composition of the book. It is here, in style, in the language base itself, that we are able to observe Jane Austen's most deft and subtle exploitation of her material.

The first sentence of the book—"It is a truth universally acknowledged, that a single man in possession of a good fortune must be in want of a wife"—again affords an instance in point. As we have said, the sen-

---

[3] The phrase and the observation are those of Mary Lascelles, in *Jane Austen and Her Art* (New York: Oxford University Press, 1939), p. 160.

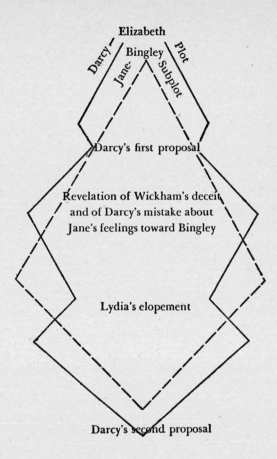

tence ironically turns itself inside out, thus: a single woman must be in want of a man with a good fortune. In this doubling of the inverse meaning over the surface meaning, a very modest-looking statement sums up the chief conflicting forces in the book: a decorous convention of love (which holds the man to be the pursuer) embraces a savage economic compulsion (the compulsion of the insolvent female to run down male "property"), and in the verbal embrace they appear as a unit. The ironic mode here is a mode of simultaneous opposition and union: civilized convention and economic primitivism unite in the sentence as they do in the action, where "feelings" and "fortune," initially in conflict, are reconciled in the socially creative union of marriage.

This is but one type of verbal manipulation with which the book luxuriates. Another we shall illustrate with a sentence from Mr. Collins' proposal to Elizabeth, where "significant form" lies in elaborate rather than in modest phrasing. Mr. Collins manages to wind himself up almost inextricably in syntax.

> "But the fact is, that being as I am, to inherit this estate after the death of your honored father, (who, however, may live many years longer,) I could not satisfy myself without resolving to chuse a wife from among his daughters, that the loss to them might be as little as possible, when the melancholy event takes place—which, however, as I have already said, may not be for several years."

Fancy syntax acts here, not as an expression of moral and intellectual refinement (as Mr. Collins intends it to act), but as an expression of stupidity, the antithesis of that refinement. The elaborate language in which Mr. Collins gets himself fairly *stuck* is a mimesis of an action of the soul, the soul that becomes self dishonest through failure to know itself, and that overrates itself at the expense of the social context, just as it overrates verbalism at the expense of meaning. We have suggested that moral life, in an Austen novel, is identified with emotional intelligence; and it is precisely through failure of intelligence—the wit to know his own limitations—that Mr. Collins appears as a moral monstrosity. Language is the mirror of his degeneracy. Against Mr. Collins' elaborate style of speech we may place the neat and direct phrasing of a sentence such as "It is a truth universally acknowledged . . ." where the balance of overt thesis and buried antithesis acts as a kind of signature of the intelligential life—its syntactical modesty conveying a very deft and energetic mental dance.

Similarly, elaborate epithet ("your honored father," "the melancholy event") is suspect—the sign not of attention but of indifference, of a moldiness of spirit which, far from being innocuous, has the capacity of mold to flourish destructively and to engulf what is clean and sound, as such epithet itself devours sense. Comedy, let us say again, "is a serious matter," and what is serious in this scene of Mr. Collins' proposal is the engulfing capacity of the rapacious Mr. Collins, from whom Elizabeth escapes narrowly. The narrowness of the escape is underlined by the fact that Elizabeth's friend, Charlotte—herself, we assume, intelligent, inasmuch as she is Elizabeth's friend—complacently offers herself as host to this mighty mold. In the civilized community which is our area of observation, emotional intelligence and quickness of moral perception—as we see them, for instance, in Elizabeth—are profoundly threatened by an all-environing imbecility. It is through style that we understand the nature of this threat; for the simplicity and directness of the governing syntax of the book prepares us to find positive values in simplicity and directness, negative values in elaboration and indirection. Even the canny intelligence of Mr. Bennet is not that emotionally informed intelligence—or, shall we say, that intelligence which informs the emotions—that we are led to look upon as desirable; and Mr. Bennet reveals his failure also in "style," a style of speech that shows a little too elaborate consciousness of the pungency of double-talk, of the verbal effect of ironic undercutting. When Elizabeth suggests that it would be imprudent to send the lightheaded Lydia to Brighton, he says,

> Lydia will never be easy till she has exposed herself in some public place or other, and we can never expect her to do it with so little expense or inconvenience to her family as under the present circumstances.

Being intelligent, Mr. Bennet learns regret for his failure, although (and we delight also in Jane Austen's "realism" here, the tenacity of her psychological grip on her characters) not too much regret—not so much that he ceases to be Mr. Bennet.

From still another point of view, the style of the book is significant of total structure; we refer here to a generalized kind of epithet used in descriptive passages. The park at Pemberley, Darcy's estate, "was very large, and contained great variety of ground"; one drove "through a beautiful wood stretching over a wide extent." What we wish to notice, in diction of this kind, is the merely approximate appropriateness of the qualifier: "large," "great variety," "beautiful wood," "wide extent." This type of diction we might again describe as "modest," or we might speak of it as flatly commonplace; but we shall want to investigate its possibilities of function in the total form of the book. The reader will observe the continued use of the same kind of diction in the passage below, describing the house; what should be noted is the use to which the description is put—its use, not to convey any sense of "naturalistic" particularity, but, rather, to reveal Darcy's taste (of which Elizabeth has been suspicious) and a subtle turn in Elizabeth's feelings about him.

> It was a large, handsome, stone building, standing well on rising ground, and backed by a ridge of high woody hills;—and in front, a stream of some natural importance was swelled into greater, but without any artificial appearance. Its banks were neither formal nor falsely adorned. Elizabeth was delighted. She had never seen a place for which nature had done more, or where natural beauty had been so little counteracted by an awkward taste. They were all of them warm in their admiration; and at that moment she felt that to be mistress of Pemberley might be something!

Wealth applied to the happiest and most dignified creation of environment —that is all we need to know about this setting, a need which the description fulfills by virtue of generalizations—"large," "standing well," "natural importance," "natural beauty," and the series of negations of what is generally understood by "artificial appearance," "falsely adorned," and so forth. More particularity of description would deflect from what is significant in the episode, namely, the effect of the scene upon Elizabeth's attitude toward her lover. Darcy himself has had in her eyes a certain artificiality, unpleasant formality, falseness; he has been lacking in that naturalness which delights her in the present scene, which is his home and which speaks intimately of him; and she has felt that his taste in the handling of human relations was very seriously "awkward." The appearance of Pemberley cannot help putting a slight pressure on her judgment of him, and the description is used with deliberate purpose for this effect. And how shrewd psychologically and warmly human is the remark, "and at that moment she felt that to be mistress of Pemberley might be something!" With all her personal integrity and exacerbated delicacy of feeling about the horrors of acquisitiveness, Elizabeth is smitten with an acquisitive temptation. (No wonder Jane Austen could not find Elizabeth's painted portrait in the galleries, though she was able to find Jane Bennet's there. Elizabeth is quite too human to have a duplicate in paint; only language is able to catch her.) In this final clause, the dramatic concern is solely with the social context—the shifting attitudes of one person toward another, as these attitudes are conditioned by the terms of a narrow, but nevertheless complex, social existence; but as the relationships between persons shift, the individual himself (as Elizabeth, here) is reinterpreted, shows a new aspect of his humanity. In this fashion, the Austen style—here a deliberately generalized and commonplace descriptive style —functions again as determination of significant form, significance in this particular case being the *rational* meaning of a physical setting.

Finally we should remark upon what is perhaps the most formative and conclusive activity of style in the book: the effect of a narrowly mercantile and materialistic vocabulary in setting up meanings. Let us go down a few lists of typical words, categorizing them rather crudely and arbitrarily, but in such a manner as to show their direction of reference.[4] The reader will perhaps be interested in adding to these merely suggestive lists, for in watching the Austen language lies the real excitement of the Austen novel. We shall set up such categories as "trade," "arithmetic," "money," "material possessions," simply in order to indicate the kind of language Jane Austen inherited from her culture and to which she was confined—and in order to suggest what she was able to do with her language, how much of the human drama she was able to get into such confines.

TRADE	ARITHMETIC	MONEY	MATERIAL POSSESSIONS	SOCIAL INTEGRATION
employed	equally	pounds	estate	town
due form	added	credit	property	society
collect	proportion	capital	owner	civil
receipt	addition	pay	house	neighborhood
buy	enumerate	fortune	manor	county
sell	figure	valuable	tenant	fashion
business	calculated	principal	substantial	breeding
supply	amount	interest	establishment	genteel
terms	amounting	afford	provided	marriage
means	inconsiderable	indebted	foundation	husband
venture	consideration	undervalue	belongs to	connection

We could add such verbal categories as those referring to "patronage," "law," "skill" (a particularly interesting one, covering such words as "design," "cunning," "arts," "schemes," and so on; a category obviously converging with the "trade" category, but whose vocabulary, as it appears in this book, is used derogatorily—the stupid people, like Mrs. Bennet, Lady Catherine de Bourgh, Wickham, and Mr. Collins, are the ones who "scheme" and have "designs").

---

4 Mr. Schorer's essay "Fiction and the 'Analogical Matrix,'" cited above, closely examines this aspect of Jane Austen's style.

In viewing in the abstract the expressive possibilities open to literary creatorship, we might assume that the whole body of the English language, as it is filed in the dictionary, is perfectly free of access to each author— that each author shares equally and at large in the common stuff of the language. In a sense this is true; the whole body of the language *is* there, virtually, in the dictionary, and anyone can consult it and use it if he wants to. But we have observed fairly frequently, if only by-the-way, in these studies, that each author does not consult the whole body of the language in selecting words for his meanings; that he is driven, as if compulsively, to the selection of a highly particular part of the language; and that the individual character of his work, its connotations and special insights, derive largely from the style he has made his own—that is to say, from the vocabulary and verbal arrangements he has adopted out of the whole gamut of words and rhetorical patterns available in the language. In making these selections, he is acting partly under the compulsions of the culture in which he has been bred and whose unconscious assumptions—as to what is interesting or valuable or necessary or convenient in life—are reflected in the verbal and rhetorical selections common in that culture; and he is acting partly also under compulsions that are individual to his own personal background, but that still maintain subtle links with the common cultural assumptions. The general directions of reference taken by Jane Austen's language, as indicated by such lists as those given above (and the lists, with others like them, could be extended for pages), are clearly materialistic. They reflect a culture whose institutions are solidly defined by materialistic interests—property and banking and trade and the law that keeps order in these matters— institutions which determine, in turn, the character of family relations, the amenities of community life, and the whole complex economy of the emotions. By acknowledgment of the fact that the materialistic assumptions of our own culture are even more pervasive than those reflected in this book, and that their governance over our emotions and our speech habits is even more grim, more sterilizing, and more restrictive, we should be somewhat aided in appreciation of the "contemporaneity" of Jane Austen herself.

But where then, we must ask, does originality lie, if an author's very language is dictated in so large a part by something, as it were, "outside" himself—by the culture into which he is accidentally born? How can there be any free play of individual genius, the free and original play with the language by which we recognize the insight and innovations of genius? The question has to be answered separately for the work of each artist, but as for Jane Austen's work we have been finding answers all along—in her exploitation of antithetical structures to convey ambivalent attitudes, in her ironic use of syntactical elaborations that go against the grain of the language and that convey moral aberrations, and finally in her direct and oblique play with an inherited vocabulary that is materialistic in reference and that she forces—or blandishes or intrigues—into spiritual duties.

The language base of the Austen novel gives us the limiting conditions of the culture. Somehow, using this language of acquisitiveness and calculation and materialism, a language common to the most admirable characters as well as to the basest characters in the book, the spiritually creative persons will have to form their destinies. The project would be so much easier if the intelligent people and the stupid people, the people who are morally alive and the people who are morally dead, had each their different language to distinguish and publicize their differences! But unfortunately for that ease, they have only one language. Fortunately for the drama of the Austen novel, there is this difficulty of the single materialistic language; for drama subsists on difficulty. Within the sterile confines of public assumptions, the Austen protagonists find with difficulty the fertility of honest and intelligent individual feeling. On a basis of communication that is drawn always from the public and savage theology of "property," the delicate lines of spiritual adjustment are explored. The final fought-for recognitions of value are recognitions of the unity of experience—a unity between the common culture and the individual development. No one more knowledgeably than this perceptive and witty woman, ambushed by imbecility, could have conducted such an exploration.

ON *The Heart of Mid-Lothian*

Ultimately, as critical readers, we are concerned with an author's conception of life. But, in a work of art, it is only through the intimate activities of aesthetic form that any conception of life is honestly put before us. The very close correlation between aesthetic structure and what we call "value" or "significance" is the chief mystery in the economy of art—a mystery simply because it is an empirical fact that we recognize again and again in our reading just as we recognize empirically the connection between touching a hot stove and getting burned or between exposure in the rain and getting wet. These are homely analogies, chosen because of the impossibility, in these simple cases, of dissociating the one term of the correlation from the other: we cannot dissociate a burn from something hot, nor a soaking from something wet. Similarly, we cannot dissociate an author's conception of life, and its "value" and "significance," from the aesthetic structure of the literary work. It is for this reason that the "world view" to be found in a finely wrought novel is fairly inexhaustible, and we can reread and reread the book with increasing extension of insight. For on first reading such a work, it is impossible to be aware of all elements, all relationships among them, all inflections given the major rhythm as it engages the minor rhythms; but as our alertness to more and more of these is freed by rereading, the view of life which the book contains becomes changed in our apprehension and appears inexhaustible because of the new aspects constantly being given to that view by newly emerging relationships.

Inasmuch as *Pride and Prejudice* has none of the more obvious attractions of fiction—exalted passions, exotic geography, and so forth—it offers itself particularly well for a test of the aesthetic coherence of the novel, and of its "view of life," as that coherence can be felt in the "parts" that are a novel's very smallest parts—the individual words that make it up; the qualities of this book must be sought with a wholly activated intelligence in the word and the phrasing, the partial and delicate exposure of attitude in an ambivalent thought, an idiosyncrasy of diction, a turn of syntax. Read in this way, the book raises in the mind a rich and subtle conception of life that does not appear on first glance at the tidily commonplace surface; but such a reading also illustrates the fact that this conception of life owes its integrity, and its value for us in making discrimination finer, precisely to the aesthetic integrity of the book. To set *The Heart of Mid-Lothian* beside *Pride and Prejudice* is to set a book colored by illicit passions, violence, riot, crowd scenes, gypsy life and the life of bandits, lynching and murder, picturesque manners in low places and high places, and an environment of crags and castles and filthy dens, beside a book whose color is solely mental; it is also to set a poorly structured book beside a finely structured book, and to witness more convincingly in this juxtaposition of two classic English novels the fact that incoherent structure equates with an incoherent world view, essentially valueless for us no matter how attractive certain single elements of the book may be, while coherent aesthetic structure equates with a coherent world view, potentially valuable to us in the degree of the complexity of those elements that are made to cohere.

   The Heart of Mid-Lothian has generally been considered the best of Scott's work, for it is a book in which he is not only the fictional historian and the novelist of "local color," but also the moral psychologist, the investigator of matters of conscience. The figure of Jeanie Deans has moved many astute critics to applause. Her story, in short, is this. Jeanie's younger sister, Effie, is accused of child murder; a curious technicality of the law provides that had Effie once admitted her pregnancy to another person, the shadow of the clandestine would be removed, the case would be dismissed through lack of material evidence, and Effie would be saved from the hangman; Jeanie is the likeliest person to whom Effie might have admitted her condition, but Jeanie's conscience forbids her to speak the necessary untruth, and at the trial Effie is condemned; whereupon Jeanie walks from Edinburgh to London to obtain pardon for her sister from the king. This is by no means a complete sketch of the action of the novel, for Scott's contract with the publisher called for a good deal greater length to the book than the matter of Jeanie Deans's heroic action could provide; and as he needed the money, he supplied the length. We must judge a novel as one whole and at its full length; we cannot excerpt a part of it and call this part the novel, or we should have to allow ourselves the privilege of "editing" every novel in the same fashion, and our standards of critical objectivity would become helplessly disorganized and criticism itself ineffectual. We cannot cut short *The Heart of Mid-Lothian* at that point where its older readers found it still so highly praiseworthy—the point where Jeanie obtains the pardon; we must judge the book at its full length without commiseration for Scott's financial needs in building Abbotsford. And, indeed, the "conception of life" which the book holds is not fully recognizable until the end. Though the moral imagination of generations of readers has been most stirred by Jeanie's original problem and her solution of it, yet the further proliferation of Jeanie's destiny and Effie's (as Scott made up his pence) casts back upon the earlier section a comment that lays Scott's own moral imagination under dubiety.

One other preliminary consideration: the portion of the book dealing with the conviction for child murder and the action of the sister in making the trip on foot to London was founded in fact (Scott's preface describes his interview with Helen Walker—the original of Jeanie); and it is possible that the reader's sense that he is reading a "true story" determines in some degree the admiration he may have for the fiction. But since it *is* a fiction that we are reading, we must exorcise from our minds whatever tendency we may have to estimate the book by its partly factual foundation and by the interest and admiration we might feel for a real Helen Walker. (Who knows how much factual "truth" any number of stories may contain, whose authors did not supply the relevant documentary notes!) We must judge Jeanie's problem as the fictional Jeanie's, not as Helen Walker's, and this portion of the novel as we do the rest of it—as fiction, not as fact.

We shall speak chiefly here of Jeanie's first problem—to lie to save a life, or not to lie—for this problem provides the main dynamics of the book. It is a problem of no trivial interest. Even though we have largely lost the objective moral code which gave such a problem its original gravity—lost it with the loss of religious sanctions—or rather, just because of the loss of a common moral code, it is a question of potentially profound interest for the modern reader. In our own time we have been made more conscious of the subtle and terrible operations of the lie than our immediate forebears could have been, for we have seen its use on the most massive scale in propaganda, and we have seen the close relationship between human destiny and the political manipulation of the lie. Through academic studies in semantics, with their concern for what constitutes "meaning" in the word; through fairly popular exposure to psychoanalytical knowledge, with its interpretation of hidden levels of meaning in our actions and speech; and through the last two decades' experience of the strategies of totalitarianism, with its witty and immensely vicious practice of deceit through the word—we have become highly conscious of the implications of "truth" and of the breakdown of truth, even though we have become proportionately more confused as to what constitutes the truth or the lie. The problem, then, of the lie, on which *The Heart of Mid-Lothian* centers, is one on which we can well afford to dwell.

But we shall want to dwell on it, not in the abstract, but in the concrete aesthetic context in which the problem is raised. The book pivots on Jeanie's decision to tell the "truth"; it is what stirs our interest initially in this main character, and what keeps her a figure of any consideration for us as the story proceeds. If the book as a whole is faultily structured, and if the conception of life that it contains seems inadequate to give organic coherence to those parts of life it attempts to interpret, we might expect that the pivotal moral problem itself would be infected by the general fault of confusion. To get Jeanie's situation firmly before us, let us speak of it in the following way. Her sensibility has been trained by the spare and rigorous code of her Cameronian father, in an extraordinarily limited environment of thought and feeling but an environment extraordinarily powerful in its controls on the individual. She is altogether doubtful of Effie's alleged crime of child murder; there is no evidence, except that Effie had been pregnant and now the child cannot be found; Effie herself denies the act movingly and convincingly; but Jeanie cannot tell a lie to save her sister's life because generations of Cameronian ancestors bind her tongue, ancestors who, after the civil war, waged wars of logic and turned a none too logical theology into a strait jacket of scruples. We look, then, upon the invincible restriction Jeanie puts on herself as an act "conditioned" by her intellectual environment and inheritance. But we look on it also as a morally independent act; for we have to look upon it thus—even taking the "conditioning" into consideration —in order to found our own moral judgment somewhere: a wholly "conditioned" action is a helpless action, relating our pity to it perhaps but not our normative judgment, and Jeanie's action is set before us certainly not to win our pity but to stir our moral interest, our awe possibly, assuredly our judgment.

With this view of the problem, let us set beside it an analogous case of conscience in Shakespeare's *Measure for Measure*. (The comparison is not unfair, for Scott's admirers have continuously compared him honorifically with Shakespeare.) *Measure for Measure* is an ambiguous play, with an ambiguity that is morally unpleasant, for it offers a conventional solution for a problem too deeply rooted in emotional and nervous responses to be solved conventionally. We are, therefore, not comparing this play as a whole with Scott's novel as a whole, to the denigration of the latter; we are comparing only the pivotal problems in these two works, for what light of judgment one may throw on the other. In *Measure for Measure,* a man of known austerity and abstinence is deputized temporarily in the main seat of government; Angelo's first act of authority is to revive an obsolete law against lechery and to condemn to death a young man—Claudio—who has got his sweetheart with child. (We may note here that, as the "crime" in this play is sexual indulgence, so the *real* "crime" in Scott's novel is also sexual indulgence—for Effie is guilty of no other.) Claudio appeals to his sister, Isabella, to plead with Angelo for his life; and Isabella's plea is made so effective by the radiance of her own purity (she is about to take orders in a religious sisterhood) that Angelo, the abstinent man, is moved with lust for her and offers her Claudio's freedom on the condition that she will sleep with him. Isabella returns to Claudio's cell to tell him the consequences of her visit to the deputy; she is certain that Claudio will reject a bargain which would save his life so dishonorably. Here (in Act III, scene 1) the greatest ambiguity enters: we see Claudio, honorable in intention but grazed by the horror of death, brooding on the possible moral irrelevance of the sexual act; he reasons—if Angelo, a man of such pure life and so great in authority, can indulge the lecherous motive, is it actually a sin? Or if a sin, is it a sin of such consequence that Isabella should refuse a moment's use of her body for the saving of her brother's life? Isabella does refuse, and Claudio must face the hangman.

In the last two acts of the play, a conventional compromise is effected: Claudio is freed and Isabella keeps her virtue; but the play does not leave us with the feeling that the problem originally set, and articulated in Claudio's brooding thought, has been solved adequately by the structure in which it inheres. Of this much, though, we are certain: that the morality and the spiritual issues involved are vital, profound and intricate and difficult. Behind Isabella's refusal is not the conceit of a prude merely, but the holy orders she is about to take, and behind these the ascetic attitude of mind, an attitude that is neither an individual's aberration nor the neurosis of a culture, but a discipline of devotion almost universal to the developed religious character and even to the developed philosophical character. In the effect of her purity upon Angelo, in awakening lust in him, is a paradox of the spiritual life—the stimulus which innocence offers to the impulse of violation; and from this point of view, her yielding to him would be an active acquiescence in the germination of the demonic. Furthermore, the problem is set in an environment of sexual ugliness—pimps and whores and that frivolity of the physical which speaks of an uglier frivolity of spirit; this on the one hand—and on the other, a profound engagement of the mind with the uncertain horrors awaiting the soul after death. Between these two—the obsession with sexual ugliness and the other obsession with the horrors of death—neither Claudio's plea that Isabella expose herself to Angelo, nor Isabella's refusal, can be lightly taken. Finally, a subtle notion of perversity—the breaking of something more primitive than a religious taboo—attaches to Angelo's proposition and to Claudio's encouragement of it.

> Is't not a kind of incest, to take life
> From thine own sister's shame?

Isabella asks. The sexual act that might save Claudio is more than dishonorable; it has the taint of the "unnatural."

We have been speaking of the *context* given to Isabella's refusal to save her brother's life through prostitution. If the same problem were presented for our contemplation in the abstract, we might give a swift and facile answer to it: we might say, for instance, that Isabella suffered from barrenness of moral imagination, conceit of virginity, egotism of the spirit. But the concrete context offered by the play forces us to think with more complexity of what is meant by abstinence and prostitution, vice and purity, spiritual life and spiritual death—forces us to think so complexly about them that we (like Shakespeare himself in this instance) cannot give an answer that carries authority for our emotions. In other

118

words, the play stretches our own moral imagination, exercises and toughens it, vitalizes it to a greater awareness of the complexity of the moral life. It succeeds in doing this by virtue of the rich and disturbing context it gives to the central dramatic motif.

In the abstract, also, we might pass a ready judgment on Jeanie Deans's refusal to save a sister's life by a lie. We might, in the abstract, approve or disapprove of her solution of the problem. Truth is of ancient nobility, and the devil has been called the Father of Lies. On the other hand, the question "What is truth?", voiced at the most passionate moment of Christian history, indicates anything but simplicity in the character of truth; and even Peter's thrice-told lie was a good deal more than an unscrupulosity of the tongue. But our concern again is not with the problem in the abstract, but with the concrete context the author provides for it. Is the question of the lie, as dealt with in this book, handled in such a way as to animate and complicate and enrich our perception of the difficulty and drama of truth?

The context gives us one possible point of view, that of the "conditioning" we have spoken of. The pressure placed on our actions by "conditions" is of the greatest dramatic and moral interest: it provided the most powerful source of ambiguity in ancient Greek tragedy, and it does so again today in the novels of Faulkner. But the "conditioning" of Jeanie Deans is not used as a source of ambiguity; it is, indeed, not *used* by Scott at all in the structure of the book. It is an element existing in the book; we are allowed to know and understand Jeanie's training in verbal scrupulosity; but we are not led thereby to penetrate into the complexity of our destiny as "conditioned" and yet morally independent creatures, as we are led to do by Sophocles and by Faulkner. Jeanie's Cameronian training is a mere bit of local color. But real confusion arises from this "mereness." Unfortunately, attitudes toward truth and falsehood are not "merely" local color; they are profoundly and universally important in our destinies. Scott *assumes* that they are important, and he *assumes* that Jeanie's decision to tell the truth contains a vital human attitude toward truth, but he neglects to explore this assumption in the aesthetic context he provides.

We cannot undertake to rewrite schematically Scott's novel, but we might speculate on a possibility of the following sort: had Jeanie been presented as the cultural product of a small sect pushed to the margins of the world, a sect that had developed a fantasy of prestige based on the singularity of its strictness of conduct, a presentation of this kind might, if taken up and made significant in the structure of the whole work, have brought Jeanie into the realm of moral interest, where men acquire guilt even in aspiring toward truth, are treasonable in ignorance and dishonorable in a passion for spiritual order; for such a presentation could have made acknowledgment of the unpredictable complexity and tragedy of serious moral choices. The context offers us also another, related, suggestion. After all, there is Effie, whose life is at stake and who is innocent of the alleged crime. How much is a life worth in scruples as to the absolute "truth" of the voiced word? Or we may turn the same point of view about: how much is a verbal truth or falsehood worth in the poundage of another person's life? How deep and how fine is the connection between "verbal" truth and other kinds of truth? These are most serious and disturbing questions, and they are the questions automatically raised by Scott's pivotal problem, which, as artist or even as intelligently conscientious craftsman, he pledges himself to explore. But, again, he refuses to explore them in the concrete terms of aesthetic structure—presumably because he does not know that they are there. His neglect of their inherence in his materials is an index of confusion. Our view, as readers, is arbitrarily deflected from what the book initially offers us to look at. Instead, we are given highwaymen and kidnaping and queens and colorful eccentrics. This deflection of vision is what we mean by disorderliness and disorganization of structure. It illustrates that dependence, spoken of early in this essay, between aesthetic coherence in the novel and a coherent view of life.

In *Pride and Prejudice*, in materials that appeared at first to be of the simplest, we witnessed extraordinary complexity cohering in a major rhythm that controlled and united all minor rhythms. In *The Heart of Mid-Lothian*, in a wealth of materials, we witness a disorganization that falsifies the materials and in which they separately fall away into unrelated genres of their own: into little ballad-like dramas, like Jeanie's going to London to see the king's face that gives grace (the motif is from the ballad "Johnnie Armstrong"), or, on a larger scale, like Effie's own early story—her seduction by a highwayman lover, her grievous pregnancy and harsh travail, her disposal of her child (a ballad on this subject would have seized advantage of the tragedy of motive here, and Effie would have done away with her child, but Scott, though a collector of ballads, himself had not really the ballad-stomach; he produces an inconceivable harridan, Meg Murdockson, to do the dirty work), her conviction for murder, and her pitiful road to the gallows, where she would have been in the company of other ballad heroines; or they fall into the picaresque genre, as do Jeanie's adventures on the way to London; or into the comic, like the scenes of the old laird's death and the young laird's wooing. These, and other materials in the book, considered separately, carry on occasion the conviction of imaginative reality, but they do not cohere in a common rhythm for the mind; their juxtaposition does not *mean* anything.

The "crime," for instance, which Effie commits is, as we have said, the same "crime" which Shakespeare treats so ambiguously in *Measure for Measure*—she yields herself to her lover's bed. But never in the book is it even implicitly suggested that this *is* the crime; only the notable punishment which Effie suffers from torment of conscience, and in which even Providence seems to be interested, by afflicting her with a barren womb, insists that we look for a crime, for where there is such punishment there must be a crime; and we can find no other but this one. We have, then, two obscurities, or rather obscurations, in this case: a crime which the book refuses to acknowledge structurally and to place in rhythm with the punishment; and an absurd obscuration of whatever meaning sexual indulgence on the part of a person like Effie might have. The ambiguous meaning of sexual indulgence in *Measure for Measure* is not *obscure* meaning; it is complex meaning, difficult meaning. Despite structural anomalies in the play that have no relevance for us here, the play does provide a significant context for the problems raised by the illicit sexual act; it gives the act an environment stressing sexual ugliness, and it places this specially created ugliness in a meaningful rhythm with the counter-horror of death and with the mana of abstinence. Thus it contrives that the sexual problem, as presented, should probe our own deepest instincts and resistances, uniquely opening them up to our view. In Effie's case, though illicit sexual indulgence contributes, so far as we can see, the only structural motivation for Effie's long punishment, it has no "meaning" except that punishment. In other words, sex must be punished, and that is all there is to it. This is to obscure whatever real problem may exist here by a particularly unpleasant and facile kind of romanticism which attempts to interest us in the punishment as a kind of snuff to take away the odor of the offending deed.

One important aspect of the "conception of life" which the book holds is that of Providential care: Providence rewards sturdy little Jeanie for her leg work and her humility of aspiration; it punishes Effie with barrenness and remorse (although, to our confusion of attitude toward this Providential conception of life, it gives Effie a *succès de furor* in London and abroad, and endows her with taste and passion and susceptibility to beauty, so that Effie's punishment seems preferable to Jeanie's reward); it provides that George Staunton's horse shall throw him and break his leg when George wishes to give himself up to the law in order to ransom Effie—for the wicked must not be flattered by the indulgence of their good impulses; and nicely it arranges that George should be killed by the hand of his own son, and even that the son himself, illegitimate issue, should come to a bad end. Providence is a watering down of Calvinistic deity, an illucid gruel-like intermixture of the person of God with theological predestination, so that God is not quite clearly there (His presence might cause the discomfort of intellectual lucidity and spiritual doubt) nor the cruelty of predestination clearly conceived, but both are cheerfully obscured in the more domestic implications of "providing" and "provision." Nevertheless, a Providential universe is haunted by Calvin as by an embarrassed conscience: where Providence provides all, individual willing is a derogation of Providential function; it is absurd to will or to do. And yet, in the Providential universe of Scott's book, the central determination of our attitudes is Jeanie Deans's immense exertion of stubborn will power in legging it to London to upset whatever work Providence may have had in mind regarding Effie. R. H. Tawney, in *Religion and the Rise of Capitalism,* speaks of "the central paradox of religious ethics" as the fact that "only those are nerved with the courage to turn the world upside down who are convinced that already, in a higher sense, it is disposed for the best by a power of which they are the humble instruments." [1] An artist like Jane Austen uses his materials in the sense that he *uses them up,* exhausts their potentialities for meaning or carries that exhaustion so far that we can respect even his failures. In Scott's book there is this staring paradox of a Providential conception of life in which self-reliance is the paramount virtue, but Scott does not use the paradox. Because he ignores it, the work is sentimental, in the sense that it sets up feelings about a Providential kind of life—feelings of hope, trust, gratitude, and humility, let us say—while concretely it exhibits a

[1] New York: Harcourt, Brace & Company, Inc., 1926, p. 109.

way of life in which Providence has no part, a way of life in which the individual determines destiny, by using his legs if not his head.

Scott's literary influence was enormous. More important than his exploitations of history was his opening up, for the novelistic craft, the possibilities lying in physical description or "local color." Scott's own "local color" provides the real entertainment of his books, but it exists in them *ab extra*. Balzac, who admired Scott, turned physical description to the uses of genius; while Scott touristed in landscape and architecture, Balzac made the physical conditions of human lives their spiritual symbol, their passion and their jail. Stendhal, who loathed Scott, used Scott's bounty with both hands; the town of Verrières, in *The Red and the Black*, the cathedral, the seminary, Julien's cave in the mountains, are the transformed gift of Scott—transformed again by the uses of genius, whereas Scott had been able to make of his gift only the small uses of talent. In other fields than literature his influence was epochal. Cardinal Newman, in his *Apologia,* gives careful attention to that releasing of the emotions to new objects and new perspectives for which Scott, among others, was responsible in a time of spiritual poverty and emotional starvation. Bernard Bosanquet says, in *The Growth of Modern Philosophy,*

> It would seem, perhaps, absurd to fix upon the most unreflective of writers, Sir Walter Scott, as the chief initiator of a philosophical influence; but I believe there is little doubt that historical humanism in England, as on the Continent, received an epoch-making impulse from his writings.[2]

We are, however, in this study, concerned with a book and not an influence. Critics have named variously Scott's defect as a novelist: he failed in conveying the sense of an abiding destiny going on beyond the characters described (V. S. Pritchett, in *The Living Novel*); he seldom or never transcended the conventional, the accepted (Sir Herbert Grierson, in his biography of Scott); to go back to Hazlitt, Scott was interested in half of life only, in the past of man and not in what he might become; or to Coleridge, Scott had diversity of fancy but suffered from the blankest absence of imagination. As so frequently happens, it is Coleridge's observation that is the most useful here. To Coleridge, imagination was the

[2] Quoted by Sir Herbert Grierson in *Sir Walter Scott, Bart.* (New York: Columbia University Press, 1938), p. 312.

faculty likest in kind to the primary faculty of perception which gives spatial and temporal and causal organization to the world; a creative faculty because synthetic in function, a maker of unities. In Scott he found a grave defect of this faculty—and it is the defect which we, too, have been tracing in our review of the aesthetic and conceptual confusions in *The Heart of Mid-Lothian,* for confusion and unity are opposed terms. Coleridge was most concerned with Scott's failure to imagine character; that is, to conceive character not as a set of circumstances and accidents (such as Jeanie's Cameronian upbringing, or her falling in with Meg's gang), but as an inwardly complex agent out of whose human complexity evolve the event and the destiny. Coleridge goes on to make the pregnant and far-reaching statement that it is precisely this defect and this failure which

> has done more for Sir Walter Scott's European, yea, plusquam-European popularity, than ever the abundance of [imagination] effected for any former writer. His age is an age of *anxiety* from the crown to the hovel, from the cradle to the coffin; all is an anxious straining to maintain life, or *appearances*—to *rise,* as the only condition of not falling.

Scott's popularity, Coleridge says, is a phase of the desire to be amused, to forget oneself, in an "age of anxiety," and he continues,

> The great felicity of Sir Walter Scott is that his own intellect supplies the place of all intellect and all character in his heroes and heroines, and *representing* the intellect of his readers, supersedes all motive for its exertion, by never appearing alien, whether as above or below.[3]

This unblinking statement, damning as it is, clarifies the air around Scott. For our own purposes, it sets in a wider field of significance the aesthetic category to which, for the sake of objectivity, we have tried to confine ourselves; for it extends to our own historical condition, our own "age of anxiety," the implications of incoherence in the work of art.

[3] *Miscellaneous Criticism* (Cambridge: Harvard University Press, 1936), p. 335.

ON *Great Expectations*

"The distinguishing quality of Dickens's people," says V. S. Pritchett,

is that they are solitaries. They are people caught living in a world of
their own. They soliloquize in it. They do not talk to one another;
they talk to themselves. The pressure of society has created fits of
twitching in mind and speech, and fantasies in the soul . . . The solitariness of people is paralleled by the solitariness of things. Fog operates as a separate presence, houses quietly rot or boisterously prosper
on their own . . . Cloisterham believes itself more important than
the world at large, the Law sports like some stale and dilapidated
circus across human lives. Philanthropy attacks people like a humor
or an observable germ. The people and the things of Dickens are all
out of touch and out of hearing of each other, each conducting its
own inner monologue, grandiloquent or dismaying. By this dissociation Dickens brings to us something of the fright of childhood . . .[1]

Some of the most wonderful scenes in *Great Expectations* are those in
which people, presumably in the act of conversation, raptly soliloquize;
and Dickens' technique, in these cases, is usually to give the soliloquizer
a fantastic private language as unadapted to mutual understanding as a
species of pig Latin. Witness Mr. Jaggers' interview with Joe Gargery, in
which the dignified lawyer attempts to compensate Joe financially for his
part in Pip's upbringing, and Joe swings on him with unintelligible pugil-
istic jargon.

"Which I meantersay . . . that if you come into my place bull-
baiting and badgering me, come out! Which I meantersay as sech if
you're a man, come on! Which I meantersay that what I say, I meantersay and stand or fall by!"

[1] *The Living Novel* (New York: Reynal & Hitchcock, 1947), p. 88.

Or Miss Havisham's interview with Joe over the question of Pip's wages; for each question she asks him, Joe persists in addressing his reply to Pip rather than herself, and his replies have not the remotest relation to the questions. Sometimes, by sheer repetition of a phrase, the words a character uses will assume the frenzied rotary unintelligibility of an idiot's obsession, as does Mrs. Joe's "Be grateful to them which brought you up by hand," or Pumblechook's mincing "May I?—May I?" The minimal uses of language as an instrument of communication and intellectual development are symbolized by Pip's progress in the school kept by Mr. Wopsle's great-aunt, where the summit of his education consists in his copying a large Old-English "D," which he assumes to be the design for a belt buckle; and by Joe's pleasure in the art of reading, which enables him to find three "J's" and three "O's" and three "J-O, Joes" in a piece of script.

> "Give me [he says] a good book, or a good newspaper, and sit me down afore a good fire, and I ask no better. Lord! when you *do* come to a J and a O, and says you, 'Here, at last, is a J-O, Joe,' how interesting reading is!"

There is, perhaps, no purer expression of solipsism in literature. The cultivation of the peculiar Dickensian values of language reaches its apogee when the convict Magwitch, with a benefactor's proud delight, asks Pip to read to him from a book in a foreign language, of which he understands no syllable.

From *Don Quixote* on, the novels that we have read in this series of studies have frequently drawn our attention to the ambiguities of language and the varieties of its expressive relationship to life—from the incongruities between Quixote's and Sancho's understanding of the meaning of words, to the hopeless lapse of verbal understanding between Walter and Toby Shandy, and to the subtly threatening divergencies of meaning in the constricted language of Jane Austen's characters. Language as a means of communication is a provision for social and spiritual order. You cannot make "order" with an integer, one thing alone, for order is definitively a relationship among things. Absolute noncommunication is an unthinkable madness for it negates all relationship and therefore all order, and even an ordinary madman has to create a kind of order for himself by illusions of communication. Dickens' soliloquizing characters, for all their funniness (aloneness is inexorably funny, like the aloneness of the man who slips on a banana peel, seen from the point of view of togetherness), suggest a world of isolated integers, terrifyingly alone and unrelated.

The book opens with a child's first conscious experience of his aloneness. Immediately an abrupt encounter occurs—Magwitch suddenly comes from behind a gravestone, seizes Pip by the heels, and suspends him upside down.

> "Hold your noise!" cried a terrible voice, as a man started up from among the graves at the side of the church porch. "Keep still, you little devil, or I'll cut your throat!"

Perhaps, if one could fix on two of the most personal aspects of Dickens' technique, one would speak of the strange languages he concocts for the solitariness of the soul, and the abruptness of his tempo. His human fragments suddenly shock against one another in collisions like those of Democritus' atoms or of the charged particles of modern physics. Soldiers, holding out handcuffs, burst into the blacksmith's house during Christmas dinner at the moment when Pip is clinging to a table leg in an agony of apprehension over his theft of the pork pie. A weird old woman clothed in decayed satin, jewels and spider webs, and with one shoe off, shoots out her finger at the bewildered child, with the command: "Play!" A pale young gentleman appears out of a wilderness of cucumber frames, and daintily kicking up his legs and slapping his hands together, dips his head and butts Pip in the stomach. These sudden confrontations between persons whose ways of life have no habitual or logical continuity with each other suggest the utmost incohesion in the stuff of experience.

Technique is vision. Dickens' technique is an index of a vision of life that sees human separatedness as the ordinary condition, where speech is speech *to* nobody and where human encounter is mere collision. But the vision goes much further. Our minds are so constituted that they insist on seeking in the use of language an exchange function, a delivery and a passing on of perceptions from soul to soul and generation to generation, binding them in some kind of order; and they insist on finding cause and effect, or *motivation,* in the displacements and encounters of persons or things. Without these primary patterns of perception we would not have what we call minds. And when these patterns are confused or abrogated by our experience, we are forced, in order to preserve some kind of psychic equilibrium, to seek them in extraordinary explanations—explanations again in terms of mutual exchange and cause and effect. Dickens saw his world patently all in pieces, and as a child's vision would offer some reasonable explanation of why such a world was that way—and, by the act of explanation, would make that world yield up a principle of order, however obscure or fantastic—so, with a child's literalism of imagination, he discovered organization among his fragments.

Dickens lived in a time and an environment in which a full-scale demolition of traditional values was going on, correlatively with the uprooting and dehumanization of men, women, and children by the millions—a process brought about by industrialization, colonial imperialism, and the exploitation of the human being as a "thing" or an engine or a part of an engine capable of being used for profit. This was the "century of progress" which ornamented its steam engines with iron arabesques of foliage as elaborate as the antimacassars and aspidistras and crystal or cut-glass chandeliers and bead-and-feather portieres of its drawing rooms, while the human engines of its welfare groveled and bred in the foxholes described by Marx in his *Capital*. (Hauntingly we see this discordance in the scene in *Great Expectations* where Miss Havisham, sitting in her satin and floral decay in the house called Satis, points her finger at the child and outrageously tells him to "play." For though the scene is a potent symbol of childish experience of adult obtuseness and sadism, it has also another dimension as a social symbol of those economically determined situations in which the human soul is used as a means for satisfactions not its own, under the gross and transparent lie that its activity is its happiness, its welfare and fun and "play"—a publicity instrument that is the favorite of manufacturers and insurance agencies, as well as of totalitarian strategists, with their common formula, "We're just a happy family.") The heir of the "century of progress" is the twentieth-century concentration camp, which makes no bones about people being "things."

Dickens' intuition alarmingly saw this process in motion, a process which abrogated the primary demands of human feeling and rationality, and he sought an extraordinary explanation for it. People were becoming things, and things (the things that money can buy or that are the means for making money or for exalting prestige in the abstract) were becoming more important than people. People were being de-animated, robbed of their souls, and things were usurping the prerogatives of animate creatures—governing the lives of their owners in the most literal sense. This picture, in which the qualities of things and people were reversed, was a picture of a daemonically motivated world, a world in which "dark" or occult forces or energies operate not only in people (as modern psycho-analytic psychology observes) but also in things: for if people turn themselves or are turned into things, metaphysical order can be established only if we think of things as turning themselves into people, acting under a "dark" drive similar to that which motivates the human aberration.

There is an old belief that it takes a demon to recognize a demon, and the saying illustrates the malicious sensibility with which things, in Dickens, have felt out and imitated, in their relationship with each other and with people, the secret of the human arrangement. A four-poster bed in an inn, where Pip goes to spend the night, is a despotic monster that straddles over the whole room,

> putting one of his arbitrary legs into the fireplace, and another into the doorway, and squeezing the wretched little washing-stand in quite a Divinely Righteous manner.

Houses, looking down through the skylight of Jaggers' office in London, twist themselves in order to spy on Pip like police agents who presuppose guilt. Even a meek little muffin has to be "confined with the utmost precaution under a strong iron cover," and a hat, set on a mantelpiece, demands constant attention and the greatest quickness of eye and hand to catch it neatly as it tumbles off, but its ingenuity is such that it finally manages to fall into the slop basin. The animation of inanimate objects suggests both the quaint gaiety of a forbidden life and an aggressiveness that has got out of control—an aggressiveness that they have borrowed from the human economy and an irresponsibility native to but glossed and disguised by that economy.

Dickens' fairly constant use of the pathetic fallacy (the projection of human impulses and feelings upon the nonhuman, as upon beds and houses and muffins and hats) might be considered as incidental stylistic embellishment if his description of people did not show a reciprocal metaphor: people are described by nonhuman attributes, or by such an exaggeration of or emphasis on one part of their appearance that they seem to be reduced wholly to that part, with an effect of having become "thinged" into one of their own bodily members or into an article of their clothing or into some inanimate object of which they have made a fetish. Dickens' devices for producing this transposition of attributes are various. To his friend and biographer, Forster, he said that he was always losing sight of a man in his diversion by the mechanical play of some part of the man's face, which "would acquire a sudden ludicrous life of its own." Many of what we shall call the "signatures" of Dickens' people— that special exaggerated feature or gesture or mannerism which comes to stand for the whole person—are such dissociated parts of the body, like Jaggers' huge forefinger which he bites and then plunges menacingly at the accused, or Wemmick's post-office mouth, or the clockwork apparatus in Magwitch's throat that clicks as if it were going to strike. The device is not used arbitrarily or capriciously. In this book, whose subject is the etiology of guilt and of atonement, Jaggers is the representative not only of civil law but of universal Law, which is profoundly mysterious in a world of dissociated and apparently lawless fragments; and his huge forefinger, into which he is virtually transformed and which seems to act like an "it" in its own right rather than like a member of a man, is the Law's mystery in all its fearful impersonality. Wemmick's mouth is not a post-office when he is at home in his castle but only when he is at work in Jaggers' London office, where a mechanical appearance of smiling is required of him. And as Wemmick's job has mechanized him into a grinning slot, so oppression and fear have given the convict Magwitch a clockwork apparatus for vocal chords.

Or this general principle of reciprocal changes, by which things have become as it were daemonically animated and people have been reduced to thing-like characteristics—as if, by a law of conservation of energy, the humanity of which people have become incapable had leaked out into the external environment—may work symbolically in the association of some object with a person so that the object assumes his essence and his "meaning." Mrs. Joe wears a large apron, "having a square impregnable bib in front, that was stuck full of pins and needles"—she has no reason to wear it, and she never takes it off a day in her life. Jaggers flourishes a large white handkerchief—a napkin that is the mysterious complement of his blood-smeared engagements. Estella—who is the star and jewel of Pip's great expectations—wears jewels in her hair and on her breast; "I and the jewels," she says, as if they were interchangeable. This device of association is a familiar one in fiction; what distinguishes Dickens' use of it is that the associated object acts not merely to *illustrate* a person's qualities symbolically—as novelists usually use it—but that it has a necessary metaphysical function in Dickens' universe: in this universe objects actually usurp human essences; beginning as fetishes, they tend to—and sometimes quite literally do—devour and take over the powers of the fetish-worshiper.

The process of conversion of spirit into matter that operates in the Dickens world is shown working out with savage simplicity in the case of Miss Havisham. Miss Havisham has been guilty of aggression against life in using the two children, Pip and Estella, as inanimate instruments of revenge for her broken heart—using them, that is, as if they were not human but things—and she is being changed retributively into a fungus. The decayed cake on the banquet table acts, as it were, by homeopathic magic—like a burning effigy or a doll stuck with pins; its decay parallels the necrosis in the human agent. "When the ruin is complete," Miss Havisham says, pointing to the cake but referring to herself, she will be laid out on the same table and her relatives will be invited to "feast on" her corpse. But this is not the only conversion. The "little quickened hearts" of the mice behind the panels have been quickened by what was Miss Havisham, carried off crumb by crumb.

The principle of reciprocal changes, between the human and the nonhuman, bears on the characteristic lack of complex "inner life" on the part of Dickens' people—their lack of a personally complex psychology. It is inconceivable that the fungoid Miss Havisham should have a complex inner life, in the moral sense. But in the *art* of Dickens (distinguishing that moral dialectic that arises not solely from the "characters" in a novel but from all the elements in the aesthetic structure) there is a great deal of "inner life," transposed to other forms than that of human character: partially transposed in this scene, for instance, to the symbolic activity of the speckle-legged spiders with blotchy bodies and to the gropings and pausings of the black beetles on Miss Havisham's hearth. Without benefit of Freud or Jung, Dickens saw the human soul reduced literally to the images occupying its "inner life."

Through the changes that have come about in the human, as humanity has leaked out of it, the atoms of the physical universe have become subtly impregnated with daemonic aptitude. Pip, standing waiting for Estella in the neighborhood of Newgate, and beginning dimly to be aware of his implication in the guilt for which that establishment stands—for his "great expectations" have already begun to make him a collaborator in the generic crime of using people as means to personal ends—has the sensation of a deadly dust clinging to him, rubbed off on him from the environs, and he tries to beat it out of his clothes. Smithfield, that "shameful place," "all asmear with filth and fat and blood and foam," seems to "stick to him" when he enters it on his way to the prison. The nettles and brambles of the graveyard where Magwitch first appears "stretch up cautiously" out of the graves in an effort to get a twist on the branded man's ankles and pull him in. The river has a malignant potentiality that impregnates everything upon it—discolored copper, rotten wood, honeycombed stone, green dank deposit. The river is perhaps the most constant and effective symbol in Dickens, because it establishes itself so readily to the imagination as a daemonic element, drowning people as if by intent, disgorging unforeseen evidence, chemically or physically changing all it touches, and because not only does it act as an occult "force" in itself but it is the common passage and actual flowing element that unites individuals and classes, public persons and private persons, deeds and the results of deeds, however fragmentized and separated. Upon the river, one cannot escape its action; it may throw the murderer and his victim in an embrace. At the end of *Great Expectations,* it swallows Compeyson, while, with its own obscure daemonic motivation, though it fatally injures Magwitch, it leaves him to fulfill the more subtle spiritual destiny upon which he has begun to enter. The river scene in this section, closely and apprehensively observed, is one of the most memorable in Dickens.

It is necessary to view Dickens' "coincidences" under the aspect of this wholesale change in the aptitudes of external nature. Coincidence is the violent connection of the unconnected. Life is full of violent connections of this sort, but one of the most rigorous conventions of fictional and dramatic art is that events should make a logically sequential pattern; for art is the discovery of order. Critics have frequently deplored Dickens' use of coincidences in his plots. But in a universe that is nervous throughout, a universe in which nervous ganglia stretch through both people and their external environment, so that a change in the human can infect the currents of the air and the sea, events and confrontations that seem to abrogate the laws of physical mechanics can logically be brought about. In this sense, the apparent coincidences in Dickens actually obey a causal order—not of physical mechanics but of moral dynamics.

What connection can there be [Dickens asks in another novel] between many people in the innumerable histories of this world, who, from opposite sides of great gulfs, have, nevertheless, been very curiously brought together!

What brings the convict Magwitch to the child Pip, in the graveyard, is more than the convict's hunger; Pip (or let us say simply "the child," for Pip is an Everyman) carries the convict inside him, as the negative potential of his "great expectations"—Magwitch is the concretion of his potential guilt. What brings Magwitch across the "great gulfs" of the Atlantic to Pip again, at the moment of revelation in the story, is their profoundly implicit compact of guilt, as binding as the convict's leg iron which is its recurrent symbol. The multiplying likenesses in the street as Magwitch draws nearer, coming over the sea, the mysterious warnings of his approach on the night of his reappearance, are moral projections as "real" as the storm outside the windows and as the crouched form of the vicious Orlick on the dark stairs. The conception of what brings people together "coincidentally" in their seemingly uncaused encounters and collisions —the total change in the texture of experience that follows upon any act, public or private, external or in thought, the concreteness of the effect of the act not only upon the conceiving heart but upon the atoms of physical matter, so that blind nature collaborates daemonically in the drama of reprisal—is deep and valid in this book.

In a finely lucid atmosphere of fairy tale, Dickens uses a kind of montage in *Great Expectations,* a superimposing of one image upon another with an immediate effect of hallucination, that is but one more way of representing his vision of a purely nervous and moral organization of reality. An instance is the scene in which Estella walks the casks in the old brewery. Estella's walking the casks is an enchanting ritual dance of childhood (like walking fence rails or railroad ties), but inexplicably present in the tableau is the suicidal figure of Miss Havisham hanging by her neck from a brewery beam. Accompanying each appearance of Estella—the star and the jewel of Pip's expectations—is a similarly disturbing ghost, an image of an unformed dread. When Pip thinks of her, though he is sitting in a warm room with a friend, he shudders as if in a wind from over the marshes. Her slender knitting fingers are suddenly horribly displaced by the marred wrists of a murderess. The technique of montage is that of dreams, which know with awful precision the affinities between the guilt of our desires and the commonplaces of our immediate perceptions.

This device, of doubling one image over another, is paralleled in the handling of character. In the sense that one implies the other, the glittering frosty girl Estella, and the decayed and false old woman, Miss Havisham, are not two characters but a single one, or a single essence with dual aspects, as if composed by montage—a spiritual continuum, so to speak. For inevitably wrought into the fascinating jewel-likeness of Pip's great expectations, as represented by Estella, is the falsehood and degeneracy represented by Miss Havisham, the soilure on the unpurchased good. The boy Pip and the criminal Magwitch form another such continuum. Magwitch, from a metaphysical point of view, is not outside Pip but inside him, and his apparition is that of Pip's own unwrought deeds: Pip, having adopted "great expectations," will live by making people into Magwitches, into means for his ends. The relationship between Joe Gargery, saintly simpleton of the folk, and Orlick, dark beast of the Teutonic marshes (who comes "from the ooze"), has a somewhat different dynamics, though they too form a spiritual continuum. Joe and Orlick are related not as two aspects of a single moral identity, but as the opposed extremes of spiritual possibility—the one unqualified love, the other unqualified hate—and they form a frame within which the actions of the others have their ultimate meaning. A commonplace of criticism is that, as Edmund Wilson puts it, Dickens was usually unable to "get the good and bad together in one character." [2] The criticism might be valid if Dickens' were a naturalistic world, but it is not very relevant to Dickens' daemonically organized world. In a naturalistic world, obeying mechanical laws, each character is organically discrete from every other, and presumably each contains a representative mixture of "the good and bad." But in Dickens' thoroughly nervous world, that does not know the laws of mechanics but knows only spiritual law, one simple or "flat" character can be superimposed upon another so that together they form the representative human complexity of good-in-evil and evil-in-good.

Two kinds of crime form Dickens' two chief themes, the crime of parent against child, and the calculated social crime. They are formally analogous, their form being the treatment of persons as things; but they are also inherent in each other, whether the private will of the parent is to be considered as depraved by the operation of a public institution, or the social institution is to be considered as a bold concert of the depravities of individual "fathers." In *Great Expectations* the private crime against

[2] *The Wound and the Bow* (Boston: Houghton Mifflin Company, 1941), p. 65.

the child is Mrs. Joe's and Pumblechook's and Wopsle's, all "foster parents" either by necessity or self-conceit; while the social crime is the public treatment of Magwitch. That the two kinds of crime are inherent in each other we are made aware of as we are led to identify Magwitch's childhood with Pip's; the brutality exercised toward both children was the same brutality, though the "parents" in the one case were private persons, and in the other, society itself. Complicating the meaning of "the crime" still further, Magwitch also has taken upon himself the role of foster parent to Pip, and whether, as parent, he acts in charity or impiousness, or both, is a major ambiguity which the drama sets out to resolve.

"The crime," in Dickens, is evidently a permutation of multiple motivations and acts, both public and private, but always with the same tendency to convert people into things, and always implying either symbolically or directly a child-parent situation. The child-parent situation has been disnatured, corrupted, with the rest of nature; or rather, since the child-parent situation is the dynamic core of the Dickens world, the radical disnaturing here is what has corrupted the rest. His plots seldom serve to canalize, with the resolution of the particular set of plotted circumstances, the hysteria submerged in his vision of a nature gone thoroughly wrong; the permutations of the crimes are too many, and their ultimate cause or root is evasive, unless one would resort to some dramatically unmanageable rationale such as original sin. The Dickens world requires an act of redemption. A symbolic act of this kind is again and again indicated in his novels, in the charity of the uncherished and sinned-against child for the inadequate or criminal father—what might be called the theme of the prodigal father, Dickens' usual modification of the prodigal son theme. But the redemptive act should be such that it should redeem not only the individual "fathers," but society at large. One might almost say—thinking of Dickens' caricatures of the living dead, with their necrotic members and organs, their identifications of themselves with inanimate objects—that it should be such as to redeem the dead. *Great Expectations* is an exception among his novels in that here the redemptive act is adequate to and structural for both bodies of thematic material— the sins of individuals and the sins of society.

Pip first becomes aware of the "identity of things" as he is held suspended heels over head by the convict; that is, in a world literally turned upside down. Thenceforth Pip's interior landscape is inverted by his guilty knowledge of this man "who had been soaked in water, and smothered in mud, and lamed by stones, and cut by flints, and stung by nettles, and torn by briars." The apparition is that of all suffering that the earth can inflict, and that the apparition presents itself to a child is as much as to say that every child, whatever his innocence, inherits guilt (as the potential of his acts) for the condition of man. The inversion of natural order begins here with first self-consciousness: the child is heir to the sins of the "fathers." Thus the crime that is always pervasive in the Dickens universe is identified in a new way—not primarily as that of the "father," nor as that of some public institution, but as that of the child—the original individual who must necessarily take upon himself responsibility for not only what is to be done in the present and the future, but what has been done in the past, inasmuch as the past is part and parcel of the present and the future. The child is the criminal, and it is for this reason that he is able to redeem his world; for the world's guilt is his guilt, and he can expiate it in his own acts.

The guilt of the child is realized on several levels. Pip experiences the psychological *form* (or feeling) of guilt before he is capable of voluntary evil; he is treated by adults—Mrs. Joe and Pumblechook and Wopsle —as if he were a felon, a young George Barnwell (a character in the play which Wopsle reads on the night when Mrs. Joe is attacked) wanting only to murder his nearest relative, as George Barnwell murdered his uncle. This is the usual nightmare of the child in Dickens, a vision of imminent incarceration, fetters like sausages, lurid accusatory texts. He is treated, that is, as if he were a thing, manipulable by adults for the extraction of certain sensations: by making him feel guilty and diminished, they are able to feel virtuous and great. But the psychological *form* of guilt acquires spiritual *content* when Pip himself conceives the tainted wish—the wish to be like the most powerful adult and to treat others as things. At the literal level, Pip's guilt is that of snobbery toward Joe Gargery, and snobbery is a denial of the human value of others. Symbolically, however, Pip's guilt is that of murder; for he steals the file with which the convict rids himself of his leg iron, and it is this leg iron, picked up on the marshes, with which Orlick attacks Mrs. Joe; so that the child does inevitably overtake his destiny, which was, like George Barnwell, to murder his nearest relative. But the "relative" whom Pip, adopting the venerable criminality of society, is, in the widest symbolic scope of intention, destined to murder is not Mrs. Joe but his "father," Magwitch—to murder in the socially chronic fashion of the Dickens world, which consists in the dehumanization of the weak, or in moral acquiescence to such murder. Pip is, after all, the ordinary mixed human being, one more Everyman in the long succession of them that literature has represented, but we see this Everyman as he develops from a child; and his destiny is directed by the ideals of his world—toward "great expectations" which involve the making of Magwitches—which involve, that is, murder. These are the possibilities that are projected in the opening scene of the book, when the young child, left with a burden on his soul, watches the convict limping off under an angry red sky, toward the black marshes, the gibbet, and the savage lair of the sea, in a still rotating landscape.

In Dickens' modification of the folk pattern of the fairy wishing, Magwitch is Pip's "fairy godfather" who changes the pumpkin into a coach. Like all the "fathers," he uses the child as a thing in order to obtain through him vicarious sensations of grandeur. In relation to society, however, Magwitch is the child, and society the prodigal father; from the time he was first taken for stealing turnips, the convict's career has duplicated brutally and in public the pathos of the ordinary child. Again, in relation to Pip, Magwitch is still the child; for, spiritually committed by his "great expectations" to that irresponsibility which has accounted for the Magwitches, Pip is projectively, at least, answerable for Magwitch's existence and for his brutalization. Pip carries his criminal father within him; he is, so to speak, the father of his father. The ambiguities of each term of the relationship are such that each is both child and father, making a fourfold relationship; and the act of love between them at the end is thus reinforced fourfold, and the redemption by love is a fourfold redemption: that is to say, it is symbolically infinite, for it serves for all the meanings Dickens finds it possible to attach to the central child-father situation, the most profound and embracing relationship that, in Dickens' work, obtains among men.

As the child's original alienation from "natural" order is essentially mysterious, a guilty inheritance from the fathers which invades first awareness, so the redemptive act is also a mysterious one. The mysterious nature of the act is first indicated, in the manner of a motif, when Mrs. Joe, in imbecile pantomime, tries to propitiate her attacker, the bestial Orlick. In Orlick is concretized all the undefined evil of the Dickens world, that has nourished itself underground and crept along walls, like the ancient stains on the house of Atreus. He is the lawlessness implied in the unnatural conversions of the human into the nonhuman, the retributive death that invades those who have grown lean in life and who have exercised the powers of death over others. He is the instinct of aggression and destruction, the daemonism of sheer external Matter as such; he is pure "thingness" emerging without warning from the ooze where he has been unconsciously cultivated. As Orlick is one form of spiritual excess—unmotivated hate—Joe Gargery is the opposed form—love without reservation. Given these terms of the spiritual framework, the redemptive act itself could scarcely be anything but grotesque—and it is by a grotesque gesture, one of the most profoundly intuitive symbols in Dickens, that Mrs. Joe is redeemed. What is implied by her humble propitiation of the beast Orlick is a recognition of personal guilt in the guilt of others, and of its dialectical relationship with love. The motif reappears in the moment of major illumination in the book. Pip "bows down," not to Joe Gargery, toward whom he has been privately and literally guilty, but to the wounded, hunted, shackled man, Magwitch, who has been guilty toward himself. It is in this way that the manifold organic relationships among men are revealed, and that the Dickens world—founded in fragmentariness and disintegration—is made whole.

ON *Vanity Fair*

Almost exactly a century separates *Tom Jones* from *Vanity Fair;* but with *Vanity Fair,* so far as technical developments in the novel are concerned, it is as if there had been none. We are in the story telling convention of the "omniscient author" sanctioned by Fielding's great example, but with a damaging difference that is due, not so much to an inherent inadequacy of that convention itself, as the spiritual incoherency of another age. It is true that the technique of omniscient authorship can allow a relaxed garrulity—what James called "the terrible fluidity of self-revelation"—for if the author can enter the story in his own voice, there is nothing to keep him from talking. After discussing Becky's adolescent designs on Jos Sedley, and her visions of shawls and necklaces and aristocratic company which she imagines will be the rewards of marriage with Jos, Thackeray comments,

> Charming Alnaschar visions! it is the happy privilege of youth to construct you, and many a fanciful young creature besides Rebecca Sharp has indulged in these delightful day-dreams ere now!

The comment is both inane and distracting—distracting our attention from the tense mental operations of Becky and turning it upon the momentarily flaccid mentality of her author. The effect is one of rather surprised irritation, as it is again when, having described Jos's wardrobe, his pains in dressing, his vanity and shyness, Thackeray remarks,

> If Miss Rebecca can get the better of *him,* and at her first entrance into life, she is a young person of no ordinary cleverness.

What we feel is that two orders of reality are clumsily getting in each other's way: the order of imaginative reality, where Becky lives, and the order of historical reality, where William Makepeace Thackeray lives. The fault becomes more striking in the following unforgivable parenthesis. Jos has just presented Amelia with flowers.

> "Thank you, dear Joseph," said Amelia, quite ready to kiss her brother, if he were so minded. (And I think for a kiss from such a dear creature as Amelia, I would purchase all Mr. Lee's conservatories out of hand.)

The picture of Thackeray himself kissing Amelia pulls Amelia quite out of the created world of *Vanity Fair* and drops her into some shapeless limbo of Thackerayan sentiment where she loses all aesthetic orientation.

Nevertheless, the conventions employed in a work of art cannot fairly be judged by themselves; they can be judged only as instrumental to a vision. The time in which Thackeray wrote was, compared with Fielding's time, itself looser in what we might call cultural composition; its values were less integrated in a common philosophical "style" or tenor of mind. In *Tom Jones,* the convention of the author's appearance in his book as "gregarious eye," stage manager, and moralist, is a strategy that is used with a highly formal regularity of rhythm, and it animates every turn of Fielding's language, as the ironic life of the language. Most important, the convention had benefited by an age's practice of and belief in form, form in manners and rhetoric and politics and philosophy—that is, by an age's coherently structured world view. The set of feelings and ideas of which Fielding acts as vehicle, when he makes his personal appearances in his book, is a set of feelings and ideas with the stamp of spiritual consistency upon them. They do not afflict us with a sense of confused perspectives between the author's person and his work, his opinions and his creation, as do Thackeray's. Whereas Thackeray seems merely to be victimized or tricked by his adopted convention into a clumsy mishandling of perspectives, Fielding manipulates the same convention deliberately to produce displacements of perspective as an organic element of composition. This is not to say that Fielding's creative perceptions are, on the whole, more penetrating and profound than Thackeray's; indeed, Thackeray's seem to reach a good deal deeper into the difficulties, compromises, and darkness of the human estate; but Fielding's have the organizing power to make an ancient oral convention of storytelling an appropriate instrument of his vision, whereas the same convention—actually one that is most sympathetic to Thackeray's gift of easy, perspicacious, ranging talk—

becomes a personal convenience for relaxation of aesthetic control, *even a means to counterfeit* his creative vision.

Becky ruminates, "I think I could be a good woman if I had five thousand a year," and adds with a sigh,

> "Heigho! I wish I could exchange my position in society, and all my relations, for a snug sum in the Three per Cent. Consols."

Here she is as true to herself psychologically as is Moll Flanders; but she is more complex than Moll, and we know perfectly that, at this promising stage in her career, the sigh is only a casual fantasy—arising chiefly out of boredom with the tedious business of cultivating the good graces of people much less intelligent than herself—and that if the "snug sum" were offered, she would not really exchange her prospects for it, for her temperament is not at present to be satisfied with snugness. There are to be pearl necklaces, presentation at court, a *succès fou* at Gaunt House. But Thackeray interprets for us.

> It may, perhaps, have struck her that to have been honest and humble, to have done her duty, and to have marched straightforward on her way, would have brought her as near happiness as that path by which she was striving to attain it.

This is a doctrine with which, in principle, we have no cause either to agree or disagree; a novel is not made of doctrines and principles, but of concretely imagined life, and whatever moral principle may be honestly adduced from that life must be intrinsic to it, concretely qualitative within it. *Vanity Fair* is strong with life, but in those concretions where it is alive there is nothing to suggest that to be "honest and humble" can possibly bring happiness. Becky is the happiest person in the book; she is alive from beginning to end, alive in intelligence and activity and *joie de vivre,* whether she is throwing Dr. Johnson's dictionary out of a coach window, in superb scorn of the humiliations of the poor, or exercising her adulterous charm on General Tufto, whether she is prancing to court to be made an "honest woman" (in stolen lace), or hiding a cognac bottle in a sordid bed. From Becky's delighted exercise in being alive, we can learn nothing about the happiness to be derived from humble dutifulness. On the other hand, from Amelia's humble dutifulness we can learn nothing that convinces us doctrinally that happiness lies in such a way of life. For it is not only that the brisk gait and vivid allure of Becky's egoistic and aggressive way of life make Amelia look tepid, tear sodden, and compromised: this effect would not occur if the book were soundly structured, if its compositional center (what James called the "commanding centre" of the composition) were entirely firm and clear.

The actually functioning compositional center of *Vanity Fair* is that node or intersection of extensive social and spiritual relationships constituted by Becky's activities: her relationships with a multitude of individuals—Jos and Amelia and George, old Sir Pitt and Rawdon and Miss Crawley and the Bute Crawleys and the Pitt Crawleys, Lady Bareacres, Lord Steyne, and so on—and, through these individuals, her relationships with large and significant blocks of a civilization: with the middle-class Sedley block, that block which is in the process of physical destruction because of its lack of shrewdness in an acquisitive culture; with the other middle-class Osborne block, that block which has displaced the Sedley block through its own acquisitive shrewdness and through the necessarily accompanying denial of the compassionate and sympathetic human impulses; with the aristocratic Crawley block, in all its complexity of impotence and mad self-destruction, and (in young Sir Pitt, with the "gooseberry eyes") canny self-renovation through connivance with the economy and morality of the dominant middle class; with the ambiguous Steyne block, that is above the economic strife and therefore free of conventional moral concerns, but in its social freedom, "stained" deeply in nerves and blood. (In the names he gives people, Thackeray plays—like many novelists —on punning suggestion, as he does in the name of the crawling Crawleys, "raw-done" Rawdon, Sharp, Steyne, O'Dowd, etc.) This social relationship, concretized through Becky's relationship with individuals, is the hub of the book's meanings, its "compositional center." But beside this violently whirling and excited center is another, a weak and unavailing epicenter, where Amelia weeps and suffers and wins—wins Dobbin and solvency and neighborhood prestige and a good middle-class house with varnished staircases. Organized around the two centers are two plots, which have as little essentially to do with each other as Thackeray's creative imagination had to do with his sentimental, morally fearful reflections. He cannot bear to allow the wonderfully animated vision of Becky's world to speak for itself, for its meaning is too frightening; he must add to it a complementary world—Amelia's—to act as its judge and corrector. One thinks, in comparison, of Balzac, who was writing almost contemporaneously. Balzac was both as skeptical and as sentimental as Thackeray, but he was a passionate rationalist as well, and a much bolder dramatic formalist. In Balzac, the weak and the suffering and the pure in heart do not win. They have no pretensions to effective moral dynamism in the evil Balzacian world, which uses them as illustrative examples of the impotence of an "honest and humble" way of life.

As the convention of the omniscient author allows Thackeray to keep up a maladroit "sound track" of personal interpolations, so it also collaborates with his confusion as to where the compositional center of his book lies; for though the Becky-world and the Amelia-world, having no common motivation, confront each other with closed entrances, so to speak, yet the author is able, by abuse of his rights of omniscience, to move facilely through these closed doors. We assume that, in Thackeray's plan, the compositional center of the book was to be the moral valence between the two worlds. But there is no valence between them, nothing in either to produce a positive effect of significance on the other. The only effect is negative: the Amelia-plot pales into a morally immature fantasy beside the vivid life of the Becky-plot. For Becky is the great morally meaningful figure, the moral symbol, in the book, and beside her there is room and meaning for Amelia only as victim—certainly not as "success figure." The word "moral," which we have used rather frequently in these studies, needs perhaps a somewhat closer attention here. Becky is not virtuous, and in speaking of her as a morally significant figure, we cannot possibly confuse her moral meaning with the meaning of "virtue." She is a morally meaningful figure because she symbolizes the morality of her world at its greatest intensity and magnitude. The greediness that has only a reduced, personal meaning in Mrs. Bute Crawley, as she nags and blunders at old Miss Crawley's deathbed, acquires, through Becky's far more intelligent and courageous greed—as she encounters international techniques for the satisfaction of greed with her own subtle and knowing and superior techniques—an extensive social meaning. The corruption that, in old Sir Pitt, has meaning at most for the senility of a caste, becomes, in Becky's prostitution and treason and murderousness, the moral meaning of a culture. For Becky's activities are designed with intelligent discrimination and lively intuition, and they are carried through not only with unflagging will power but with joy as well. By representing her world at its highest energetic potential, by alchemizing all its evil but stupid and confused or formless impulses into brilliantly controlled intention, she endows her world with meaning. The meaning is such as to inspire horror; but the very fact that we conceive this horror intellectually and objectively is an acknowledgment of Becky's morally symbolic stature.

There is a French criticism of the English novel, that, in the English novel's characteristic concern with the social scene, it fails to explore "the deeper layers of personality." One understands the motivation of this criticism, if one compares representative French and English novels of approximately the same periods, although the criticism itself does not seem to be well thought out. *The Pilgrim's Progress* is populated with social "types," sparsely limned sketches that isolate certain traits, whereas, almost contemporaneously, Madame de Lafayette's *La Princesse de Clèves* is concentrated upon a depth illumination of the tortured psyche of a delicate woman who, in a loveless marriage, is moved by an illicit passion. Even *Clarissa Harlowe,* which is commonly thought of as an exhaustive representation of a young woman's emotions, is, because of its mythical qualities, rather more of a vision into the social soul than into that of a credible individual; and the difference is brought out by comparison with the almost contemporaneous *Manon Lescaut,* by the Abbé Prevost, in which the subject has certain affinities with that of *Clarissa* (except that it is the girl, here, who is the libertine, and the young man who is the afflicted one), but which is again—like so many French novels —a concentrated depth drawing of personal psychology rather than a social vision. One could pursue a number of other examples in the same way. But the difference is a relative difference only. For the "deeper layers of personality" are meaningless unless they can be related, at least by inference, to aspects of life that have some social generality; while social life is meaningless unless it finds embodiment in individuals. A more significant difference between classical French novels and classical English novels is one of method. The English novel has tended traditionally to symbolize certain phases of personality through the concrete image (Christian as the "man in rags" with a burden on his back; the Philosopher Square standing among Molly's "other female utensils" when the curtain falls in the bedroom; Clarissa, with streaming eyes and disheveled bosom, prostrating herself before Lovelace; Jaggers washing his hands or Miss Havisham beside the rotten bridecake); while the French novel has tended traditionally to a discursive analysis of feeling and motive, as has the French drama. Image and analysis are merely two different ways of mirroring what goes on in the soul. The methods are never exclusive; and we find such significant exceptions to the general tendency as Flaubert's *Madame Bovary,* where the image dominates, and Conrad's *Lord Jim,* where analysis dominates.

Let us illustrate, from *Vanity Fair,* the method of the image and what it is able to imply as to the "deeper layers of personality." Characteristically, in this book, the social concern is paramount. We have spoken of the various "blocks" of this civilization, some slipping into rubble by the crush of the others or by internal decay, some thrusting themselves up by the neighboring defaultment. But governing all the movements is one ethos of aggressive egoism, articulated through the acquisition of cash and through the prestige fantasies born of cash. Becky herself is a member of no particular class and confined to no particular "block." (Significantly, she is the daughter of a Bohemian artist and a French music-hall singer.) She is more mobile than any of the other characters, because of her freedom from caste, and thus is able to enter into a great variety of class relationships: this is the peculiar novelistic virtue of the picara and picaro, and the enduring source of virility of the picaresque form—the protagonist's freedom of movement. Still acting under the same ethos as that governing the whole civilization, Becky is able to represent its tendencies without class pretenses. Thus Becky, like Moll Flanders, though a strongly individualized character, is the type of a whole civilization, a small-scale model of a world, a microcosm in which the social macrocosm is subtilized and intensified and made significant. With this predominantly social bearing of the novel, the characters—even Becky—tend to be depicted in a relatively "external" way: that is, there is relatively little discussion of the nuances of their feelings and their motivations; they are not self-analytical characters, as characters in French novels tend to be, nor do they spend much time in deliberate analysis of each other; they appear to us physically, in action; and—with some generalized interpretive help from the author himself (whose interpretations, as we have noted, we cannot always trust)—we enter into their motives and states of feeling by our own intuition. Examples are manifold. There is Becky's meeting of George's eyes in the mirror as she and Amelia, Jos and George, are leaving for Vauxhall: a flashing, accidental illumination of his vanity and vulnerability—and though here might be an excellent opportunity for Becky to engage in psychological speculations and deliberations, little of the kind occurs. There is the physical flash, the illumination by image only, and Becky has George's number. And yet later, when George and Amelia, Becky and Rawdon, meet on their honeymoon trips at Brighton, and Becky with almost unconscious slyness encourages George to make love to her, the early image of the meeting of eyes in a mirror plays on the reader's understanding of motivation, as it does again when we see Becky in overt sexual aggressiveness at the Brussels ball. There has been no need of discursive analysis of motive; the image does the work.

Or—another instance of the work of the image—there is Jos, in his obesity and his neckcloths and his gorgeous waistcoats. We should not expect Jos to analyze himself, nor anyone else to have an interest in analyzing what he feels, for he is below the level of what is rationally interesting; and yet, from the physical picture alone, we are made intuitively aware of deeply disturbed "layers of personality" in Jos. He is one of the most complicated psychological portraits in the book (more complicated, for instance, than that of another voluptuary, the Marquis of Steyne, who has more refined opportunities than Jos and a better head), extremely unpleasant, with suggestions of impalpable submerged perversities, pathetic, with a pathos that is at the same time an outrage to our feeling for what is humanly cognizable in pathos—for Jos is a glandularly suffering animal, with the "human" so hidden in his tortured fat that we feel it to be obscene, while we must still recognize it as human. Jos offering his neck to Isidore's razor (in the passage we have quoted in the general introduction to the present volume) is a complex image of a kind of fear so muddied, an image of a psychological state so profoundly irrational, that we react to it with an impulse of horrified laughter—the intuitive horror having no other outlet than in a sense of the absurd. At the same time that these physical images of Jos flash to the mind's eye an impression of something deep and possible in individual personality, they are made by Thackeray to represent to the social reason an extremely significant phase of a culture. We see in Jos's obesity the sickness of a culture, the sickness due to spiritual gourmandism, or, in simpler but still metaphorical words, to "overeating"; in his shyness of women, the repressions and abnormalities of a sick culture; in his stupidity and febrile conceit, the intellectual numbing and tubercular euphoria of a culture. Thus the physical image, here, mirrors most fearful depths of the personal and, at the same time, most threatening perspectives of the social life.

We shall cite a few more illustrations of this method of the "image," as Thackeray uses it, keeping in mind its double significance, its significance for personal psychology (the "deeper layers of personality") and its social significance. But in preparation for these particular citations, we should speak of one singularly important theme of *Vanity Fair,* and that is a theme which we shall call the theme of the "fathers." In the eighteenth-century novels that we have read, the "father" has appeared in a light that is rather different from the light that is thrown on the "father" in nineteenth-century novels. There is Squire Allworthy, for instance, who, as "father," though he may have his failures of insight, is still an affirmative moral reference in the *Tom Jones* system of values; he is idealized, but this itself is significant of the fact that the "father" still represents a moral ideal. In the eighteenth century, the idea of the "father" was not, on the whole, ambiguous, or suggestive of doubts or deficiencies or culpability—that is, as this idea is reflected in literature. Mr. Harlowe, in *Clarissa,* is the most exceptional example; but even here, the daughter's return to her "Father's house," on the elevated stage of the divine, is an affirmation and sanction of the usual parental-filial relationship of authority and obedience which is esteemed to be universally valid; Mr. Harlowe made a mistake, but so did Clarissa make a mistake; informed by Clarissa's passion, it is to be hoped that no other daughters or fathers will ever make such mistakes. In *Tristram Shandy,* the "father," Walter Shandy, is a freak, yet he is presented only under the aspect of general human freakishness, pleasant and interesting eccentricity, and we are led in no way to think of him in terms of parental culpability; indeed, as "father," he takes his responsibility most enormously—to be the right kind of father and to bring up the right kind of son are his devouring concern; the inquiries and devotions of fatherhood—as to conditions of conception, size of the son's nose, the son's name, his education—form the whole shape of Walter Shandy's mental activities, his very eccentricity. Similarly in Smollett's *Humphry Clinker,* where the "father" (an uncle, in this case) is a querulous hypochondriac, leading his life in a tone of objection to everything, we are "on his side," we object when he objects, with a grain of salt for his elderly fury; and the book has its moral equipoise in the rightness of this "father's" perceptions.

We see, in the notion of the father in eighteenth-century literature, a reflection of social trust: of trust in and reliance upon and devotion to a general social system of values—that coherent "world view" of the eighteenth century that we have spoken of earlier in this essay. For, under our anciently inherited patriarchal organization of the family, an organization that inevitably extended itself into political organization and philosophic organization, the "father-imago" has acquired vast symbolic extension beyond domestic life and into general social life: our "fathers" are not only our individual fathers but all those who have come before us—society as it has determined our conditions of existence and the problems we have to confront. *Vanity Fair,* with its panorama of western European international society as backdrop to the heroine's activities, is full of "fathers," sick fathers, guilty fathers.

Curiously enough, we have seen the inception of the theme of the "fathers" in Jane Austen, despite her eighteenth-century social sensibility; and it is—along with her inception of modern technique in the handling of the "point of view"—a striking mark of her modernity. In *Pride and Prejudice,* the father, Mr. Bennet, is anything but the morally idealized figure of Squire Allworthy; and even as an "eccentric" or "humorous" character (in the older sense), he casts moral shadows that, for instance, Walter Shandy—another "eccentric"—does not cast. Mr. Bennet, as father, is guilty. In Dickens' *Great Expectations,* we have seen that the theme of the "father" dominates the meanings of the book, and we have seen how many inflections Dickens is able to get out of this theme. Crossing language boundaries, we find in Stendhal's *The Red and the Black* (1830) various implementations of the same theme: Julien's revolt against the peasant grossness of his own father, and his finding of a "spiritual father" in a Jansenist monk, who himself is under suspicion from the religious institution to which he belongs (here the father who is worthy of respect is himself virtually a social outcast). In Balzac's *Père Goriot*—whose title is indicative of the "father" theme—the actual father, Goriot, is a degenerative victim of corrupt social ideas, while the "spiritual father" of the hero is an out-and-out criminal. Turgenev's *Fathers and Sons* announces the same theme by its title; and again here the "fathers" are inadequate. In Dostoevski's *The Brothers Karamazov,* the sons' murder of the father is the focus of plot, and we have the famous question, on the part of Ivan Karamazov, "Who doesn't desire his father's death?" The title of D. H. Lawrence's *Sons and Lovers* indicates again the modern preoccupation with the parental-filial relationship. Joyce's *Portrait of the Artist* and his *Ulysses* carry out the same preoccupation: in the former, the hero's actual father goes to pieces and the family disintegrates with him; in the latter, the hero's "spiritual father" is a Jew, emotionally an alien in the Dublin of the book, without integration with the social body, and as lost and wandering as the son.

It is significant of the vital intuitiveness of Thackeray's *Vanity Fair* that the theme of the "fathers" should have such importance: in this book, an immensely impressive female, herself quite fatherless, manages to articulate in her career the most meaningful social aspects of the "father" theme. We need, in this view of the book, to free ourselves from the narrower Freudian aspects of the theme and to think in terms of Thackeray's broad social perspective, where the "fathers" are such variants as Mr. Sedley, Mr. Osborne, old Sir Pitt, even the Marquis of Steyne: in other words, such variants as to include all the older, authoritative, and determinative aspects of society.

And now, with this general notion of the significance of the theme of parental authority, we can consider what Thackeray manages to get out of the "image" of old Mr. Osborne and his daughters coming down the stairs, in their evening ritual, to dinner.

> The obedient bell in the lower regions began ringing the announcement of the meal. The tolling over, the head of the family thrust his hands into the great tail-pockets of his great blue coat and brass buttons, and without waiting for a further announcement, strode downstairs alone, scowling over his shoulder at the four females.
>
> "What's the matter now, my dear?" asked one of the other, as they rose and tripped gingerly behind the sire.
>
> "I suppose the funds are falling," whispered Miss Wirt; and so, trembling and in silence, this hushed female company followed their dark leader.

In the lines just before this there is one other, inconspicuous, touch: in the drawing room where they are waiting for dinner is a chronometer "surmounted by a cheerful brass group of the sacrifice of Iphigenia." The depths which are suggested by this picture, but quite as if accidentally, are the depths of Greek tragedy and, still further back, of Freud's dim, subhuman, imagined "primitive horde": the "dark leader" with his "hushed female company," and the ridiculous but furious Victorian clock "cheerfully" symbolizing the whole. Antiquity's dark brooding over the monstrous nature of man is made to take on, in this incidental image of a family's going to dinner, the unwholesomeness and perversity that have

149

been added to man's classical monstrosity by "falling funds," a drop in the stock market.

There is the recurrent incident in the hall outside the bedroom where old Miss Crawley is sick, Becky tending her, everyone—including Becky —waiting for and speculating on the "reversionary spoils."

> Captain Rawdon got an extension of leave on his aunt's illness, and remained dutifully at home. He was always in her ante-chamber. (She lay sick in the state bedroom into which you entered by the little blue saloon.) His father was always meeting him there; or if he came down the corridor ever so quietly, his father's door was sure to open, and the hyaena face of the old gentleman to glare out. What was it set one to watch the other so? A generous rivalry, no doubt, as to which should be most attentive to the dear sufferer in the state bedroom. Rebecca used to come out and comfort both of them—or one or the other of them rather.

Short and unemphasized as the passage is (outside of one ironic line, it consists only of an image, the image of Rawdon opening a door and looking into the corridor, of the old man's "hyaena face" instantly looking out from an opposite door, of Becky coming down the hall to "comfort" them), it contains a pregnant and disturbing meaning, both for personal psychology and for social psychology. Later, when Becky will attempt to inform Sir Pitt about her clandestine marriage, but without telling him the name of her husband, he will be uproariously amused; but as soon as she tells him the name—his son, Rawdon—he goes mad with inexplicable fury. We look back mentally to the incidents in the hall outside Miss Crawley's sickroom, where son and father glare at each other, and where Becky comes to comfort them *separately,* holding each in suspense as to her amorous favor. And we look forward also to that horrible line in Becky's letter to Rawdon (after the disclosure to Sir Pitt), where she says, "I might have been somebody's mamma, instead of— Oh, I tremble, I tremble . . ." What is contained here is probably the most excruciatingly primitive father-son battle in literature, with one of the most sensitively feminine but perversely sentimental reflections upon it. How are we to say, in such a case, whether what we are observing is the "deeper layers of personality" or the social scene?

And then there is the description of the turmoil surrounding old Sir

Pitt's death. It consists of a succession of images: Miss Horrocks flitting in ribbons through "the halls of their fathers"; again Miss Horrocks

> of the guilty ribbons, with a wild air, trying at the presses and escritoires with a bunch of keys.—

while upstairs they are "trying to bleed" Sir Pitt (the "trying to" suggests unknown but repulsive derangements); the servant girl screaming and making faces at him in private while he whimpers. The cumulation of these images, scattered and casual as they are, makes the face of a gorgon of destiny. The personal and social idea of the "father" (an idea which is inextricably both personal and social) is made the nasty companion of the ribbon-flitting Miss Horrocks; when Sir Pitt gives the family pearls to Lady Jane ("Pretty pearls—never gave 'em to the ironmonger's daughter"), marital relationships, with all they mean for the security created for us by our elders, are referred back retrospectively to Sir Pitt's chronic tipsiness and Lady Crawley's worsted knitting—an "enormous interminable piece of knitting"—

> She worked that worsted day and night . . . She had not character enough to take to drinking . . . ;

drawers are tried while the "father" is bled; and finally—so great is the prestige of this "father" and baronet—the servant girl has full amplitude to scream obscenities and make faces at him, for he has turned into "a whimpering old idiot put in and out of bed and cleaned and fed like a baby."

The burden of Thackeray's intuition into personal psychology and its social meaning falls on images like these, and they are innumerable in *Vanity Fair*. But the greatness of *Vanity Fair* is not in scattered images, sensitive as these are. They are all gathered up in Becky Sharp. Becky does for Jos, murderously, at the end; and what she does to Jos is only cancerously implicit in himself and the civilization that has made him; she is the darkness—shining obsidianly in an intelligent personality—in old Mr. Osborn's dense sadism against his daughters and his corruption of the meaning of paternal responsibility toward his son; she manipulates the insane father-son conflict between Sir Pitt and Rawdon; and she is the "guilty ribbons" of Miss Horrocks (instead of a servant's ribbons she has a courtesan's pearls) and at the same time the whimpering idiocy of the dying Sir Pitt (paralleling his repulsive attack of mortality, she inflicts a similarly repulsive mortality on Jos)—for she is at once all the imperatively aggressive, insanely euphoric impulses of a morally sick civilization, and an individual condensation of that civilization. We question whether we would understand her at all, or be charmed by her buoyancy or appalled by her destructiveness, if her impulses were not memorabilia of our own and her civilization our heritage.

ON *Wuthering Heights*

Emily Brontë's single novel is, of all English novels, the most treacherous for the analytical understanding to approach. It is treacherous not because of failure in its own formal controls on its meaning—for the book is highly wrought in form—but because it works at a level of experience that is unsympathetic to, or rather, simply irrelevant to the social and moral reason. One critic has spoken of the quality of feeling in this book as "a quality of suffering":

> It has anonymity. It is not complete. Perhaps some ballads represent it in English, but it seldom appears in the main stream, and few writers are in touch with it. It is a quality of experience the expression of which is at once an act of despair and an act of recognition or of worship. It is the recognition of an absolute hierarchy. This is also the feeling in Aeschylus. It is found amongst genuine peasants and is a great strength. Developing in places which yield only the permanent essentials of existence, it is undistracted and universal.[1]

We feel the lack of "completeness," which this critic refers to, in the nature of the dramatic figures that Emily Brontë uses: they are figures that arise on and enact their drama on some ground of the psychic life where ethical ideas are not at home, at least such ethical ideas as those that inform our ordinary experience of the manners of men. They have the "anonymity" of figures in dreams or in religious ritual. The attitude toward life that they suggest is rather one of awed contemplation of an unregenerate universe than a feeling for values or disvalues in types of human intercourse. It is an attitude that is expressed in some of the great Chinese paintings of the Middle Ages, where the fall of a torrent from an enormous

[1] G. D. Klingopulos, "The Novel as Dramatic Poem (II): 'Wuthering Heights,'" in *Scrutiny* XIV:4 (1946–1947).

height, or a single huge wave breaking under the moon, or a barely indicated chain of distant mountains lost among mists, seems to be animated by some mysterious, universal, half-divine life which can only be "recognized," not understood.

The strangeness that sets *Wuthering Heights* apart from other English novels does not lie alone in the attitude that it expresses and the level of experience that it defines, for something of the same quality of feeling exists, for instance, in Conrad's work. Its strangeness is the perfect simplicity with which it presents its elemental figures almost naked of the web of civilized habits, ways of thinking, forms of intercourse, that provides the familiar background of other fiction. Even Conrad's adventurers, no matter how far they may go into the "heart of darkness," carry with them enough threads of this web to orient them socially and morally. We can illustrate what we mean by this simplicity, this almost nakedness, if we compare Emily Brontë's handling of her materials with Richardson's handling of materials that, in some respects, are similar in kind. For example, the daemonic character of Heathcliff, associated as it is with the wildness of heath and moors, has a recognizable kinship with that of Lovelace, daemonic also, though associated with town life and sophisticated manners. Both are, essentially, an anthropomorphized primitive energy, concentrated in activity, terrible in effect. But Emily Brontë insists on Heathcliff's gypsy lack of origins, his lack of orientation and determination in the social world, his equivocal status on the edge of the human. When Mr. Earnshaw first brings the child home, the child is an "it," not a "he," and "dark almost as if it came from the devil"; and one of Nelly Dean's last reflections is, "Is he a ghoul or a vampire?" But Richardson's Lovelace has all sorts of social relationships and determinations, an ample family, economic orientation, college acquaintances, a position in a clique of young rakes; and Richardson is careful, through Lovelace's own pen, to offer various rationalizations of his behavior, each in some degree cogent. So with the whole multifold *Clarissa*-myth: on all sides it is supported for the understanding by historically familiar morality and manners. But *Wuthering Heights* is almost bare of such supports in social rationalization. Heathcliff might *really* be a demon. The passion of Catherine and Heathcliff is too simple and undeviating in its intensity, too uncomplex, for us to find in it any echo of practical social reality. To say that the motivation of this passion is "simple" is not to say that it is easy to define: much easier to define are the motivations that are some-

what complex and devious, for this is the familiar nature of human motivations. We might associate perfectly "simple" motivations with animal
nature or extrahuman nature, but by the same token the quality of feeling involved would resist analysis.

But this nakedness from the web of familiar morality and manners
is not quite complete. There is the framework formed by the convention
of narration (the "point of view"): we see the drama through the eyes of
Lockwood and Nelly Dean, who belong firmly to the world of practical
reality. Sifted through the idiom of their commonplace vision, the drama
taking place among the major characters finds contact with the temporal
and the secular. Because Lockwood and Nelly Dean have witnessed the
incredible violence of the life at the Heights, or rather, because Nelly
Dean has witnessed the full span and capacity of that violence and because Lockwood credits her witness, the drama is oriented in the context
of the psychologically familiar. There is also another technical bulwark
that supports this uneasy tale in the social and moral imagination, and
that is its extension over the lives of two generations and into a time of
ameliorated and respectable manners. At the end, we see young Cathy
teaching Hareton his letters and correcting his boorishness (which, after
all, is only the natural boorishness consequent on neglect, and has none
of the cannibal unregeneracy of Heathcliff in it); the prospect is one of
decent, socially responsible domesticity. For this part of the tale, Lockwood alone is sufficient witness; and the fact that now Nelly Dean's experienced old eyes and memory can be dispensed with assures us of the
present reasonableness and objectivity of events, and even infects retro-
spection on what has happened earlier—making it possible for the dream-
rejecting reason to settle complacently for the "naturalness" of the entire
story. If ghosts have been mentioned, if the country people swear that
Heathcliff "walks," we can, with Lockwood at the end, affirm our skepti-
cism as to "how anyone could ever imagine unquiet slumbers for the
sleepers in that quiet earth."

Let us try to diagram these technical aspects of the work, for the compositional soundness of *Wuthering Heights* is owing to them. We may
divide the action of the book into two parts, following each other chronologically, the one associated with the earlier generation (Hindley and
Catherine and Heathcliff, Edgar and Isabella Linton), the other with
the later generation (young Cathy and Linton and Hareton). The first
of these actions is centered in what we shall call a "mythological romance"

—for the astonishingly ravenous and possessive, perfectly amoral love of Catherine and Heathcliff belongs to that realm of the imagination where myths are created. The second action, centered in the protracted effects of Heathcliff's revenge, involves two sets of young lives and two small "romances": the childish romance of Cathy and Linton, which Heathcliff manages to pervert utterly; and the successful assertion of a healthy, culturally viable kind of love between Cathy and Hareton, asserted as Heathcliff's cruel energies flag and decay. Binding the two "actions" is the perduring figure of Heathcliff himself, demon-lover in the first, paternal ogre in the second. Binding them also is the framing narrational convention or "point of view": the voices of Nelly Dean and Lockwood are always in our ears; one or the other of them is always present at a scene, or is the confidant of someone who was present; through Lockwood we encounter Heathcliff at the beginning of the book, and through his eyes we look on Heathcliff's grave at the end. Still another pattern that binds the two actions is the repetition of what we shall call the "two children" figure—two children raised virtually as brother and sister, in a vibrant relationship of charity and passion and real or possible metamorphosis The figure is repeated, with variation, three times, in the relationships of the main characters. Of this we shall speak again later. The technical continuities or patterning of the book could, then, be simplified in this way:

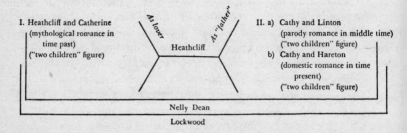

What, concretely, is the effect of this strict patterning and binding? What does it "mean"? The design of the book is drawn in the spirit of intense compositional rigor, of *limitation;* the characters act in the spirit of passionate immoderacy, of *excess.* Let us consider this contrast a little more closely. Essentially, *Wuthering Heights* exists for the mind as a tension between two kinds of reality: the raw, inhuman reality of anonymous natural energies, and the restrictive reality of civilized habits, manners, and codes. The first kind of reality is given to the imagination in the violent figures of Catherine and Heathcliff, portions of the flux of nature, children of rock and heath and tempest, striving to identify themselves as human, but disrupting all around them with their monstrous appetite for an inhuman kind of intercourse, and finally disintegrated from within by the very energies out of which they are made. It is this vision of a reality radically alien from the human that the ancient Chinese landscape paintings offer also. But in those ancient paintings there is often a tiny human figure, a figure that is obviously that of a philosopher, for instance, or that of a peasant—in other words, a human figure decisively belonging to and representing a culture—who is placed in diminutive perspective beside the enormously cascading torrent, or who is seen driving his water buffalo through the overwhelming mists or faceless snows; and this figure is outlined sharply, so that, though it is extremely tiny, it is very definite in the giant surrounding indefiniteness. The effect is one of contrast between finite and infinite, between the limitation of the known and human, and the unlimitedness of the unknown and the nonhuman. So also in *Wuthering Heights:* set over against the wilderness of inhuman reality is the quietly secular, voluntarily limited, safely human reality that we find in the gossipy concourse of Nelly Dean and Lockwood, the one an old family servant with a strong grip on the necessary emotional economies that make life endurable, the other a city visitor in the country, a man whose very disinterestedness and facility of feeling and attention indicate the manifold emotional economies by which city people particularly protect themselves from any disturbing note of the ironic discord between civilized life and the insentient wild flux of nature in which it is islanded. This second kind of reality is given also in the romance of Cathy and Hareton, where book learning and gentled manners and domestic charities form a little island of complacence. The tension between these two kinds of reality, their inveterate opposition and at the same time their *continuity* one with another, provides at once the content and the form of *Wuthering Heights*. We see the tension graphically in the diagram given above. The inhuman excess of Heathcliff's and Catherine's passion, an excess that is carried over into the second half of the book by Heathcliff's revenge, an excess everywhere present in language [2]—in verbs and modifiers and metaphors that seethe with a brute fury—this excess is held within a most rigorous pattern of repeated motifs and of what someone has called the "Chinese box" of Nelly Dean's and Lockwood's interlocution. The form of the book, then—a form that may be expressed as a tension between the impulse to excess and the impulse to limitation or economy—*is* the content. The form, in short, is the book itself. Only in the fully wrought, fully realized, work of art does form so exhaust the possibilities of the material that it identifies itself with these possibilities.

If there has been any cogency in what we have said above, we should ask now how it is that the book is able to represent dramatically, in terms of human "character," its vision of the inhuman. After all, Catherine and Heathcliff *are* "characters," and not merely molecular vibrations in the primordial surge of things; indeed, they are so credibly characterized that Hollywood has been able to costume and cosmeticize them. As "characters," what are they? As lovers, what kind of love is theirs? They gnash and foam at each other. One could borrow for them a line from a poem by John Crowe Ransom describing lovers in hell: "Stuprate, they rend each other when they kiss." This is not "romantic love," as that term has popular meaning; and it is not even sexual love, naturalistically considered —the impulse to destruction is too pure in it, too simple and direct. Catherine says she *is* Heathcliff, and the implication is not of the possibility of a "mating," for one does not "mate" with oneself. Similarly, after her death, when Heathcliff howls that he cannot live without his *life,* he cannot live without his *soul* (and Nellie says that he "howled, not like a man, but like a savage beast"), the relationship and the destiny suggested are not those of adult human lovers, because the complex attendant motivations of adult life are lacking. But the emotional implications of Catherine's and Heathcliff's passion are never "adult," in the sense of there being in that passion any recognition of the domestic and social responsibilities, and the spiritual complexities, of adult life. Whatever could happen to these two, if they could be happily together, would be something altogether asocial, amoral, savagely irresponsible, wildly impulsive: it would be the enthusiastic, experimental, quite random activity of child-

[2] Mark Schorer examines this aspect of *Wuthering Heights* in his essay "Fiction and the 'Analogical Matrix,'" in *Critiques and Essays on Modern Fiction* (New York: The Ronald Press Company, 1952).

hood, occult to the socialized adult. But since no conceivable *human* male and female, not brutish, not anthropologically rudimentary, could be together in this way as adults, all that we can really imagine for the grown-up Catherine and Heathcliff, as "characters" on the human plane, is what the book gives of them—their mutual destruction by tooth and nail in an effort, through death, to get back to the lost state of gypsy freedom in childhood.

Caught in the economical forms of adult life—concepts of social and intellectual "betterment" (such as lead Catherine to marry Edgar Linton), the frames of wealth and property ownership (which Heathcliff at first exploits in order to "raise" himself to Catherine's standard, and then as an engine of revenge against both the Earnshaws and the Lintons), marital relationships, and parenthood—they are, for the imagination, "humanized," endowed with "character," at least to the extent that we see their explosive confusions, resistances, and misery convulsing the forms usual to human adulthood. Their obsession, their prime passion, is also "human" although it is utterly destructive of the values signified by that word: the passion to lose the self in some "otherness," whether in complete identification with another person (an identification for which "mating" is a surrogate only of a temporary and lapsing kind), or by absorption into "nature"—but it is a passion that is tabooed for the socialized adult, disguised, held in check by the complex cultural economies, safely stabled in the unconscious, at best put to work in that darkness to turn the mill of other objectives. This regressive passion is seen in uncompromised purity in Catherine and Heathcliff, and it opens the prospect of disintegration—disintegration into the unconsciousness of childhood and the molecular fluidity of death—in a word, into anonymous natural energy.

If the story of Catherine and Heathcliff had not been a story told by an old woman as something that had had its inception many years ago, if the old woman who tells the story had not been limited in imagination and provincial in her sympathies, if the story had been dramatized immediately in the here-and-now and not at a temporal remove and through a dispassioned intermediator, it is doubtful that it would resonate emotionally for us or carry any conviction—even any "meaning." Because of the very fact that the impulses it represents are taboo, they can conveniently be observed only at a remove, as someone else's, as of the past, and from the judicial point of view of conventional manners. The

159

"someone else's" and the "long ago" are the mind's saving convention for making a distance with itself such as will allow it perspective. Thus the technical *displacement* of Heathcliff's and Catherine's story into past time and into the memory of an old woman functions in the same way as dream displacements: it both censors and indulges, protects and liberates.

Significantly, our first real contact with the Catherine-Heathcliff drama is established through a dream—Lockwood's dream of the ghost-child at the window. Lockwood is motivated to dream the dream by the most easily convincing circumstances; he has fallen asleep while reading Catherine's diary, and during his sleep a tempest-blown branch is scratching on the windowpane. But why should Lockwood, the well-mannered urbanite, dream *this*?

> I pulled its wrist on to the broken pane, and rubbed it to and fro till the blood ran down and soaked the bedclothes . . .

The image is probably the most cruel one in the book. Hareton's hanging puppies, Heathcliff's hanging the springer spaniel, Hindley's forcing a knife between Nelly's teeth or throwing his baby over the staircase, Catherine's leaving the blue print of her nails on Isabella's arm, Heathcliff stamping on Hindley's face—these images and others like them imply savagery or revengefulness or drunkenness or hysteria, but always a motivating set of emotional circumstances. But this is the punctilious Lockwood—whose antecedents and psychology are so insipid that we care little about them—who scrapes the dream-waif's wrist back and forth on broken glass till the blood runs down and soaks the bedclothes. The cruelty of the dream is the gratuitousness of the violence wrought on a child by an emotionally unmotivated vacationer from the city, dreaming in a strange bed. The bed is an old-fashioned closet bed ("a large oak case . . . it formed a little closet" with a window set in it): its paneled sides Lockwood has "pulled together" before going to sleep. The bed is like a coffin (at the end of the book, Heathcliff dies in it, behind its closed panels); it had been Catherine's bed, and the movable panels themselves suggest the coffin in which she is laid, whose "panels" Heathcliff bribes the sexton to remove at one side. Psychologically, Lockwood's dream has only the most perfunctory determinations, and nothing at all of result for the dreamer himself, except to put him uncomfortably out of bed.

But poetically the dream has its reasons, compacted into the image of the daemonic child scratching at the pane, trying to get from the "outside" "in," and of the dreamer in a bed like a coffin, released by that deathly privacy to indiscriminate violence. The coffin-like bed shuts off any interference with the wild deterioration of the psyche. Had the dream used any other agent than the effete, almost epicene Lockwood, it would have lost this symbolic force; for Lockwood, more successfully than anyone else in the book, has shut out the powers of darkness (the pun in his name is obvious in this context); and his lack of any dramatically thorough motivation for dreaming the cruel dream suggests those powers as existing autonomously, not only in the "outsideness" of external nature, beyond the physical windowpane, but also within, even in the soul least prone to passionate excursion.

The windowpane is the medium, treacherously transparent, separating the "inside" from the "outside," the "human" from the alien and terrible "other." Immediately after the incident of the dream, the time of the narrative is displaced into the childhood of Heathcliff and Catherine, and we see the two children looking through the window of the Lintons' drawing room.

> "Both of us were able to look in by standing on the basement, and clinging to the ledge, and we saw—ah! it was beautiful—a splendid place carpeted with crimson, and crimson-covered chairs and tables, and a pure white ceiling bordered by gold, a shower of glass-drops hanging in silver chains from the centre, and shimmering with little soft tapers. Old Mr. and Mrs. Linton were not there; Edgar and his sister had it entirely to themselves. Shouldn't they have been happy? We should have thought ourselves in heaven!"

Here the two unregenerate waifs look *in* from the night on the heavenly vision of the refinements and securities of the most privileged human estate. But Heathcliff rejects the vision: seeing the Linton children blubbering and bored there (*they* cannot get *out!*), he senses the menace of its limitations; while Catherine is fatally tempted. She is taken in by the Lintons, and now it is Heathcliff alone outside looking through the window.

> "The curtains were still looped up at one corner, and I resumed my station as a spy; because, if Catherine had wished to return, I intended

shattering their great glass panes to a million of fragments, unless they
let her out. She sat on the sofa quietly . . . the woman-servant brought
a basin of warm water, and washed her feet; and Mr. Linton mixed a
tumbler of negus, and Isabella emptied a plateful of cakes into her
lap . . . Afterwards, they dried and combed her beautiful hair . . ."

Thus the first snare is laid by which Catherine will be held for a human
destiny—her feet washed, cakes and wine for her delectation, her beautiful hair combed (the motifs here are limpid as those of fairy tale, where
the changeling in the "otherworld" is held there mysteriously by bathing
and by the strange new food he has been given to eat). By her marriage
to Edgar Linton, Catherine yields to that destiny; later she resists it tor-
mentedly and finds her way out of it by death. Literally she "catches her
death" by throwing open the window.

> "Open the window again wide: fasten it open! Quick, why don't
> you move?" [she says to Nelly].
> "Because I won't give you your death of cold," I answered.
> "You won't give me a chance of life, you mean," she said . . .

In her delirium, she opens the window, leans out into the winter wind, and
calls across the moors to Heathcliff,

> "Heathcliff, if I dare you now, will you venture? . . . Find a way,
> then! . . . You are slow! . . . you always followed me!"

On the night after her burial, unable to follow her (though he digs up
her grave in order to lie beside her in the coffin from which the side
panels have been removed), he returns to the Heights *through the window*
—for Hindley has barred the door—to wreak on the living the fury of
his frustration. It is years later that Lockwood arrives at the Heights
and spends his uncomfortable night there. Lockwood's outcry in his dream
brings Heathcliff *to the window,* Heathcliff who has been caught ineluc-
tably in the human to grapple with its interdictions long after Catherine
has broken through them. The treachery of the window is that Catherine,
lost now in the "other," can look through the transparent membrane
that separates her from humanity, can scratch on the pane, but cannot
get "in," while Heathcliff, though he forces the window open and howls
into the night, cannot get "out." When he dies, Nelly Dean discovers
the window swinging open, the window of that old-fashioned coffin-like

162

bed where Lockwood had had the dream. Rain has been pouring in during the night, drenching the dead man. Nelly says,

> I hasped the window; I combed his black long hair from his forehead; I tried to close his eyes: to extinguish, if possible, that frightful, life-like gaze of exultation before any one else beheld it. They would not shut: they seemed to sneer at my attempts . . .

Earlier, Heathcliff's eyes have been spoken of as "the clouded windows of hell" from which a "fiend" looks out. All the other uses of the "window" that we have spoken of here are not figurative but perfectly naturalistic uses, though their symbolic value is inescapable. But the fact that Heathcliff's eyes refuse to close in death suggests the symbol in a metaphorical form (the "fiend" has now got "out," leaving the window open), elucidating with simplicity the meaning of the "window" as a separation between the daemonic depths of the soul and the limited and limiting lucidities of consciousness, a separation between the soul's "otherness" and its humanness.

There is still the difficulty of defining, with any precision, the quality of the daemonic that is realized most vividly in the conception of Heathcliff, a difficulty that is mainly due to our tendency always to give the "daemonic" some ethical status—that is, to relate it to an ethical hierarchy. Heathcliff's is an archetypal figure, untraceably ancient in mythological thought—an imaged recognition of that part of nature which is "other" than the human soul (the world of the elements and the animals) and of that part of the soul itself which is "other" than the conscious part. But since Martin Luther's revival of this archetype for modern mythology, it has tended to forget its relationship with the elemental "otherness" of the outer world and to identify itself solely with the dark functions of the soul. As an image of soul work, it is ethically relevant, since everything that the soul does—even unconsciously, even "ignorantly" (as in the case of Oedipus)—offers itself for ethical judgment, whereas the elements and the animals do not. Puritanism perpetuated the figure for the imagination; Milton gave it its greatest aesthetic splendor, in the fallen angel through whom the divine beauty still shone; Richardson introduced it, in the person of Lovelace, to an infatuated middle class; and always the figure was ethically relevant through the conception of "sin" and "guilt." (Let us note here, however, the ambivalence of the figure, an ambivalence that the medieval devil does not have. The medieval devil is

a really ugly customer, so ugly that he can even become a comedy figure
—as in the medieval moralities. The daemonic archetype of which we are
speaking here is deeply serious in quality because of his ambivalence:
he is a fertilizing energy and profoundly attractive, and at the same time
horribly destructive to civilized institutionalism. It is because of his
ambivalence that, though he is the "enemy," ethically speaking, he so
easily takes on the stature and beauty of a hero, as he does in the Satan
of *Paradise Lost*.) In Byron's *Manfred*, the archetype underwent a rather
confusing sea-change, for Manfred's crime is, presumably, so frightful
that it cannot be mentioned, and the indefinable nature of the crime blurs
the edges of the figure and cuts down its resonance in the imagination
(when we guess that the crime might be incest, we are disposed to find this
a rather paltry equation for the Byronic incantation of guilt); nevertheless, the ethical relevancy of the figure remains. Let us follow it a little
further, before returning to Emily Brontë's Heathcliff. In the later nineteenth century, in the novels of Dostoevski, it reappears with an enormous
development of psychological subtlety, and also with a great strengthening and clarification of its ethical significance. In the work of André Gide,
it undergoes another sea-change: the archetypal daemonic figure now becomes the principle of progress, the spirit of free investigation and creative experience; with this reorientation, it becomes positively ethical rather
than negatively so. In Thomas Mann's *Doctor Faustus*, it reverts to its
earlier and more constant significance, as the type of the instinctive part
of the soul, a great and fertilizing power, but ethically unregenerate and
therefore a great danger to ethical man.

Our interest in sketching some phases of the history of this archetype
has been to show that it has had, in modern mythology, constantly a
status in relation to ethical thought. The exception is Heathcliff. Heathcliff is no more ethically relevant than is flood or earthquake or whirlwind. It is as impossible to speak of him in terms of "sin" and "guilt" as
it is to speak in this way of the natural elements or the creatures of the
animal world. In him, the type reverts to a more ancient mythology and
to an earlier symbolism. *Wuthering Heights* so baffles and confounds the
ethical sense because it is not informed with that sense at all: it is profoundly informed with the attitudes of "animism," by which the natural
world—that world which is "other" than and "outside of" the consciously
individualized human—*appears* to act with an energy similar to the
energies of the soul; to be permeated with soul energy but of a mysterious

and alien kind that the conscious human soul, bent on securing itself through civilization, cannot identify itself with as to purpose; an energy that can be propitiated, that can at times be canalized into humanly purposeful channels, that *must* be given religious recognition both for its enormous fertility and its enormous potential destructiveness. But Heathcliff does have human shape and human relationships; he is, so to speak, "caught in" the human; two kinds of reality intersect in him—as they do, with a somewhat different balance, in Catherine; as they do, indeed, in the other characters. Each entertains, in some degree, the powers of darkness—from Hindley, with his passion for self-destruction (he, too, wants to get "out"), to Nelly Dean, who in a sense "propitiates" those powers with the casuistry of her actions, and even to Lockwood, with his sadistic dream. Even in the weakest of these souls there is an intimation of the dark Otherness, by which the soul is related psychologically to the inhuman world of pure energy, for it carries within itself an "otherness" of its own, that inhabits below consciousness.

The imagery of the windowpane is metamorphic, suggesting a total change of mode of being by the breaking-through of a separating medium that exists between consciousness and the "other." The strangest and boldest and most radiant figuration that Emily Brontë has given to her subject is the "two children" figure, also a metamorphic figure of breakthrough and transformation. The *type* or classic form of this figure is a girl with golden hair and a boy with dark hair and shadowed brow, bound in kinship and in a relationship of charity and passion, and with a metamorphosis of some kind potential in the relationship. The beautiful dark boy will be brightened, made angelic and happy, by the beautiful golden girl: this, apparently, is what *should* happen. But the dynamics of the change are not perfectly trustworthy. In one of Emily Brontë's poems, describing a child who might be the child Heathcliff, the ambivalent dark boy will evidently sink further into his darkness.

> *I love thee, boy; for all divine,*
> *All full of God thy features shine.*
> *Darling enthusiast, holy child,*
> *Too good for this world's warring wild,*
> *Too heavenly now but doomed to be*
> *Hell-like in heart and misery.*[3]

[3] *The Complete Poems of Emily Jane Brontë*, edited by C. W. Hatfield (New York: Columbia University Press, 1941), p. 121.

In the 1850 printing of the Brontë poems (the printing supervised by the Brontë sisters) two companion pieces appear under the title "The Two Children," in the first of which the dark boy is still unchanged.

> *Frowning on the infant,*
> *Shadowing childhood's joy,*
> *Guardian angel knows not*
> *That melancholy boy . . .*[4]

In the second of these companion pieces, the golden child is evoked, and now the change in the dark one is promised.

> *Child of Delight! with sunbright hair,*
> *And seablue, seadeep eyes;*
> *Spirit of Bliss, what brings thee here,*
> *Beneath these sullen skies?*
>
> *Thou shouldest live in eternal spring,*
> *Where endless day is never dim;*
> *Why, Seraph, has thy erring wing*
> *Borne thee down to weep with him?*

She answers that she is "not from heaven descended," but that she has seen and pitied "that mournful boy."

> *And I swore to take his gloomy sadness,*
> *And give to him my beamy joy . . .*[5]

Here, with the change of the dark child, the golden child will be changed also, for she will take his "gloomy sadness." In another set of verses, the light-dark contrast is turned around bewilderingly.

> *And only he had locks of light,*
> *And she had raven hair;*
> *While now, his curls are dark as night,*
> *And hers as morning fair.*[6]

What really seems to be implied by all these shifts is not a mere exchange of characteristics but a radical identification of the two children, so that each can appear in the mode of the other, the bright one in the mode of darkness and the dark one in the mode of light.

[4] *Ibid.*, p. 229.
[5] *Ibid.*, p. 230.
[6] *Ibid.*, p. 174.

166

In still another of those poems that dramatize affairs in the kingdom of Gondal that occupied Emily Brontë's youthful fantasy, a brooding phantom figure haunts the moonlit grounds of a castle. Its face is "divinely fair," but on its "angel brow"

> *Rests such a shade of deep despair*
> *As nought divine could ever know.*

Apparently the cause of his death was adoration of another man's wife ("Lord Alfred's idol queen"), and it is for this reason that his spirit is "shut from heaven—an outcast for eternity." The woman for whom he died is represented as an "infant fair," looking from a golden frame in a portrait gallery.

> *And just like his its ringlets bright,*
> *Its large dark eye of shadowy light,*
> *Its cheeks' pure hue, its forehead white,*
> *And like its noble name.*

A deliberate confusion of the planes of reality—a shifting into the life inside the picture frame (like the shifts "through the window" in *Wuthering Heights*), and with it a shifting from despairing adulthood into childhood—is suggested with the following questions:

> *And did he never smile to see*
> *Himself restored to infancy?*
>
> *Never part back that golden flow*
> *Of curls, and kiss that pearly brow,*
> *And feel no other earthly bliss*
> *Was equal to that parent's kiss?* [7]

The suggestions are those of metamorphic changes, but all under the aspect of frustration: the despairing lover cannot get through the picture frame where the child is. Other motifs here are reminiscent of those of *Wuthering Heights*. The spectral lover is an ambivalent figure, of divine beauty, but an outcast from heaven. Kinship is suggested between him and the child in the picture ("And just like his its ringlets bright . . . And like its noble name"), and one is left to imagine that "Lord Alfred's idol queen" was his sister, wherefore the frustration of their love. The last stanza quoted above remarks ambiguously on the parental feeling

[7] *Ibid.,* pp. 177–178.

167

involved in the relationship: is it not the infant who is the "parent" here? Parental charity is the feeling of the golden "guardian angel" for her dark charge in "The Two Children" poems, as it is, in a degree, of Catherine for Heathcliff during their childhood, and of young Cathy first for Linton and then for Hareton. The fact that, in the poem, both the infant and the spectral lover have golden hair seems, in this elusive fantasy, to be a mark of perversion of the metamorphic sequence, at least of its having gone awry (as in the case, too, of young Cathy and Linton, who is not dark but fair).

In the relationship of Catherine and Heathcliff, the fantasy has its typical form. She is golden, he is dark. His daemonic origin is always kept open, by reiterations of the likelihood that he is really a ghoul, a fiend, an offspring of hell, and not merely so in behavior. And Catherine also, like the guardian child in "The Two Children" poems, is "not from heaven descended": she has furious tantrums, she lies, she bites, her chosen toy is a whip. They are raised as brother and sister; there are three references to their sleeping in the same bed as infants. She scolds and orders and mothers and cherishes him ("much too fond of him" as a child, Nelly says). The notions of somatic change and discovery of noble birth, as in fairy tale, are deliberately played with; as, when Catherine returns from her first sojourn at the Lintons' and Heathcliff asks Nelly to "make him decent," he says, comparing himself with Edgar,

> "I wish I had light hair and a fair skin, and was dressed and behaved as well, and had a chance of being as rich as he will be!"

and Nelly answers,

> "You're fit for a prince in disguise . . . Were I in your place, I would frame high notions of my birth . . ."

(If Heathcliff is really of daemonic origin, he is, in a sense, indeed of "high birth," a "prince in disguise," and might be expected, like the princes of fairy tale, to drop his "disguise" at the crisis of the tale and be revealed in original splendor: the dynamics of the "two children" figure also points to that potential transformation.) Some alluring and astonishing destiny seems possible for the two. *What* that phenomenon might be or mean, we cannot know, for it is frustrated by Catherine's marriage to Edgar, which dooms Heathcliff to be "hell-like in heart and misery."

Catherine's decision dooms her also, for she is of the same daemonic substance as Heathcliff, and a civilized marriage and domesticity are not sympathetic to the daemonic quality.

With the second generation, the "two children" figure is distorted and parodied in the relationship of Catherine's daughter and Heathcliff's son. Young Cathy, another "child of delight, with sunbright hair," has still some of the original daemonic energy, but her "erring wing" has brought her down to "weep with" a *pale-haired* and pallid little boy whose only talents are for sucking sugar candy and torturing cats. She does her best, as infant mother, to metamorphose him, but he is an ungrateful and impossible subject. Her passionate charity finally finds her "married" to his corpse in a locked bedroom. With Cathy and Hareton Earnshaw, her cousin on her mother's side, the "two children" are again in their right relationship of golden and dark, and now the pathos of the dark child cures the daemon out of the golden one, and the maternal care of the golden child raises the dark one to civilized humanity and makes of him a proper husband.

In these several pairs, the relation of kinship has various resonances. Between Catherine and Heathcliff, identity of "kind" is greatest, although they are foster brother and sister only. The foster kinship provides an imaginative implicit reason for the unnaturalness and impossibility of their mating. Impassioned by their brother-and-sisterlike identity of kind, they can only destroy each other, for it is impossible for two persons to *be* each other (as Catherine says she "is" Heathcliff) without destruction of the physical limitations that individualize and separate. In Emily Brontë's use of the symbolism of the incest motive, the incestual impulse appears as an attempt to make what is "outside" oneself identical with what is "inside" oneself—a performance that can be construed in physical and human terms only by violent destruction of personality bounds, by rending of flesh and at last by death.

With Catherine's daughter and young Linton, who are cousins, the implicit incestuousness of the "two children" figure is suggested morbidly by Linton's disease and by his finally becoming a husband only as a corpse. With Cathy and Hareton Earnshaw, also cousins, Victorian "ameliorism" finds a way to sanction the relationship by symbolic emasculation; Cathy literally teaches the devil out of Hareton, and "esteem" between the two takes the place of the old passion for identification. With this successful metamorphosis and mating, the daemonic quality

169

has been completely suppressed, and, though humanity and civilization have been secured for the "two children," one feels that some magnificent bounty is now irrecoverable. The great magic, the wild power, of the original two has been lost.

We are led to speculate on what the bounty might have been,[8] had the windowpane not stood between the original pair, had the golden child and the dark child not been secularized by a spelling book. Perhaps, had the ideal and impossible eventuality taken place, had the "inside" and the "outside," the bright child and the dark one, become identified in such a way that they could freely assume each other's modes, then perhaps the world of the animals and the elements—the world of wild moor and barren rock, of fierce wind and attacking beast, that is the strongest palpability in *Wuthering Heights*—would have offered itself completely to human understanding and creative intercourse. Perhaps the dark powers that exist within the soul, as well as in the outer elemental world, would have assumed the language of consciousness, or consciousness would have bravely entered into companionship with those dark powers and transliterated their language into its own. Emily Brontë's book has been said to be nonphilosophical—as it is certainly nonethical; but all philosophy is not ethics, and the book seizes, at the point where the soul feels itself cleft within and in cleavage from the universe, the first germs of philosophic thought, the thought of the duality of human and nonhuman existence, and the thought of the cognate duality of the psyche.

[8] A stimulating and enlightening interpretation of the book is to be found in Richard Chase's "The Brontës, or Myth Domesticated," in *Forms of Modern Fiction,* edited by William Van O'Connor (Minneapolis: University of Minnesota Press, 1948).

ON *Adam Bede*

In Chapter 17 of *Adam Bede,* "the story pauses a little" and George Eliot sets forth her aim as a novelist, an aim which she describes as "the faithful representing of commonplace things," of things *as they are,* not "as they never have been and never will be"; and we are reminded of a similar aim as expressed by Defoe's Moll Flanders, who said, "I am giving an account of what was, not of what ought or ought not to be." It is the vocation of the "realistic" novelist to represent life in this way; it is at the furthest possible remove from the work of marvel making that we have just witnessed in *Wuthering Heights;* but, as Defoe brought us to a consideration of the shaping changes which the "real" undergoes as it is submitted to art, even to the most "realistic" art, so George Eliot brings us back to the same consideration of the transforming effect of composition upon things-as-they-are. Her strongest effort, she says, is to avoid an "arbitrary picture," and

> to give a faithful account of men and things as they have mirrored themselves in my mind. The mirror is doubtless defective; the outlines will sometimes be disturbed, the reflection faint or confused; but I feel as much bound to tell you as precisely as I can what that reflection is, as if I were in the witness-box, narrating my experience on oath.

We cannot avoid observing that the "mirror" is at times defective, but since it is for the most part clear and well lighted we are not primarily concerned with the defects; more interesting is the analogy of the mirror itself—the novelist's mind as a mirror from whose "reflections" of "men and things" he draws his account. Men and things, then, do not leap to his page directly out of the "real" but, before they get there, take a journey through the "mirror." But the mirror which the mind offers is not at all like other mirrors; even—leaving out of consideration defective glasses—very clear minds are not like very clear mirrors. Dangerous as analogies are, a spoon would be a better one, where, in the concave, as we tip it toward us, we see our head compressed and a half-moon scooped out of it on top as if it were a dime-store flowerpot for our viney hair, our body tapered to vanishing at the hips, and the whole upside down; or, in the convex, our eyelids are as large as foreheads, our forehead is as small as an eyelid, our cheeks hang down from our face like shoulders, and our shoulders hide under them like little ears. The "mirror" of the mind shapes what it sees. It does not passively "reflect" things-as-they-are, but creates things-as-they-are. Though we can clearly discriminate the quality of intention shown by a realistic art—and it usually reduces finally to a choice of materials from the field of the quotidian, the commonplace, the mediocre—yet its aim of veraciousness is necessarily one of veraciousness to what the artist sees in the shape-giving, significance-endowing medium of his own mind, and in this sense the mythopoeic art of *Wuthering Heights* is as veracious as the realistic art of *Adam Bede*.

The singularity of the world of *Wuthering Heights* is its innocence of "good" and "evil" in any civilized ethical meaning of these terms; it is a world shaped by kinetic rather than by ethical forces, and its innocence is that of the laws of dynamics (Catherine's fatal choice, for instance, is essentially a choice of stasis and a denial of motion; it is as if an electron or a star should "choose" to stand still). *Adam Bede* offers the radical contrast of a world shaped through and through by moral judgment and moral evaluation. We are prone, perhaps, to think of a perfectly amoral vision, such as Emily Brontë's, as a vision not of things-as-they-are but as a subjective creation of things-as-they-never-were-but-might-be, and, on the other hand, to think of an ethical vision, such as George Eliot's, as closer to things-as-they-are, more "objective," because of our own familiar addiction to moral judgments (however inapropos or cliché) and our difficulty in turning ethics out of doors. But, on a thought, it should be clear that a through and through ethically shaped world is as "created" a world as the other. The question is not one of *whether* things are really this way or that way, for either vision touches responsive similitudes within us, and God knows what things really are. The question is one of different organizations and different illuminations of the infinite possible qualities of things-as-they-are.

Technique is that which selects among the multitude of possible qualities, organizes them in the finite world of the novel, and holds them in a shape that can catch the light of our own awareness, which, without shapes to fall upon, is ignorant. Technique is like the concave or convex surface of the spoon, and the different turnings and inclinations to which it is liable; technique elongates or foreshortens, and while the rudimentary relationships of common experience remain still recognizable, it reveals astonishing bulges of significance, magnifies certain parts of the anatomy of life, of whose potentialities we had perhaps not been aware, humbles others. The massively slow movement of *Adam Bede* is one such shape-making technique. It is true that we are generally persuaded of the *actual* slow movement of rural life, and it is rural life —the life of villagers, tenant farmers, and peasantry—that George Eliot describes; but Dickens, in the first part of *Great Expectations,* is also dealing with people in a rural community, and yet the tempo or "pace" which he sets for these lives is one of shockingly abrupt accelerations.

> "Hold your noise!" cried a terrible voice, as a man started up from among the graves at the side of the church porch. "Keep still, you little devil, or I'll cut your throat!"

Emily Brontë deals with even more rurally isolated lives, but here the movement is one of furious assault: beasts attack, the tempest whirls and suffocates, emotions express themselves in howls, biting, kicking, trampling, bloodletting, homicidal and suicidal violence. In the context of this comparison let us set almost any random paragraph from *Adam Bede.* The movement is one of a massive leisureliness that gathers up as it goes a dense body of physical and moral detail, adding particle to particle and building layer upon layer with sea-depth patience.

> In the large wicker-bottomed arm-chair in the left-hand chimney-nook sat old Martin Poyser, a hale but shrunken and bleached image of his portly black-haired son—his head hanging forward a little, and his elbows pushed backwards so as to allow the whole of his fore-arm to rest on the arm of the chair. His blue handkerchief was spread over his knees, as was usual indoors, when it was not hanging over his head; and he sat watching what went forward with the quiet *outward* glance of healthy old age, which, disengaged from any interest in an inward drama, spies out pins upon the floor, follows one's minutest motions with an unexpectant purposeless tenacity, watches the flickering of the flame or the sun-gleams on the wall, counts the quarries on the

173

floor, watches even the hand of the clock, and pleases itself with detecting a rhythm in the tick.

And here are the Poysers going to church.

> There were acquaintances at other gates who had to move aside and let them pass: at the gate of the Home Close there was half the dairy of cows standing one behind the other, extremely slow to understand that their large bodies might be in the way; at the far gate there was the mare holding her head over the bars, and beside her the liver-coloured foal with its head towards its mother's flank, apparently still much embarrassed by its own straddling existence. The way lay entirely through Mr. Poyser's own fields till they reached the main road leading to the village, and he turned a keen eye on the stock and the crops as they went along, while Mrs. Poyser was ready to supply a running commentary on them all . . .
>
> The damp hay that must be scattered and turned afresh to-morrow was not a cheering sight to Mr. Poyser, who during hay and corn harvest had often some mental struggles as to the benefits of a day of rest; but no temptation would have induced him to carry on any field-work, however early in the morning, on a Sunday; for had not Michael Holdsworth had a pair of oxen "sweltered" while he was ploughing on Good Friday? That was a demonstration that work on sacred days was a wicked thing; and with wickedness of any sort Martin Poyser was quite clear that he would have nothing to do, since money got by such means would never prosper.
>
> "It a'most makes your fingers itch to be at the hay now the sun shines so," he observed, as they passed through the "Big Meadow." "But it's poor foolishness to think o' saving by going against your conscience. There's that Jim Wakefield, as they used to call 'Gentleman Wakefield,' used to do the same of a Sunday as o' week-days, and took no heed to right or wrong, as if there was nayther God nor devil. An' what's he come to? Why, I saw him myself last market-day a-carrying a basket wi' oranges in't."
>
> "Ah, to be sure," said Mrs. Poyser, emphatically, "you make but a poor trap to catch luck if you go and bait it wi' wickedness. The money as is got so's like to burn holes i' your pocket. I'd niver wish us to leave our lads a sixpence but what was got i' the rightful way. And as for the weather, there's One above makes it, and we must put up wi't: it's nothing of a plague to what the wenches are."
>
> Notwithstanding the interruption in their walk, the excellent habit which Mrs. Poyser's clock had of taking time by the forelock,

had secured their arrival at the village while it was still a quarter to two, though almost every one who meant to go to church was already within the churchyard gates.

It would be difficult to quote at less length for these illustrations, for a leisurely pace can be illustrated only by its own leisureliness.

But what does "pace" mean? Of what is it the expressive signature? We have examined slightly, in the study of *Great Expectations,* what the tempo of that book means—how its abrupt shocks of timing, its ballet-like leaps, express the mysterious movements of a non-naturalistic world in which guilt has an objective being as palpable as that "fearful man, all in coarse grey, with a great iron on his leg" who starts up from among the graves; a world in which the secret inner life of the spirit does not wait on the slow processes of analysis and of naturalistic cause and effect, but suddenly appears before one on the staircase with hands stretched out, saying, "My boy! my dear boy!"; in short, an absurd world, quite contradicting commonsense, and one, therefore, in which things and people do not walk by the clock but dance pantomimic dances in the outrageous tempo of the absurd. In *Wuthering Heights,* the pace of assault is so deeply at the core of the book's feeling that comment seems superfluous: we cannot imagine this novel as moving otherwise than by violent attack—than by verbs of "snatching," "grinding," "crashing," "smashing," "thundering," "choking," "burning," "torturing," "murdering": for such excess is of the nature of that nonhuman Otherworld which, in Emily Brontë's vision, erupts grotesquely into the limited, the civilized, the moral, the static. And now, before attempting to define the expressive value of a very different kind of pace, let us consider somewhat more closely the types of material that, in *Adam Bede,* present themselves with the patient rhythms of day and night, of the seasons, of planting and harvest, of the generations of men, and of the thoughts of simple people who are bound by deep tradition to soil and to community.

We enter the description of Hall Farm in Chapter 6 at "the drowsiest time of the year, just before hay-harvest," and at "the drowsiest time of the day, too, for it is close upon three by the sun, and it is half-past three by Mrs. Poyser's handsome eight-day clock." If the reader will turn back to the passage quoted above, describing old Martin Poyser, he will find the clock again: old Martin watches its hands, not through engagement with time but through disengagement from it; he pleases himself with "detecting a rhythm in the tick" as he does with watching the sun-gleams on the wall and counting the quarries on the floor. And again, in the passage describing the Poysers on their way to church, we are told of "the excellent habit which Mrs. Poyser's clock had of taking time by the forelock," so that, despite interruptions in their walk, they arrive at the village "while it was still a quarter to two." The mechanism of the eight-day clock works in sympathy with the week, with the rhythm of workdays and Sabbath, and we are reminded in the same passage of that other scheduling of man's time which holds him to Sabbath observance no matter if the hay wants turning, for, as Mrs. Poyser says, "as for the weather, there's One above makes it, and we must put up wi't." We shall return to the clock, but we wish to note now the *kind* of life that this great mass of slow time carries with it. It is a kind of life that is signified by that wonderful kitchen at Hall Farm, with its polished surfaces of oak table and, of course, the oak clockcase—not "any of your varnished rubbish," but polished with "genuine 'elbow polish' "—the great round pewter dishes ranged on the shelves above the long deal dinner table, the jasper-shining hobs of the grate, mellow oak and bright brass; and it is signified by the Hall Farm dairy,

> such coolness, such purity, such fresh fragrance of new-pressed cheese, of firm butter, of wooden vessels perpetually bathed in pure water; such soft coloring of red earthenware and creamy surfaces, brown wood and polished tin, grey limestone and rich orange-red rust on the iron weights and hooks and hinges.

It is a kind of life that is signified, too, by the funeral of Thias Bede, that deeply reverend magical rite at which

> none of the old people held books—why should they? not one of them could read. But they knew a few "good words" by heart, and their withered lips now and then moved silently, following the service without any very clear comprehension indeed, but with a simple faith in its efficacy to ward off harm and bring blessing . . .

while old Lisbeth is comforted in her grief by "a vague belief that the psalm was doing her husband good," for

> it was part of that decent burial which she would have thought it a greater wrong to withhold from him than to have caused him many

unhappy days while he was living. The more there was said about her husband, the more there was done for him, surely the safer he would be.

It is a kind of life that is signified by the chapter describing the schoolmaster, Bartle Massy, and his pupils—the stone sawyer, the brickmaker, the dyer—

> three big men, with the marks of their hard labour about them, anxiously bending over the worn books, and painfully making out, "The grass is green," "The sticks are dry," "The corn is ripe" . . . It was almost as if three rough animals were making humble efforts to learn how they might become human.

Bartle Massy himself has no critical place in the plot, but, like the schoolmaster in Goldsmith's "The Deserted Village," he is one more significant member of a community; and his kindness, his depth of feeling, his long habits of sacrifice and self-discipline, even his eccentricity, are of the richest texture of the community life. For it is the community that is the protagonist of this novel, the community as the repository of certain shared and knowledgeable values that have been developed out of ages of work and care and common kindness. The kitchen at Hall Farm shines in the sun, the dairy is clean and fragrant, Lisbeth's grief is alleviated by the funeral, and Bartle Massy's pupils make their toilsome efforts "to learn how they might become human," because of a moral development that has been made possible only by slow and difficult centuries of accreted recognitions, limitations, modulations, techniques.

Therefore the eight-day clock, with its minute rhythms for an old man's ear, with its rhythm for the daily work that starts at half past four, when the mowers' bottles have to be filled and the baking started, and with its weekly rhythm for the Sabbath. The clock is a monument not to time merely as time, but to the assured and saving values stored up through ages of experience. In one of her books George Eliot says, "There is no private life which has not been determined by a wider public life." In *Adam Bede,* this is the mute recognition by which the community lives: as imaginatively realized here, it is a recognition that personal good has communal determinations, that it is contingent upon the preservation of common values. But the statement bears also its converse, which might be phrased thus: "There is no public life which has not been determined by the narrower private life"; for the story of *Adam Bede* is a story of the irreparable damage wrought on the community by a private moment's frivolity.

Mrs. Poyser's clock at Hall Farm, the clock which has sublimated all time into good, is set for daylight saving (it has the "excellent habit" of "taking time by the forelock"). Not so the clocks of the gentlefolk at the Chase. Throughout that Thursday when Arthur twice meets Hetty in the wood, the clock is watched irritably. It is "about ten o'clock" when Arthur, time irritable and bored on his hands, goes to the stables; the "twelve o'clock sun" sees him galloping toward Norburne to see a friend; but Hetty is on his mind, and "the hand of the dial in the courtyard had scarcely cleared the last stroke of three" when he is again home; so that "it was scarcely four o'clock" when he is waiting at the gate of the wood. Hetty comes daily to learn lace mending of Mrs. Pomfret, the maid at the Chase, at four o'clock, and she tells Arthur that she always sets out for the farm "by eight o'clock." They exchange a look: "What a space of time those three moments were, while their eyes met and his arms touched her!" Arthur meditates irresolutely "more than an hour" on the false impression he feels he has created in the girl; but "the time must be filled up," and he dresses for dinner, "for his grandfather's dinner-hour was six"; meanwhile Hetty too is watching the clock, and at last "the minute-hand of the old-fashioned brazen-faced timepiece was on the last quarter of eight." In the shadows of the wood he kisses her. Then he pulls out his watch: "I wonder how late it is . . . twenty minutes past eight—but my watch is too fast." Back at the farm, Mrs. Poyser exclaims,

> "What a time o'night this is to come home, Hetty . . . Look at the clock, do; why, it's going on for half-past nine, and I've sent the gells to bed this half-hour, and late enough too . . ."
>
> "I did set out before eight, aunt," said Hetty, in a pettish tone, with a slight toss of her head. "But this clock's so much before the clock at the Chase, there's no telling what time it'll be when I get here."
>
> "What! you'd be wanting the clock set by gentle-folks's time, would you? an' sit up burnin' candle, an' lie a-bed wi' the sun a-bakin' you like a cowcumber i' the frame? The clock hasn't been put forrard for the first time to-day, I reckon."

ON *Adam Bede*

The pace of *Adam Bede* is set to Mrs. Poyser's clock, to all that slow toil and patient discipline that have made daylight—and living—valuable. Slower, organically, invisibly slow, are the months of Hetty's pregnancy; the Poysers' clock, the clock at the Chase, do not keep this time, with their eights and nines and half past nines. This other, deep, hidden, animal time drags the whole pace down to that of poor Hetty's "journey in despair," a blind automatism of animal night where the ticking of the human clock cannot be heard.

Hetty's very fragility is her claim to the saving disciplines of a traditional way of life. It is by her mediocrity that their value is tested, for without them she is abandoned to chaos. There is probably no other work that explores human suffering at the organic level with such deep authority as the chapter describing Hetty's journey from Oxford to Stonyshire. It is a suffering that has no issue in "illumination," no spiritual value for the sufferer, for Hetty is not the kind of character that sustains "illumination" through suffering. If she were, we should not have had the particular insight that *Adam Bede* affords into the moral meaning of time and tradition in the lives of simple people. Hetty is lost because she is more fragile than the others and therefore more dependent on the community disciplines (far more fragile, because of her class, than "Chad's Bess" of the village, for instance, who, with her looseness and silliness and—like Hetty—with false garnets in her ears, has a secure and accustomed place in the village life); lost from the only values that can support her mediocrity, she sinks into the chaos of animal fear, which, in the human being, is insanity. Other novelists have explored other kinds of suffering; one might draw up a chart or a dissertation, of no mean interest, that would show the hierarchies of human suffering as represented in literature and their psychological, ethical, and spiritual significance; surely Hetty's would be at the bottom of the scale (even lower, one would think, than that of some of the least human characters in Faulkner's novels, for Faulkner is interested in the "illumination" of which even idiots are capable). But its lowness and blindness in the scale of human suffering is its moving power. For Hetty is very human, very real, and if knowledge of suffering did not include hers, it would not include the broadest and commonest layer of human existence.

It is improbable that any but an English novelist would have interested himself in Hetty as a figure of tragic pathos. Flaubert would have despised her: the luxury fantasies of Emma Bovary (a French Hetty) have a richness and complexity of cultural experience, and a play of sensibility, that make Hetty's dreams of standing beside Arthur Donnithorne as a bride look thin indeed; and the fatality of Hetty's pregnancy would not have occurred to the author of *Madame Bovary,* nor all the mess of child murder, for these are quite English habits of interest (as we have been able to witness those habits in *The Heart of Mid-Lothian*—to whose plot *Adam Bede* is confessedly indebted—and shall again in Hardy's *Tess*); though Emma Bovary's adulterous experiences give her a far wider range of opportunity than Hetty's few moments with Arthur Donnithorne allow, Emma's child is a child by marriage and its existence has ironic rather than tragic significance; and the interest of Emma's adulteries is an interest in the adulterous psychology rather than an interest in spermatic and ovarian operations. Dostoevski could not have used Hetty, for she has less of God in her, a more meager spiritual capacity, than his imbeciles and whores; she is not capable even of that kind of "recognition" which leads the abused child in *The Possessed* and the carpenter in *Crime and Punishment* to hang themselves.

But the massy line of the book is deflected toward the end. ("The mirror," George Eliot says, "is doubtless defective; the outlines will sometimes be disturbed, the reflection faint or confused.") By Mrs. Poyser's clock, Hetty's last-minute reprieve cannot really be timed with a time integral to the rest of the novel, nor can Adam's marriage with Dinah. Henry James says of these events that he doubts very much "whether the author herself had a clear vision" of them, and suggests that the reason may be that George Eliot's perception

> was a perception of nature much more than of art, and that these particular incidents do not belong to nature (to my sense at least); by which I do not mean that they belong to a very happy art . . . they are a very good example of the view in which a story must have marriages and rescues in the nick of time, as a matter of course.[1]

We should add Arthur Donnithorne's return in his interesting and picturesque ill-health. Hetty's reprieve, the marriage of Dinah and Adam, Arthur's reconstruction through such suffering as Arthur is able to suffer—these are no compensation for and no real "illumination" of the tragedy

[1] *Partial Portraits* (London, 1911), p. 53.

of Hetty. They are the artificial illumination which so many Victorian novels indulged in, in the effort to justify to man God's ways or society's ways or nature's ways. But still there is left the ticking of the oak-cased clock, rubbed by human "elbow-polish," that paces the book through its greater part: the realization of value, clean as the clock-tick, radiant as the kitchen of Hall Farm, fragrant as the dairy; and the tragic realization of the loss of however simple human values, in Hetty's abandoned footsteps as she seeks the dark pool and caresses her own arms in the desire for life.

ON *The Egoist*

With Meredith's *The Egoist* we enter into a critical problem that we have not before faced in these studies. That is the problem offered by a writer of recognizably impressive stature, whose work is informed by a muscular intelligence, whose language has splendor, whose "view of life" wins our respect, and yet for whom we are at best able to feel only a passive appreciation which amounts, practically, to indifference. We should be unjust to Meredith and to criticism if we should, giving in to the inertia of indifference, simply avoid dealing with him and thus avoid the problem along with him. He does not "speak to us," we might say; his meaning is not a "meaning for us"; he "leaves us cold." But do not the challenge and the excitement of the critical problem as such lie in that ambivalence of attitude which allows us to recognize the intelligence and even the splendor of Meredith's work, while, at the same time, we experience a lack of sympathy, a failure of any enthusiasm of response?

The difficulty is not that the Meredithian prose places too much demand upon the reader's attentiveness. There is no "too much" of this kind that a work of art can require of us. *Tristram Shandy* requires as much or more. Even *Pride and Prejudice,* for all its simplicity of surface, asks that we read with as alert an attentiveness to the word. Henry James offers more sinuous verbal paths than Meredith, paths that demand more of concentration inasmuch as they may be marked only by commas or question marks or dots that signify a suspension or attenuation of the track of communication, where Meredith would set up crusty substantives for the mind's grasp to help it around corners. "The enjoyment of a work of art," James said,

> the acceptance of an irresistible illusion, constituting, to my sense, our highest experience of "luxury," the luxury is not greatest, by my conse-

> quent measure, when the work asks for as little attention as possible.
> It is greatest, it is delightfully, divinely great, when we feel the surface,
> like the thick ice of the skater's pond, bear without cracking the
> strongest pressure we throw on it.[1]

And, indeed, it seems to be precisely where Meredith offers the toughest
stylistic going that we enjoy him the most. This is true at least of *The
Egoist,* if not of later work. Curiously, our very sense of a *virtue* of excrescence in the style is symptomatic of that failure of thoroughly significant communication which we feel in Meredith. It is symptomatic, but let
us insist that it is not the failure itself; for to be felt as excrescence, even
fine excrescence, style must be related to *something else* in the work to
which it seems to be perilously appended—just as building ornament is
sensed as excrescent only as we see it in relation to the building.

Nor is the difficulty a lack of sensitive craft and pattern. *The Egoist*
is a beautifully planned novel. Its pace is assured and powerful; from the
opening incident, when Willoughby, on the terrace with Constantia Dur-
ham, snubs the marine lieutenant and tosses off, "I'll send him a check,"
to the last, when he deliciously misfires his revenge in all directions at
once, events march their complicated route with a large inevitability. The
spatial, or plastic, conception of the book is as fine as its movement in
time: Willoughby's fantastic rigidity is set around, like a Maypole, with a
gay and urgent dance on ribbons; the flat-footed, muscle-bound, blown-
jowled monolith of his self-importance is host to a lawn festival of delicate
searchings, bright scurryings, mobile strategies of the intelligences whose
living occasions he has tried to halter at his center.

Nor should we confuse Meredith's failure with his deliberate limitation of the comic drama to the scope of a lawn festival, or, as he says, in
his "Prelude" on the Comic Spirit, to

> human nature in the drawing-room of civilized men and women,
> where we have no dust of the struggling outer world, no mire, no
> violent crashes . . .

In this "Prelude," he merely puts into manifesto a limitation which Jane
Austen made; and in our reading of *Pride and Prejudice* we have sufficiently examined that limitation so that we should not need, now, to bring

[1] In *The Art of the Novel,* James's Critical Prefaces edited by R. P. Blackmur (New
York: Charles Scribner's Sons, 1934), p. 304.

any question against a novelist on the grounds that he confines his interest to "human nature in the drawing-room." Human nature is as human there as anywhere else, its opportunities as full and as menacing as in a slum or a coal mine or a dust bowl or a snake pit. It is perhaps strategic to remind ourselves of this fact again here, before we go on to Henry James, for our understanding of James would indeed be stultified if we retained still any facile notion that "life" is deeper and thicker in certain material conditions than in others, among the masses than among the classes, on a street corner than in a drawing room, in a chamber pot than in a porcelain cup.

Mr. Wilson Follett, in his introduction to the Modern Library edition of *The Egoist,* approaches Meredith's dwindled reputation in another way, from the point of view of certain vast generational changes in philosophical and psychological assumptions as to the nature of personality. He says,

> The central fact, the change behind all changes, is the modern annihilation of the Will, both as a valid concept and as a working tool. Up to our own generation man had embraced the belief . . . that he was at least partly the master of his own fate; and, acting on that belief, he had often made his conviction actually work. It had the important pragmatic sanction that it made him feel at home in his world, a world of moral choice. It is among the ruins of that world that we now grope. We see ourselves as lost and rootless in a universe without meaning—victims of malevolently blind forces, in and outside ourselves, that predetermine our actions and reduce our will and our vaunted reason to mere delusive reflexes, behavioristic phenomena. Meredith represents a world of Will, a society of lives modifiable by Will; and that fact alone is enough to give our time the sensation of being divided from him by a span computable in nothing less than light-years.[2]

How, then, are we to understand the fact that George Eliot's universe, where moral choice traces its significant reign, is not similarly divided from us? Or, to use a modern example, how are we to justify our response of excited intelligence and conviction to a book like Albert Camus's *La Peste,* where the vocation of man, even man in despair, is seen as altruistic *willing?* It might, indeed, be argued that, in a world denuded of values

[2] New York: 1947, pp. xii–xiii. Reprinted with permission.

and meanings, dramas in which the will is an operative factor would have a greater poignancy of significance—at least potentially—than they could have in a world which took for granted the measurable effects of willing. It might be argued that, as the conception of the will has become more complicated, complicated by our knowledge that we act under "blind forces" which are our will while yet we will against them, dramas of human relationships under the aspect of personally willed modification would have a more intense interest for us because we would find in them a more complex significance, a greater ambiguity, than would be possible if the personal will were thought of as morally univocal and psychologically undivided. The fiction that has attracted us most in an "absurd" world whose expressive signature is the concentration camp is fiction in which the will, though viewed variously, is still the moral center of the composition: this is true—to take extreme cases—of those fictions in which the personal will is defeated, "absurdly" defeated, as in Kafka and Hardy; it is true of Hemingway's fictions, where the very meagerness of the area within the Nothing where the will can operate is the sign of its tragic nobility; it is true of those fictions that explore the possibilities of self-knowledge (knowledge of what it is that we "will," or of the will's capacity for modification, or of its need for reteaching by experience of the emotions and instincts it has neglected or denied), as in Conrad and James and much of Thomas Mann; it is true of those that explore the epic corruption of the will, as in Melville and Dostoevski. Generational changes in assumptions as to what the will is, how it works, whether it is practically operative or not, do not explain our distance from Meredith, for—so far as moral significance in fiction is concerned—our interest is still intensely in the concept of the will. It is probable that indifference to a work of art (after we have considered the work well) is never explained by the *kind* of "world view" or "life view" that it holds, no matter how alien from our own, but only by the lack of self-substantial coherency of that view of things as represented in the aesthetic form.

In connection with Meredith's view of the human world as a place where choices made by the personal will perceptibly affect reality, *The Egoist* offers, in its major elements, special reasons for a rapport with the modern reader which is nevertheless lacking. There are, in the book, two chief modes in which the effective will appears, represented by Willoughby's immalleable self-will, aspiring to a simplification of the universe on his own measure, and by Clara Middleton's delicate, mobile, searching will, aspiring to air, opportunity, multiplicity. As for Willoughby's effectiveness,

> *Through very love of self himself he slew,*

as his epitaph has it—certainly a pronounced victory of volition. The "comic drama of the suicide" illustrated by Willoughby's career is a drama that, in clinical rather than in English country-house materials, is fairly obsessive to modern interest. It is a drama that Dr. Karl Menninger has traced, uncomically, in *Man against Himself*. We find the note of it in W. H. Auden's poem "September 1, 1939."

> *The windiest militant trash*
> *Important Persons shout*
> *Is not so crude as our wish:*
> *What mad Nijinsky wrote*
> *About Diaghilev*
> *Is true of the normal heart;*
> *The error bred in the bone*
> *Of each woman and each man*
> *Craves what it cannot have,*
> *Not universal love,*
> *But to be loved alone.*[3]

Of the craving "to be loved alone" Meredith's Willoughby makes the necessary conversion into self-love, since we cannot be loved alone by anybody but ourselves. With Clara,

> He dragged her through the labyrinths of his penetralia, in his hungry coveting to be loved more and still more, more still, until imagination gave up the ghost, and he talked to her plain hearing like a monster.

Willoughby is the fetus in full panoply, clothing himself "at others' expense," enjoying, or seeking to enjoy, "without incurring the immense debtorship for a thing done," possessing "without obligation to the object possessed." These phrases are Meredith's description of the sentimentalist, Willoughby being the prime example; they are also descriptive of an embryo. Willoughby is the monster of the womb, imposing on drawing room and lawn his unearned adulthood, his fetal vaporousness supported by name, wealth, and "a leg," and his demands for osmotic nourish-

---

[3] *The Collected Poetry of W. H. Auden* (New York: Random House, Inc., 1945), p. 58.

ment as if society were but one huge placenta designed for his shelter and growth. With Willoughby we *should* have the utmost rapport, for we have learned fiercely to understand him, through our so broadly ramified education in the fetal and infantile proclivities of the adult.

Willoughby must be delivered, but unfortunately not as in a normal birth, from the womb to the world, for he has been wearing the world as a custom-made womb. His delivery is the delivery of other people from him, from the extravagance of their courtesy in allowing him to occupy them. Willoughby is the difficult occasion for other people to dis-entrail themselves, by the exercise of intelligence, from a strangling, homomorphic Cause; he is the occasion in revolt against which individuality and variety of will are realized. By courtesy, faith, habit, and social exigency Clara Middleton and Vernon Whitford and Laetitia Dale find themselves in the kissing arms of this octopus, fanned on by the aunts, by Dr. Middleton's taste in port, and by a society of submarine fantasies and chattering twilight expectations. They extricate themselves, with difficulty, by learning to recognize meaning in experience and by acting on the recognition. "The drama of Meredith's characters," Ramon Fernandez says,

> is always and essentially the drama of an exacting sensibility. They begin by going straight ahead, in the direction of life, along the road of action. Their first acts, however rich and generous they may be, are simple, normal, not to say conventional . . . Since they can live only by acting, they act at first in perfect harmony with the circle in which tradition has caused them to be born. But then sensibility, at the first collision, is awakened. They feel confusedly that they can no longer live in the conditions which at first they accepted. And there they are, thrown back upon themselves, attentive, on the alert, seeking anxiously among the echoes of experience the key to the enigma which shall deliver them. To live for them is to seek to think, but to think in order to be able afresh to breathe, act, and bloom.[4]

The nobility, the interest, the viability of this conception of character we cannot but acknowledge, and we make the acknowledgment the more readily as Meredith's view of life touches off with electric irony, and almost as if allegorically, certain grim features, both psychological and political, of our own condition.

[4] *Messages* (New York: Harcourt, Brace & Company, Inc., 1927), p. 175.

Why, then, do we find ourselves indifferent? "Not a difficulty met," James said of Meredith, speaking as a novelist about a novelist,

> not a figure presented, not a scene constituted—not a dim shadow condensing once into audible or visible reality—making you hear for an instant the tap of its feet on the earth.[5]

This is perhaps to go too far, particularly between novelists who are so much akin—in respect at least of stylistic elaboration, the social setting, the delicate development of a consciousness of values—as James is to Meredith in *The Egoist*. But it is indicative. Willoughby is a victim in wax model, Virginia Woolf said, not flesh and blood: he "is turned slowly round before a steady fire of scrutiny and criticism which allows no twitch on the victim's part to escape it" [6]—a process that, on description, looks as unfair as other destructive magical rites, as unfair as torture for confession. The fact is that Willoughby is treated as a perfectly lonely aberration, a freak; nobody (neither we as readers nor anyone in the book) knows how he came about, how he happened, what he is for, what connection there might be between his psychological peculiarities and the human soul at large. We do not really supply the connections when we say, "There is a Willoughby in each of us," for though the statement seems valid enough, its validity lies outside the book and not structurally within it: *within* the book there are no Willoughbys except Willoughby. Meredith makes similarly extraneous statements about Willoughby's human representativeness, but they remain dogmatic, without internal aesthetic corroboration. From the earliest note we have of his youth,

> "When he was a child he one day mounted a chair, and there he stood in danger, would not let us touch him, because he was taller than we, and we were to gaze. Do you remember him, Eleanor? 'I am the sun of the house!' It was inimitable!"

he is uncaused, a prodigy; and his career in maturity has only an external relatedness—a relatedness of exploitation—to other people; he is an obstacle to them, an ingratiating and portentous obstacle, but quite definitively outside of them, not inside. That we are not, *aesthetically*, given

[5] Quoted by Siegfried Sassoon, in *Meredith* (New York: The Viking Press, Inc., 1948), p. 232.
[6] *The Second Common Reader* (New York: Harcourt, Brace & Company, Inc., 1932), pp. 252–253.

any insight as to what subtle internal bonds there might be between Willoughby and society—what, in the social soul, was itself Willoughby in order to fertilize this monster—or as to what taint of identity there might be between the soul of Willoughby and the soul of anybody else, makes us restless with his image, powerfully as that image is drawn, for he has evidently much too important a symbolic potential to be left so without spiritual relations, so unproliferative of the possible meanings he might have either for the constitution of the body politic or for that of the private psyche.

Like the giant of *Jack and the Beanstalk,* he is an external menace only, not a suffered portion of self or of the cultural conditions of self. That giant's feet did not touch the earth, because, after the scramble of escape, the stalk was cut down at a single blow. At the end of *The Egoist,* a dozen people—all the world—take whacks with free conscience at the beanstalk. Jane Austen's Mr. Collins, in *Pride and Prejudice,* is a monster quite in the fetal style of Willoughby, but Mr. Collins has the spiritual support of a society of other monsters with common economic causes, and the menace that he offers is one that, graded from grotesque obviousness to inconspicuous subtlety, is distributed through the social organism, pervasive in the private soul, providing the common stuff of the very language—thus truly dangerous because unconsciously environing. Mr. Collins—that is, the representative qualities of Mr. Collins, the complacencies of egoism backed by desperations of economic footing and caste, in a culture contracted to their measure—cannot really be escaped, even by happy marriages and removals, but must be dealt with alertly at every moment as the condition of existence.

Henry James's Osmond, in *The Portrait of a Lady,* also affords parallels with Willoughby, and again the difference in treatment is significant of Meredith's failure to give his egoist a spiritual context. *The Egoist* is of the year 1877; *The Portrait of a Lady,* 1881. We should not wish to force an unwarranted meaning upon these dates, but they do provide a curious comment on the parallels between the two books, particularly in view of James's opinion of Meredith. Health, wealth, and beauty are the qualifications Willoughby demands in his bride; she must also

> come to him out of cloistral purity . . . out of an egg-shell, some-
> what more astonished at things than a chick . . . and seeing him with
> her sex's eyes first of all men.

It is a note sounded also by Osmond, in James's *Portrait,* and we hear in it almost the same comic exaggeration. He asks, concerning Isabel, who has been suggested to him as a possible bride,

> "Is she beautiful, clever, rich, splendid, universally intelligent and un-precedentedly virtuous? It's only on those conditions that I care to make her acquaintance."

Contempt for "the world" is the breath of life to both Willoughby and Osmond; their need to scorn it and set themselves and their possessions apart from it is the inspiration of their existence, on the principle that "the world" must admire where it is scorned and pay to the scorner the tribute of its own helpless vulgarity. For Willoughby,

> The breath of the world, the world's view of him, was partly his vital breath, his view of himself . . . [He was] born to look down upon a tributary world, and to exult in being looked to. Do we wonder at his consternation in the prospect of that world's blowing foul upon him? Princes have their obligations to teach them they are mortal, and the brilliant heir of a tributary world is equally enchained by the homage it brings him . . .

And for Osmond,

> To surround his interior with a sort of invidious sanctity, to tantalise society with a sense of exclusion, to make people believe his house was different from every other, to impart to the face that he presented to the world a cold originality—this was the ingenious effort of the personage to whom Isabel had attributed a superior morality . . . under the guise of caring only for intrinsic values Osmond lived ex-clusively for the world . . .

These parallelisms—and others—almost suggest that James deliber-ately used the pattern conceived by Meredith. But how much more he discovered in it! The difference lies in a sense of spiritual context. Wil-loughby appears without "internal relations" with the society he domi-nates or with the individuals whose self-development he attempts to suffocate; he is, moreover, personally valueless, a formal abstraction of conceit without any other palpable qualification than a "leg." Osmond is incomparably a subtler evil, for he does represent values, and when he says—in the magnificent scene in which he forbids Isabel to go to England—

> "I think we should accept the consequences of our actions, and what I value most in life is the honour of a thing!"

the gravity of his sincerity, speaking, as Isabel realizes, in the name of "something sacred and precious," is in perfect measure with his blasphemy against *precisely the same values* as his wife interprets them. The menace that he offers is a menace within Isabel herself, in her recognition of the spiritual density and integrity of a man so corrupt. Osmond speaks her own language, for it is in "the honour of a thing" and in accepting "the consequences of her actions" that she finds her own moral identity; the menace, the confusion that cripples decision, lies in the formal similarity of their moral aspirations and the appalling dissimilarity of the interpretations these yield to each. Osmond has roots and ramifications: he is supported not only by human accomplices in his peculiarly subtle guilt, but by ages of value growth thoroughly intelligential, by Rome itself, by Europe, by Isabel's own passion for a finer experience. It is Osmond's spiritual context, his "internal relations" with society and with individuals, that make him so meaningful a figure. It is Willoughby's lack of such context that makes him a *bibelot* of literature.

The prose style of *The Egoist,* intensely nervous and packed, constantly inventive, has somewhat the same status of an abnormal and eccentric growth as does Willoughby, and in this sense Siegfried Sassoon's remark that the phraseology of the book "is an artifice which seems appropriate" [7] has an unintended rightness. The style is beautifully wrought, as is the figure of Willoughby himself; we cannot deny it its qualities of virtu. Again and again the vivid and witty image concretizes a state of mind. There is Willoughby's agony over the threatened defection of Clara.

> The fact that she was a healthy young woman returned to the surface of his thoughts like the murdered body pitched into the river, which will not drown, and calls upon the elements of dissolution to float it.

Or the quality of his pathos with Laetitia:

[7] *Op. cit.,* p. 208.

> As his desire was merely to move her without an exposure of himself, he had to compass being pathetic as it were under the impediments of a mailed and gauntleted knight, who can not easily heave the bosom, or show it heaving.

Or his torments of decision:

> Laocoon of his own serpents, he struggled to a certain magnificence of attitude in the muscular net of constrictions he flung round himself.

It is of this kind of stylistic virtuosity that Ramon Fernandez speaks when he says that Meredith's "artifice" consists

> in representing the most concrete possible equivalent for a mental movement . . . Meredith fills in the intervals of the action with little symbolical actions because he is anxious above all not to let his thought and that of the reader lose their dramatic rhythm.[8]

His images, Fernandez says, thus constitute "a defense system against abstraction." Since the definitive and suicidal characteristic of the egoist is his abstraction from the living world, a style so full of concrete images and tough little verbal dramas has its peculiar logic here, for it keeps the egoist within our ken; he might otherwise lose his liveliness and dissolve into his own sentimental vapor. Yet, attractive as is this rationalization of style, one asks if there is not a fallacy in throwing so much of the burden of concreteness upon style and if the concreteness most necessary to fiction does not lie in that spiritual *contextualism* of lives which we have noticed as lacking in *The Egoist*. Where such context strongly exists and style subserves it, is not the concreteness there too—the concreteness that makes the created world of a novel excitedly meaningful "for us"? Where it does not exist, and style is called upon to substitute for it by energy and picture, is not style forced into an unnatural position where it figures as a kind of "egoist" itself—a separated, self-willed, self-regarding element? In what is surely one of the most abstract vocabularies in fiction, and one of the least "image-making" of styles, Jane Austen evoked a concrete world that is meaningful "for us" because, like a world, it exists in the autonomy of its own internal relations.

On Meredith's style is imposed a somewhat desperate function of

[8] *Op. cit.*, p. 171.

keeping author, characters, and reader in a state of awareness, not so much of what is going on, but of each other, a function of keeping us awake to the fact that we are reading a brilliant book by an exceptionally intelligent author about highly burnished characters—all of which the style makes us ever so ready to admit. One thinks of Milton here, for Meredith's style has its brilliance as Milton's has its "grandness," and in reading Milton one has to hang on by the words and the astonishing verbal manipulation if sometimes by nothing else. What Desmond McCarthy said of Meredith might be said of Milton: "It must be remembered in reading Meredith that half his touches are not intended to help you to realize the object so much as to put power into the form." [9] The statement applied to Meredith makes only a fumbling kind of sense, inasmuch as it divides the "form" from the "object," and what we see as failure in Meredith is just this division of form and object, the division of the elegant pattern and splendid style of the book from potential meaning, from potential relationships between characters and thus potential relationships with ourselves. Applied to Milton, it has a good deal more sense, and the difference lies here. One feels that, in a highly special and deeply meaningful way, the Miltonic style *is* "the object"; one feels that the verbal manipulation is the mind's desperate exhibition of its independence and strength, working on the plastic stuff of the word in a frightful vacuum of other stuff adequately tough to reward the worker's gift and exertion—the mind is with its "back to the wall," so to speak, in the position of Lucifer; one feels that this is the moral kinetics which, in Milton, is profoundly "the object," and that the "power" of Milton's language is the same as that satanic power which moved a causeway through empty space from hell to earth. We cannot say so much of Meredith. Style is here a brilliant manner, and, with some embarrassment—for we would not be without the pleasures Meredith provides—we would quote Dr. Middleton on style in the author's own admirably intelligent style:

> "You see how easy it is to deceive one who is an artist in phrases. Avoid them, Miss Dale; they dazzle the penetration of the composer. That is why people of ability like Mrs. Mountstuart see so little; they are bent on describing brilliantly."

[9] Quoted by Siegfried Sassoon, *op. cit.*, p. 210.

ON *Tess of the D'Urbervilles*

It was Hardy who said of Meredith that "he would not, or could not —at any rate did not—when aiming to represent the 'Comic Spirit,' let himself discover the tragedy that always underlies comedy if you only scratch deeply enough." Hardy's statement does not really suggest that comedy is somehow tragedy *manqué*, that writers of comedy would write tragedies if they only "scratched deeply enough." What he says is what Socrates said to Aristophanes and Agathon at the end of the *Symposium* —that the genius of tragedy is the same as that of comedy. It is what Cervantes knew, whose great comic hero, Quixote, walks in the same shades with Orestes and Oedipus, Hamlet and Lear. It is what Molière knew. Even Jane Austen knew it. The precariousness of moral consciousness in its brute instinctual and physical circumstances, its fragility as an instrument for the regeneration of the will: this generic disproportion in the human condition comedy develops by grotesque enlargement of one or another aberrated faculty; tragedy, by grotesque enlargement of the imbalance between human motive and the effect of action. The special point to our purpose is, however, another: neither tragic figure nor comic figure is merely phenomenal and spectacular if it truly serves the function common to both genres—the catharsis; acting as scapegoats for the absurdity of the human dilemma, they are humanity's thoughtful or intuitive comment on itself. We return, thus, deviously by way of the kinship of tragedy and comedy, to the matter of "internal relations." The human condition, whether in the "drawing-room of civilized men and women" or on a wild heath in ancient Britain, shows, if scratched deeply enough, the binding ironies that bind the spectacular destiny of the hero with the unspectacular common destiny; and it is in the internal relations of the

195

art form, the aesthetic structure, that these bonds have symbolic representation. The aesthetic failure of *The Egoist* is thus a diagnostic mark of a crucial failure of vision, a weakness and withdrawal of vision before the common dilemma and the common destiny.

To turn to one of Hardy's great tragic novels is to put "internal relations" in the novel to peculiar test, for there is perhaps no other novelist, of a stature equal to Hardy's, who so stubbornly and flagrantly foisted upon the novel elements resistant to aesthetic cohesion. We shall want to speak of these elements first, simply to clear away and free ourselves from the temptation to appraise Hardy by his "philosophy"—that is, the temptation to mistake bits of philosophic adhesive tape, rather dampened and rumpled by time, for the deeply animated vision of experience which our novel, *Tess,* holds. We can quickly summon examples, for they crop out obviously enough. Before one has got beyond twenty pages one finds this paragraph on the ignominy and helplessness of the human estate:

> All these young souls were passengers in the Durbeyfield ship—entirely dependent on the judgment of the two Durbeyfield adults for their pleasures, their necessities, their health, even their existence. If the heads of the Durbeyfield household chose to sail into difficulty, disaster, starvation, disease, degradation, death, thither were these half-dozen little captives under hatches compelled to sail with them—six helpless creatures, who had never been asked if they wished for life on any terms, much less if they wished for it on such hard conditions as were involved in being of the shiftless house of Durbeyfield. Some people would like to know whence the poet whose philosophy is in these days deemed as profound and trustworthy as his song is sweet and pure, gets his authority for speaking of "Nature's holy plan."

Whenever, in this book, Hardy finds either a butt or a sanction in a poet, one can expect the inevitable intrusion of a form of discourse that infers proofs and opinions and competition in "truth" that belongs to an intellectual battlefield alien from the novel's imaginative concretions. On the eve of the Durbeyfield family's forced deracination and migration, we are told that

> to Tess, as to some few millions of others, there was ghastly satire in the poet's lines:

> *Not in utter nakedness*
> *But trailing clouds of glory do we come.*

> To her and her like, birth itself was an ordeal of degrading personal compulsion, whose gratuitousness nothing in the result seemed to justify, and at best could only palliate.

Aside from the fact that no circumstances have been suggested in which Tess could have had time or opportunity or the requisite development of critical aptitudes to brood so formidably on Wordsworth's lines, who are those "few millions" who are the "like" of Tess? as, who are the "some people" in the previous quotation? and in what way do these statistical generalizations add to the already sufficient meaning of Tess's situation? At the end of the book, with the "Aeschylean phrase" on the sport of the gods, we feel again that intrusion of a commentary which belongs to another order of discourse. The gibbet is enough. The vision is deep and clear and can only be marred by any exploitation of it as a datum in support of abstraction. We could even do without the note of "ameliorism" in the joined hands of Clare and Tess's younger sister at the end: the philosophy of an evolutionary hope has nothing essential to do with Tess's fate and her common meaning; she is too humanly adequate for evolutionary ethics to comment upon, and furthermore we do not believe that young girls make ameliorated lives out of witness of a sister's hanging.

What philosophical vision honestly inheres in a novel inheres as the signifying form of a certain concrete body of experience; it is what the experience "means" because it is what, structurally, the experience *is*. When it can be loosened away from the novel to compete in the general field of abstract truth—as frequently in Hardy—it has the weakness of any abstraction that statistics and history and science may be allowed to criticize; whether true or false for one generation or another, or for one reader or another, or even for one personal mood or another, its status as truth is relative to conditions of evidence and belief existing outside the novel and existing there quite irrelevant to whatever body of particularized life the novel itself might contain. But as a structural principle active within the particulars of the novel, local and inherent there through a maximum of organic dependencies, the philosophical vision has the unassailable truth of living form.

We wish to press this difference a bit further by considering—deliberately in a few minor instances, for in the minor notation is the furthest reach of form—the internality and essentiality of Hardy's vision, just as we have previously considered instances of its externalization and devitalization. Significantly, his "ideas" remain the same in either case. They are abruptly articulated in incident, early in the book, with the death of Prince, appearing here with almost ideographical simplicity.

> The morning mail-cart, with its two noiseless wheels, speeding along these lanes like an arrow, as it always did, had driven into [Tess's] slow and unlighted equipage. The pointed shaft of the cart had entered the breast of the unhappy Prince like a sword, and from the wound his life's blood was spouting in a stream, and falling with a hiss into the road.
>
> In her despair Tess sprang forward and put her hand upon the hole, with the only result that she became splashed from face to skirt with the crimson drops . . .

The mail cart leaves, and she remains alone on the road with the ruin.

> The atmosphere turned pale; the birds shook themselves in the hedges, arose, and twittered; the lane showed all its white features, and Tess showed hers, still whiter. The huge pool of blood in front of her was already assuming the iridescence of coagulation; and when the sun rose, a million prismatic hues were reflected in it. Prince lay alongside still and stark, his eyes half open, the hole in his chest looking scarcely large enough to have let out all that had animated him.

With this accident are concatenated in fatal union Tess's going to "claim kin" of the D'Urbervilles and all the other links in her tragedy down to the murder of Alec. The symbolism of the detail is naïve and forthright to the point of temerity: the accident occurs in darkness and Tess has fallen asleep—just as the whole system of mischances and cross-purposes in the novel is a function of psychic and cosmic blindness; she "put her hand upon the hole"—and the gesture is as absurdly ineffectual as all her effort will be; the only result is that she becomes splashed with blood—as she will be at the end; the shaft pierces Prince's breast "like a sword"—Alec is stabbed in the heart with a knife; with the arousal and twittering of the birds we are aware of the oblivious manifold of nature stretching infinite and detached beyond the isolated human figure; the iridescence of the coagulating blood is, in its incongruity with the dark human trouble, a note of the same indifferent cosmic chemistry that has brought about the accident; and the smallness of the hole in Prince's chest, that looked "scarcely large enough to have let out all that had animated him," is the minor remark of that irony by which Tess's great cruel trial appears as a vanishing incidental in the blind waste of time and space and biological repetition. Nevertheless, there is nothing in this event that has not the natural "grain" of concrete fact; and what it signifies—of the complicity of doom with the most random occurrence, of the cross-purposing of purpose in a multiple world, of cosmic indifference and of moral desolation—is a local truth of a particular experience and irrefutable as the experience itself.

In the second chapter of *Tess* the gathering for the May-day "club-walking" is described, a debased "local Cerealia" that has lost its ancient motive as fertility rite and that subsists as a social habit among the village young people. Here Clare sees Tess for the first time, in white dress, with peeled willow wand and bunch of white flowers. But it is too late for him to stop, the clock has struck, he must be on his way to join his companions. Later, when he wants to marry Tess, he will tell his parents of the "pure and virtuous" bride he has chosen, when her robe is no longer the white robe of the May-walking but the chameleon robe of Queen Guinevere,

> *That never would become that wife*
> *That had once done amiss.*

In the scene of the May-walking, the lovers are "star-crossed" not by obscure celestial intent but by ordinary multiplicity of purposes and suitabilities; but in the submerged and debased fertility ritual—ironically doubled here with the symbolism of the white dress (a symbolism which Clare himself will later debase by his prudish perversity)—is shadowed a more savage doom brought about by a more violent potency, that of sexual instinct, by which Tess will be victimized. Owing its form entirely to the vision that shapes the whole of Tess's tragedy, the minor incident of the May-walking has the assurance of particularized reality and the truth of the naturally given.

Nothing could be more brutally factual than the description of the swede field at Flintcomb-Ash, nor convey more economically and transparently Hardy's vision of human abandonment in the dissevering earth.

> The upper half of each turnip had been eaten off by the live-stock, and it was the business of the two women to grub out the lower or earthy half of the root with a hooked fork called a hacker, that this might

be eaten also. Every leaf of the vegetable having previously been consumed, the whole field was in color a desolate drab; it was a complexion without features, as if a face, from chin to brow, should be only an expanse of skin. The sky wore, in another color, the same likeness; a white vacuity of expression with the lineaments gone.

The visitation of the winter birds has the same grain of local reality, and yet all the signifying and representative disaster of Tess's situation—its loneliness, its bleak triviality, its irrelevance in the dumb digestion of earth—is focused in the mirroring eyes of the birds.

> . . . strange birds from behind the North Pole began to arrive silently . . . gaunt spectral creatures with tragical eyes—eyes which had witnessed scenes of cataclysmal horror in inaccessible polar regions, of a magnitude such as no human being had ever conceived, in curdling temperatures that no man could endure; which had beheld the crash of icebergs and the slide of snow-hills by the shooting light of the Aurora; been half blinded by the whirl of colossal storms and terraqueous distortions; and retained the expression of feature that such scenes had engendered. These nameless birds came quite near to Tess and Marian, but of all they had seen which humanity would never see they brought no account. The traveller's ambition to tell was not theirs, and, with dumb impassivity, they dismissed experiences which they did not value for the immediate incidents of this upland—the trivial movements of the two girls in disturbing the clods with their fragile hackers so as to uncover something or other that these visitants relished as food.

There is the same sensitive honesty to the detail and expression of fact, the same inherence of vision in the particulars of experience, in the description of the weeds where Tess hears Clare thrumming his harp.

> The outskirt of the garden in which Tess found herself had been left uncultivated for some years, and was now damp and rank with juicy grass which sent up mists of pollen; and tall blooming weeds, emitting offensive smells—weeds whose red and yellow and purple hues formed a polychrome as dazzling as that of cultivated flowers. She went stealthily as a cat through this profusion of growth, gathering cuckoo-spittle on her skirts, brushing off snails that were climbing the apple-tree stems, staining her hands with thistle-milk and slug-slime, and rubbing off upon her naked arms sticky blights that, though snow-

white on the tree-trunks, made blood-red stains on her skin; thus she drew quite near to Clare, though still unobserved of him.

The weeds, circumstantial as they are, have an astonishingly cunning and bold metaphorical function. They grow at Talbothays, in that healing procreative idyl of milk and mist and passive biology, and they too are bountiful with life, but they stain and slime and blight; and it is in this part of Paradise (an "outskirt of the garden"—there are even apple trees here) that the minister's son is hidden, who, in his conceited impotence, will violate Tess more nastily than her sensual seducer: who but Hardy would have dared to give him the name Angel, and a harp too? It is Hardy's incorruptible feeling for the actual that allows his symbolism its amazingly blunt privileges and that at the same time subdues it to and absorbs it into the concrete circumstance of experience, real as touch.

The dilemma of Tess is the dilemma of morally individualizing consciousness in its earthy mixture. The subject is mythological, for it places the human protagonist in dramatic relationship with the nonhuman and orients his destiny among preternatural powers. The most primitive antagonist of consciousness is, on the simplest premise, the earth itself. It acts so in *Tess,* clogging action and defying conscious motive; or, in the long dream of Talbothays, conspiring with its ancient sensuality to provoke instinct; or, on the farm at Flintcomb-Ash, demoralizing consciousness by its mere geological flintiness. But the earth is "natural," while, dramatically visualized as antagonist, it transcends the natural. The integrity of the myth thus depends, paradoxically, upon naturalism; and it is because of that intimate dependence between the natural and the mythological, a dependence that is organic to the subject, that Hardy's vision is able to impregnate so deeply and shape so unobtrusively the naturalistic particulars of the story.

In *Tess,* of all his novels, the earth is most actual as a dramatic factor —that is, as a factor of causation; and by this we refer simply to the long stretches of earth that have to be trudged in order that a person may get from one place to another, the slowness of the business, the irreducible reality of it (for one has only one's feet), its grimness of soul-wearying fatigue and shelterlessness and doubtful issue at the other end of the journey where nobody may be at home. One thinks, in immediate comparison, of Egdon Heath in *The Return of the Native*. Except for one instance—when Mrs. Yeobright has a far walk to Clym's cottage, and Clym, unforewarned, fails to meet her, and she turns away—the heath in *The Return* exists peripherally and gratuitously in relation to the action, on the one hand as the place where the action happens to happen (an action has to happen somewhere), and on the other, as a metaphor—a metaphorical reflection of the loneliness of human motive, of the inertia of unconscious life, of the mystery of the enfolding darkness; but it is not a dramatically causative agent and its particular quality is not *dramatically* necessary. In *The Mayor of Casterbridge,* the Roman ruins round about the town of Casterbridge are a rather more complicated metaphor, for they are works of man that have fallen into earth; they speak mutely of the anonymity of human effort in historical as well as in geological time; their presence suggests also the classic pattern of the Mayor's tragedy, the ancient repetitiveness of self-destruction; and they provide thus a kind of guarantee or confirming signature of the heroism of the doomed human enterprise. But the Mayor could have had his tragedy in a town with no Roman ruins about it at all; they are, even more than Egdon Heath, gratuitous, and their gratuitousness leads Hardy into some pedantry of documentation to support their metaphorical standing in the story. In *Tess* the earth is *primarily not a metaphor but a real thing* that one has to move on in order to get anywhere or do anything, and it constantly acts in its own motivating, causational substantiality by being there in the way of human purposes to encounter, to harass them, detour them, seduce them, defeat them.

In the accident of Prince's death, the road itself is, in a manner of speaking, responsible, merely by being the same road that the mail cart travels. The seduction of Tess is as closely related, causally, to the distance between Trantridge and Chaseborough as it is to Tess's naïveté and to Alec's egoism; the physical distance itself causes Tess's fatigue and provides Alec's opportunity. The insidiously demoralizing effect of Tess's desolate journeys on foot as she seeks dairy work and field work here and there after the collapse of her marriage, brutal months that are foreshortened to the plodding trip over the chalk uplands to Flintcomb-Ash, is, again, as directly as anything, an effect of the irreducible *thereness* of the territory she has to cover. There are other fatal elements in her ineffectual trip from the farm to Emminster to see Clare's parents, but fatal above all is the distance she must walk to see people who can have no foreknowledge of her coming and who are not at home when she gets there. Finally, with the uprooting and migration of the Durbeyfield family on Old Lady Day, the simple fatality of the earth as earth, in its measure-lessness and anonymousness, with people having to move over it with no place to go, is decisive in the final event of Tess's tragedy—her return to Alec, for Alec provides at least a place to go.

The dramatic motivation provided by natural earth is central to every aspect of the book. It controls the style: page by page *Tess* has a wrought density of texture that is fairly unique in Hardy; symbolic depth is communicated by the physical surface of things with unhampered transparency while the homeliest conviction of fact is preserved ("The upper half of each turnip had been eaten off by the live-stock"); and one is aware of style not as a specifically verbal quality but as a quality of observation and intuition that are here—very often—wonderfully identical with each other, a quality of lucidity. Again, it is because of the *actual* motivational impact of the earth that Hardy is able to use setting and atmosphere for a symbolism that, considered in itself, is so astonishingly blunt and rudimentary. The green vale of Blackmoor, fertile, small, enclosed by hills, lying under a blue haze—the vale of birth, the cradle of innocence. The wide misty setting of Talbothays dairy, "oozing fatness and warm ferments," where the "rush of juices could almost be heard below the hiss of fertilization"—the sensual dream, the lost Paradise. The starved uplands of Flintcomb-Ash, with their ironic mimicry of the organs of generation, "myriads of loose white flints in bulbous, cusped, and phallic shapes," and the dun consuming ruin of the swede field—the mockery of impotence, the exile. Finally, that immensely courageous use of setting, Stonehenge and the stone of sacrifice. Obvious as these symbolisms are, their deep stress is maintained by Hardy's naturalistic premise. The earth exists here as Final Cause, and its omnipresence affords constantly to Hardy the textures that excited his eye and care, but affords them wholly charged with dramatic, causational necessity; and the symbolic values of setting are constituted, in large part, by the responses required of the characters themselves in their relationship with the earth.

Generally, the narrative system of the book—that is, the system of episodes—is a series of accidents and coincidences (although it is important to note that the really great crises are psychologically motivated: Alec's seduction of Tess, Clare's rejection of her, and the murder). It is accident that Clare does not meet Tess at the May-walking, when she was "pure" and when he might have begun to court her; coincidence that the mail cart rams Tess's wagon and kills Prince; coincidence that Tess and Clare meet at Talbothays, *after* her "trouble" rather than before; accident that the letter slips under the rug; coincidence that Clare's parents are not at home when she comes to the vicarage; and so on. Superficially it would seem that this type of event, the accidental and coincidental, is the very least credible of fictional devices, particularly when there is an accumulation of them; and we have all read or heard criticism of Hardy for his excessive reliance upon coincidence in the management of his narratives; if his invention of probabilities and inevitabilities of action does not seem simply poverty-stricken, he appears to be too much the puppeteer working wires or strings to make events conform to his "pessimistic" and "fatalistic" ideas. It is not enough to say that there is a certain justification for his large use of the accidental in the fact that "life is like that"— chance, mishap, accident, events that affect our lives while they remain far beyond our control, are a very large part of experience; but art differs from life precisely by making order out of this disorder, by finding causation in it. In the accidentalism of Hardy's universe we can recognize the profound truth of the darkness in which life is cast, darkness both within the soul and without, only insofar as his accidentalism *is not itself accidental* nor yet an ideology-obsessed puppeteer's manipulation of character and event; which is to say, only insofar as the universe he creates has aesthetic integrity, the flesh and bones and organic development of a concrete world. This is not true always of even the best of Hardy's novels; but it is so generally true of the construction of *Tess*—a novel in which the accidental is perhaps more preponderant than in any other Hardy— that we do not care to finick about incidental lapses. The naturalistic premise of the book—the condition of earth in which life is placed—is the most obvious, fundamental, and inexorable of facts; but because it is the physically "given," into which and beyond which there can be no penetration, it exists as mystery; it is thus, even as the basis of all natural manifestation, itself of the quality of the supernatural. On the earth, so conceived, coincidence and accident constitute order, the prime terrestrial order, for they too are "the given," impenetrable by human *ratio,* accountable only as mystery. By constructing the *Tess*-universe on the solid ground (one might say even literally on the "ground") of the earth as Final Cause, mysterious cause of causes, Hardy does not allow us to forget that what is most concrete in experience is also what is most inscrutable, that an overturned clod in a field or the posture of herons standing in a water mead or the shadows of cows thrown against a wall by evening sunlight are as essentially fathomless as the procreative yearning, and this in turn as fathomless as the sheerest accident in event. The accidentalism and coincidentalism in the narrative pattern of the book stand, thus, in perfectly orderly correlation with the grounding mystery of the physically concrete and the natural.

But Hardy has, with very great cunning, reinforced the *necessity* of this particular kind of narrative pattern by giving to it the background of the folk instinctivism, folk fatalism, and folk magic. If the narrative is conducted largely by coincidence, the broad folk background rationalizes coincidence by constant recognition of the mysteriously "given" as what "was to be"—the folk's humble presumption of order in a rule of mishap. The folk are the earth's pseudopodia, another fauna; and because they are so deeply rooted in the elemental life of the earth—like a sensitive animal extension of the earth itself—they share the authority of the natural. (Whether Hardy's "folk," in all the attributes he gives them, ever existed historically or not is scarcely pertinent; they exist here.) Their philosophy and their skills in living, even their gestures of tragic violence, are instinctive adaptations to "the given"; and because they are indestructible, their attitudes toward events authoritatively urge a similar fatalism upon the reader, impelling him to an imaginative acceptance of the doom-wrought series of accidents in the foreground of the action.

We have said that the dilemma of Tess is the dilemma of moral consciousness in its intractable earthy mixture; schematically simplified, the signifying form of the *Tess*-universe is the tragic heroism and tragic ineffectuality of such consciousness in an antagonistic earth where events shape themselves by accident rather than by moral design; and the *mythological* dimension of this form lies precisely in the earth's antagonism—for what is persistently antagonistic appears to have its own intentions, in this case mysterious, supernatural, for it is only thus that the earth can seem to have "intentions." The folk are the bridge between mere earth and moral individuality; of the earth as they are, separable conscious ego does not arise among them to weaken animal instinct and confuse response—it is the sports, the deracinated ones, like Tess and Clare and Alec, who are morally individualized and who are therefore able to suffer isolation, alienation, and abandonment, or to make others so suffer; the folk, while they remain folk, cannot be individually isolated, alienated, or lost, for they are amoral and their existence is colonial rather than personal. (There is no finer note of this matter—fine in factual and symbolic precision, and in its very inconspicuousness—than the paragraph describing the loaded wagons of the migrating families:

> The day being the sixth of April, the Durbeyfield wagon met many other wagons with families on the summit of the load, which was built on a well-nigh unvarying principle, as peculiar, probably, to the rural laborer as the hexagon to the bee. The groundwork of the arrangement was the position of the family dresser, which, with its shining handles, and finger marks, and domestic evidences thick upon it, stood importantly in front, over the tails of the shaft-horses, in its erect and natural position, like some Ark of the Covenant which must not be carried slightingly.

Even in the event of mass uprooting, the folk character that is preserved is that of the tenacious, the colonial, the instinctive, for which Hardy finds the simile of the hexagon of the bee, converting it then, with Miltonic boldness, to its humanly tribal significance with the simile of the Ark of the Covenant.) Their fatalism is communal and ritual, an instinctive adaptation as accommodating to bad as to good weather, to misfortune as to luck, to birth as to death, a subjective economy by which emotion is subdued to the falling out of event and the destructiveness of resistance is avoided. In their fatalism lies their survival wisdom, as against the death direction of all moral deliberation. There is this wisdom in the cheerful compassion of the fieldwomen for Tess in her time of trouble: the trouble "was to be." It is in Joan Durbeyfield's Elizabethan ditties of lullaby:

> *I saw her lie do-own in yon-der green gro—ve;*
> *Come, love, and I'll tell you where.*

—the kind of ditty by which women of the folk induce maturity in the child by lulling him to sleep with visions of seduction, adultery, and despair. It is in the folk code of secrecy—as in Dairyman Crick's story of the widow who married Jack Dollop, or in Joan's letter of advice to her daughter, summoning the witness of ladies the highest in the land who had had their "trouble" too but who had not told. Tess's tragedy turns on a secret revealed, that is, on the substitution in Tess of an individualizing morality for the folk instinct of concealment and anonymity.

While their fatalism is a passive adaptation to the earthy doom, the folk magic is an active luxury: the human being, having a mind, however incongruous with his animal condition, has to do something with it—and if the butter will not come and someone is in love in the house, the coexistence of the two facts offers a mental exercise in causation (though this is not really the "rights o't," about the butter, as Dairyman Crick himself observes; magical lore is not so dainty); yet the magic is no less a survival wisdom than the fatalism, inasmuch as it does offer mental exercise in causation, for man cannot live without a sense of cause. The magic is a knowledgeable mode of dealing with the unknowledgeable, and it is adaptive to the dooms of existence where moral reason is not adaptive, for moral reason seeks congruence between human intention and effect and is therefore always inapropos (in Hardy's universe, tragically inapropos), whereas magic seeks only likenesses, correspondences, analogies, and these are everywhere. Moral reason is in complete incommunication with the "given," for it cannot accept the "given" as such, cannot accept accident, cannot accept the obscure activities of instinct, cannot accept doom; but magic can not only accept but rationalize all these, for the correspondences that determine its strategies are themselves "given"—like is like, and that is the end of the matter. As the folk fatalism imbues the foreground accidents with the suggestion of necessity, the folk magic imbues them with the suggestion of the supernaturally motivated; and motivation of whatever kind makes an event seem "necessary," suitable, fitting. The intricate interknitting of all these motifs gives to Hardy's actually magical view of the universe and of human destiny a backing of concrete life, as his evocation of the earth as Cause gives to his vision the grounding of the naturalistic.

The folk magic is, after all, in its strategy of analogy, only a specialization and formalization of the novelist's use of the symbolism of natural detail, a symbolism of which we are constantly aware from beginning to end. Magical interpretation and prediction of events consist in seeing one event or thing as a "mimicry" of another—a present happening, for instance, as a mimicry of some future happening; that is, magic makes a system out of analogies, the correlative forms of things. Poets and novelists do likewise with their symbols. Burns's lines: "And my fause luver staw my rose, / But ah! he left the thorn wi' me," use this kind of mimicry, common to poetry and magic. When a thorn of Alec's roses pricks Tess's chin, the occurrence is read as an omen—and omens properly belong to the field of magic; but the difference between this symbol which is an omen, and the very similar symbol in Burns's lines, which acts only reminiscently, is a difference merely of timing—the one "mimics" a

seduction which occurs later, the other "mimics" a seduction and its consequences which have already occurred. And there is very little difference,
functionally, between Hardy's use of this popular symbol as an *omen*
and his symbolic use of natural particulars—the chattering of the birds
at dawn after the death of Prince and the iridescence of the coagulated
blood, the swollen udders of the cows at Talbothays and the heavy fertilizing mists of the late summer mornings and evenings, the ravaged
turnip field on Flintcomb-Ash and the visitation of the polar birds. All
of these natural details are either predictive or interpretive or both, and
prediction and interpretation of events through analogies are the profession of magic. When a piece of blood-stained butcher paper flies up in the
road as Tess enters the gate of the vicarage at Emminster, the occurrence is
natural while it is ominous; it is realistically observed, as part of the
"given," while it inculcates the magical point of view. Novelistic symbolism
is magical strategy. In *Tess,* which is through and through symbolic, magic
is not only an adaptive specialization of the "folk," but it also determines
the reader's response to the most naturalistic detail. Thus, though the story
is grounded deeply in a naturalistic premise, Hardy's use of one of the commonest tools of novelists—symbolism—enforces a magical view of life.

Logically accommodated by this view of life is the presentation of
supernatural characters. Alec D'Urberville does not appear in his full
otherworldly character until late in the book, in the episode of the planting fires, where we see him with pitchfork among flames—and even then
the local realism of the planting fires is such as almost to absorb the
ghostliness of the apparition. The usual form of his appearance is as a
stage villain, complete with curled mustache, checked suit, and cane; and
actually it seems a bit easier for the reader to accept him as the Evil
Spirit itself, even with a pitchfork, than in his secular accouterments of
the villain of melodrama. But Hardy's logic faces its conclusions with
superb boldness, as it does in giving Angel Clare his name and his harp
and making him a minister's son; if Alec is the Evil One, there will be
something queer about his ordinary tastes, and the queerness is shown
in his stagy clothes (actually, this melodramatic stereotype is just as valid
for a certain period of manners and dress as our own stereotype of the
gunman leaning against a lamppost and striking a match against his
thumbnail). Alec is the smart aleck of the Book of Job, the one who goes
to and fro in the earth and walks up and down in it, the perfectly deracinated one, with his flash and new money and faked name and ag-

gressive ego. If he becomes a religious convert even temporarily it is because he is not really so very much different from Angel (the smart aleck of the Book of Job was also an angel), for extreme implies extreme, and both Angel and Alec are foundered in egoism, the one in idealistic egoism, the other in sensual egoism, and Angel himself is diabolic enough in his prudery. When Alec plays his last frivolous trick on Tess, lying down on one of the slabs in the D'Urberville vaults and springing up at her like an animated corpse, his neuroticism finally wears, not the stagy traditional externals of the Evil Spirit, but the deeply convincing character of insanity—of that human evil which is identifiable with madness. Both Angel and Alec are metaphors of extremes of human behavior, when the human has been cut off from community and has been individualized by intellectual education or by material wealth and traditionless independence.

Between the stridencies of Angel's egoism and Alec's egoism is Tess —with her Sixth Standard training and some anachronistic D'Urberville current in her blood that makes for spiritual exacerbation just as it makes her cheeks paler, "the teeth more regular, the red lips thinner than is usual in a country-bred girl": incapacitated for life by her moral idealism, capacious of life through her sensualism. When, after Alec's evilly absurd trick, she bends down to whisper at the opening of the vaults, "Why am I on the wrong side of this door?" her words construct all the hopelessness of her cultural impasse. But her stabbing of Alec is her heroic return through the "door" into the folk fold, the fold of nature and instinct, the anonymous community. If both Alec and Angel are spiritually impotent in their separate ways, Tess is finally creative by the only measure of creativeness that this particular novelistic universe holds, the measure of the instinctive and the natural. Her gesture is the traditional gesture of the revenge of instinct, by which she joins an innumerable company of folk heroines who stabbed and were hanged—the spectacular but still anonymous and common gesture of common circumstances and common responses, which we, as habitual readers of newspaper crime headlines, find, unthinkingly, so shocking to our delicate notions of what is "natural." That she goes, in her wandering at the end, to Stonehenge, is an inevitable symbolic going—as all going and doing are symbolic—for it is here that the earthiness of her state is best recognized, by the monoliths of Stonehenge, and that the human dignity of her last gesture has the most austere recognition, by the ritual sacrifices that have been made on these stones.

ON *The Portrait of a Lady*

To go from Hardy's *Tess* to James's *The Portrait of a Lady* is to go from Stonehenge to St. Peter's and from a frozen northern turnip field, eyed hungrily by polar birds, to the Cascine gardens where nightingales sing. Though both books concern the "campaign" of a young woman—a campaign that, expressed most simply, is a campaign *to live*—a greater difference of atmosphere could scarcely be imagined nor of articulation of what it means *to live*. The gaunt arctic birds in *Tess* have witnessed, with their "tragical eyes," cataclysms that no human eye might see, but of which they retain no memory. The birds offer a symbol of Tess's world: a world inimical to consciousness, where one should have no memory (Tess's fatal error is to remember her own past), where the eye of the mind should remain blank, where aesthetic and moral perceptivity is traumatic. The nightingales that sing to Isabel Archer and her lover in the "grey Italian shade" also offer a symbol of a world: they are the very voice of memory, of an imperishable consciousness at once recreating and transcending its ancient, all-human knowledge. It is to the tutelage of the European memory that Isabel Archer passionately surrenders herself in her campaign *to live,* that is, to become conscious; for, in James's world, the highest affirmation of life is the development of the subtlest and most various consciousness. In doing so, she must—like the girl in the barbarous legend of the nightingale, who, likewise in a foreign land, read an obscene crime in the weaving of a tapestry—come into knowledge of an evil which, in its own civilized kind, is as corrupting and implacable as that in the old tale. But consciousness here, as an activity nourished by knowledge, transcends the knowledge which is its content: and this too is in analogy with the ancient symbolic tale, where knowledge of evil is transcended, in the very doom of its reiteration, by the bird's immortal song.

The Portrait is not, like *Tess,* a tragedy, but it is as deeply informed with the tragic view of life: that tragic view whose essence is contained in the words, "He who loses his life shall find it," and "Except a corn of wheat fall into the ground and die, it abideth alone: but if it die, it bringeth forth much fruit." We associate tragic seriousness of import in a character's destiny with tension between the power of willing (which is "free") and the power of circumstances ("necessity") binding and limiting the will; and if either term of the tension seems lacking, seriousness of import fails. Apparently, no two authors could be at further antipodes than James and Hardy in the respective emphases they place on these terms. In Hardy, the protagonist's volition founders at every move on a universally mechanical, mysteriously hostile necessity; it is only in Tess's last acts, of blood sacrifice and renunciation of life, that her will appallingly asserts its freedom and that she gains her tragic greatness. In James's *Portrait,* and in his other novels as well, the protagonist appears to have an extraordinarily unhampered play of volition. This appearance of extraordinary freedom from the pressure of circumstances is largely due to the "immense deal of money" (the phrase is taken from an early page of *The Portrait*) with which James endows his world—for, in an acquisitive culture, money is the chief symbol of freedom. The vague rich gleams of money are on every cornice and sift through every vista of the world of *The Portrait,* like the muted gold backgrounds of old Persian illuminations; and the human correlative of the money is a type of character fully privileged with easy mobility upon the face of the earth and with magnificent opportunities for the cultivation of aesthetic and intellectual refinements. It is by visualizing with the greatest clarity the lustrously moneyed tones of the James universe that we make ourselves able to see the more clearly what grave, somber shapes of illusion and guilt he organizes in this novel. The tension between circumstances and volition, "necessity" and "freedom," is demonstrated at the uppermost levels of material opportunity where, presumably, there is most freedom and where therefore freedom becomes most threatening—and where necessity wears its most insidious disguise, the disguise of freedom.

In following the previous studies, the reader will perhaps have been impressed with the fact that the novel as a genre has shown, from *Don*

Quixote on, a constant concern with the institutions created by the circulation of money and with the fantasies arising from the having of it, or, more especially, the not having it; a concern not always so direct as that of *Moll Flanders* and *Vanity Fair*, but almost inevitably implicit at least, expressed in indirect forms of aspiration and encitement to passion. As the definitively middle-class literary genre, the novel purchased its roots in a money-conscious social imagination. The wealth shining on the James world is a kind of apogee of the novel's historical concern with money, showing itself, in *The Portrait*, as a grandly sweeping postulate of possession: as if to say, "Here, now, is all the beautiful money, in the most liberating quantities: what ambition, what temptation, what errors of the will, what evil, what suffering, what salvation still denote the proclivities of the human even in a world so bountifully endowed?"

The "international myth" [1] that operates broadly in James's work, and that appears, in this novel, in the typical confrontation of American innocence and moral rigor with the tortuosities of an older civilization, gives its own and special dimension to the moneyed prospect. James came to maturity in a post-Civil War America euphoric with material achievement. In terms of the Jamesian "myth," American wealth is now able to buy up the whole museum of Europe, all its visible "point" of art objects and culture prestige, to take back home and set up in the front yard (we need look no further, for historical objectification of this aspect of the "myth," than to William Randolph Hearst's epic importation of various priceless chunks of Europe to California). If the shadows of the physically dispossessed—the sweat and the bone-weariness and the manifold anonymous deprivation in which this culture-buying power had its source—are excluded from James's money-gilded canvas, the shadow of spiritual dispossession is the somber shape under the money outline. We are not allowed to forget the aesthetic and moral impoverishment that spread its gross vacuum at the core of the American acquisitive dream— the greed, the obtuse or rapacious presumption, the disvaluation of values that kept pace to pace with material expansion. James's characteristic thematic contrasts, here as in other novels, are those of surface against depth, inspection against experience, buying power against living power, the American tourist's cultural balcony against the European abyss of

---

[1] Discussion of James's "international myth" will be found in *The Question of Henry James,* edited by F. W. Dupee (New York: Henry Holt & Company, Inc., 1945), and Philip Rahv's *Image and Idea* (New York: New Directions, 1949).

history and memory and involved motive where he perilously or callously teeters. In *The Portrait,* the American heroine's pilgrimage in Europe becomes a fatally serious spiritual investment, an investment of the "free" self in and with the circumstantial and binding past, a discovery of the relations of the self with history, and a moral renovation of history in the freedom of the individual conscience. It is a growing of more delicate and deeper-reaching roots and a nourishment of a more complex, more troubled, more creative personal humanity. It is, in short, what is ideally meant by "civilization," as that word refers to a process that can take place in an individual.

The postulate of wealth and privilege is, in revised terms, that of the second chapter of Genesis (the story of Adam in the garden)—that of the optimum conditions which will leave the innocent soul at liberty to develop its potentialities—and, as in the archetype of the Fall of Man, the postulate is significant not as excluding knowledge of good and evil, but as presenting a rare opportunity for such knowledge. It is the bounty poured on Isabel Archer (significantly, the man who gives her the symbolical investiture of money is a man who is fatally ill; significantly, also, she is under an illusion as to the giver) that makes her "free" to determine her choice of action, and thus morally most responsible for her choice; but it is the very bounty of her fortune, also, that activates at once, as if chemically, the proclivity to evil in the world of privilege that her wealth allows her to enter—it is her money that draws Madame Merle and Osmond to her; so that her "freedom" is actualized as imprisonment, in a peculiarly ashen and claustral, because peculiarly refined, suburb of hell. Isabel's quest had, at the earliest, been a quest for happiness—the naïvely egoistic American quest; it converts into a problem of spiritual salvation, that is, into a quest of "life"; and again the Biblical archetype shadows forth the problem. After eating of the fruit of the tree of knowledge of good and evil, how is one to regain access to the tree of life?

The great fairy tales and saints' legends have identified life with knowledge. For the fairy-tale hero, the fruit of the tree of life that is the guerdon of kingdom is the golden fleece or the golden apples that his wicked stepmother or usurping uncle have sent him in quest of; and to achieve the guerdon he must go through all tormenting knowledge—of serpents, floods, fire, ogres, enchantment, and even of his own lusts and murderous capacities. The ordeal of the heroes of saints' legends is also an ordeal of knowledge of evil, and the guerdon is life. As do these

ancient tales, *The Portrait* identifies life with the most probing, dangerous, responsible awareness—identifies, as it were, the two "trees," the tree
of the Fall and the tree of the Resurrection. The heroine's voluntary
search for fuller consciousness leads her, in an illusion of perfect freedom
to choose only "the best" in experience, to choose an evil; but it is this
that, by providing insight through suffering and guilt, provides also access to life—to the fructification of consciousness that is a knowledge of
human bondedness. At the very end of the book, Caspar Goodwood gives
passionate voice to the illusion of special privileges of choice and of a
good to be had by exclusion and separateness: he says to Isabel,

> "It would be an insult to you to assume that you care for . . . the bot-
> tomless idiocy of the world. We've nothing to do with all that; we're
> quite out of it . . . We can do absolutely as we please; to whom under
> the sun do we owe anything? What is it that holds us, what is it that
> has the smallest right to interfere . . . ? The world's all before us—
> and the world's very big."

Isabel answers at random, "The world's very small." What attitude of
mind takes her back to Rome, back to old evil and old servitude, is not
described; we know only that she does go back. But it is evident that she
does so because the "small" necessitous world has received an extension,
not in the horizontal direction of imperial mobility that Caspar Goodwood suggests, but an invisible extension in depth, within her own
mind—an extension into the freedom of personal renunciation and inexhaustible responsibility. The knowledge she has acquired has been
tragic knowledge, but her story does not stop here, as it would if it were
a tragedy—it goes on out of the pages of the book, to Rome, where we
cannot follow it; for the knowledge has been the means to "life," and having learned to live, she must "live long," as she says. It is only the process
of the learning that the portrait frame itself holds.

The title, *The Portrait,* asks the eye to see. And the handling of the
book is in terms of seeing. The informing and strengthening of the eye of
the mind is the theme—the ultimate knowledge, the thing finally "seen,"
having only the contingent importance of stimulating a more subtle and
various activity of perception. The dramatization is deliberately "scenic,"
moving in a series of recognition scenes that are slight and low-keyed at
first, or blurred and erroneous, in proportion both to the innocence of
the heroine and others' skill in refined disguises and obliquities; then, to-

ward the end, proceeding in swift and livid flashes. For in adopting as his compositional center the growth of a consciousness, James was able to use the bafflements and illusions of ignorance for his "complications," as he was able to use, more consistently than any other novelist, "recognitions" for his crises. Further, this action, moving through errors and illuminations of the inward eye, is set in a symbolic construct of things to be seen by the physical eye—paintings and sculptures, old coins and porcelain and lace and tapestries, most of all buildings: the aesthetic riches of Europe, pregnant with memory, with "histories within histories" of skills and motivations, temptations and suffering. The context of particulars offered to physical sight (and these may be settings, like English country houses or Roman ruins, or objects in the setting, like a porcelain cup or a piece of old lace draped on a mantel, or a person's face or a group of people—and the emphasis on the visual is most constant and notable not in these particulars, extensive as they are, but in the figurative language of the book, in metaphors using visual images as their vehicle) intensifies the meaning of "recognition" in those scenes where *sight* is *insight,* and provides a concrete embodiment of the ambiguities of "seeing."

In James's handling of the richly qualitative setting, it is characteristically significant that he suggests visual or scenic traits almost always in such a way that the emphasis is on *modulations of perception in the observer.* The "look" of things is a response of consciousness and varies with the observer; the "look" of things has thus the double duty of representing external stimuli, by indirection in their passage through consciousness, and of representing the observer himself. For instance, when Ralph takes Isabel through the picture gallery in the Touchett home, the "imperfect" but "genial" light of the bracketed lamps shows the pictures as "vague squares of rich colour," and the look of the pictures is Isabel's state at the moment—her eager and innately gifted sensibility and her almost complete ignorance, her conscious orientation toward an unknown "rich" mode of being that is beautiful but indeterminate. Let us take another example from late in the book. Directly after that conversation with Madame Merle when Isabel learns, with the full force of evil revelation, Madame Merle's part in her marriage, she goes out for a drive alone.

> She had long before this taken old Rome into her confidence, for in a
> world of ruins the ruin of her happiness seemed a less unnatural catas-
> trophe. She rested her weariness upon things that had crumbled for

centuries and yet still were upright; she dropped her secret sadness into the silence of lonely places, where its very modern quality detached itself and grew objective, so that as she sat in a sun-warmed angle on a winter's day, or stood in a mouldy church to which no one came, she could almost smile at it and think of its smallness. Small it was, in the large Roman record, and her haunting sense of the continuity of the human lot easily carried her from the less to the greater. She had become deeply, tenderly acquainted with Rome: it interfused and moderated her passion. But she had grown to think of it chiefly as the place where people had suffered. This was what came to her in the starved churches, where the marble columns, transferred from pagan ruins, seemed to offer her a companionship in endurance and the musty incense to be a compound of long-unanswered prayers.

Here the definition of visible setting—churches and marble columns and ruins, and comprehending all these, Rome—though it is full, is vague and diffuse, in the external sense of the "seen"; but in the sense that it is a setting evoked by Isabel's own deepened consciousness, it is exactly and clearly focused. It is Rome *felt*, felt as an immensity of human time, as a great human continuum of sadness and loneliness and passion and aspiration and patience; and it has this definition by virtue of Isabel's personal ordeal and her perception of its meaning. The "vague squares of rich colour" have become determinate.

The theme of "seeing" (the theme of the developing consciousness) is fertile with ironies and ambiguities that arise from the natural symbolism of the act of seeing, upon which so vastly many of human responses and decisions are dependent. The eye, as it registers surfaces, is an organ of aesthetic experience, in the etymological sense of the word "aesthetic," which is a word deriving from a Greek verb meaning "to perceive"—to perceive through the senses. James provides his world with innumerable fine surfaces for this kind of perception; it is a world endowed with the finest selective opportunities for the act of "seeing," for aesthetic cultivation. But our biological dependence upon the eye has made it a symbol of intellectual and moral and spiritual perception, forms of perception which are—by the makers of dictionaries—discriminated radically from aesthetic perception. Much of James's work is an exploration of the profound identity of the aesthetic and the moral. (In this he is at variance with the makers of dictionaries, but he has the companionship of Socrates' teacher Diotima, as her teaching is represented by Plato in the

Symposium. Diotima taught that the way to spiritual good lay through the hierarchies of the "beautiful," that is, through graduations from one form of aesthetic experience to another.) Aesthetic experience proper, since it is acquired through the senses, is an experience of *feeling.* But so also moral experience, when it is not sheerly nominal and ritualistic, is an experience of *feeling.* Neither one has reality—has psychological depth —unless it is "felt" (hence James's so frequent use of phrases such as "felt life" and "the very *taste* of life," phrases that insist on the feeling-base of complete and integrated living). Furthermore, both aesthetic and moral experience are nonutilitarian. The first distinction that aestheticians usually make, in defining the aesthetic, is its distinction from the useful; when the aesthetic is converted to utility, it becomes something else, its value designation is different—as when a beautiful bowl becomes valuable not for its beauty but for its capacity to hold soup. So also the moral, when it is converted to utility, becomes something else than the moral —becomes even immoral, a parody of or a blasphemy against the moral life (in our richest cultural heritage, both Hellenic and Christian, the moral life is symbolically associated with utter loss of utility goods and even with loss of physical life—as in the Gospel passage, "Leave all that thou hast and follow me," or as in the career of Socrates, or as in Sophocles' *Antigone*). Moral and aesthetic experience have then in common their foundation in feeling and their distinction from the useful. The identity that James explores is their identity in the most capacious and most integrated—the most "civilized"—consciousness, whose sense relationships (aesthetic relationships) with the external world of scenes and objects have the same quality and the same spiritual determination as its relationships with people (moral relationships). But his exploration of that ideal identity involves cognizance of failed integration, cognizance of the many varieties of one-sidedness or one-eyedness or blindness that go by the name of the moral or the aesthetic, and of the destructive potentialities of the human consciousness when it is one-sided either way. His ironies revolve on the ideal concept of a spacious integrity of feeling: feeling, ideally, is *one*—and there is ironic situation when feeling is split into the "moral" and the "aesthetic," each denying the other and each posing as *all.*

There is comic irony in Henrietta Stackpole's moral busybodyness as she flutters and sputters through Europe obtaining feature materials for her home-town newspaper, "featuring" largely the morally culpable un-Americanism of Europeans to serve her readers as a flattering warning against indulgence in the aesthetic. Henrietta is a stock James comedy character, and she is essential. Without Henrietta's relative incapacity to "see" more than literal surfaces, the significant contrast between surface and depth, between outward and inward "seeing," between undeveloped and developed consciousness, would lose a needed demonstration. (But let us say for Henrietta that, like Horatio in *Hamlet,* she is employed by the dramatist for as many sorts of purposes as his scenes happen to demand; when a foil of obtuseness is wanted, Henrietta is there, and when a foil of good interpretive intelligence or plain charitable generosity is wanted, Henrietta is also there. She is the type of what James technically called the *ficelle,* a wholly subordinate character immensely useful to take in confidences from the principals and to serve other functions of "relief"—"relief" in that sense in which the lower level of a relievo provides perspective for the carved projections.) In Mrs. Touchett, what appears at first as the comic irony of absolute aesthetic insensitivity accompanied by a rugged moral dogmatism ("she had a little moral account-book—with columns unerringly ruled and a sharp steel clasp—which she kept with exemplary neatness") becomes at the end of the book, with her son's death, the tragic irony of that kind of ambiguous misery which is an inability to acknowledge or realize one's own suffering, when suffering is real but the channels of feeling have become nearly atrophied by lack of use. At the midday meal, when Isabel and Mrs. Touchett come together after the night of Ralph's death,

> Isabel saw her aunt not to be so dry as she appeared, and her old pity for the poor woman's inexpressiveness, her want of regret, of disappointment, came back to her. Unmistakably she would have found it a blessing to-day to be able to feel a defeat, a mistake, even a shame or two. [Isabel] wondered if [her aunt] were not even missing those enrichments of consciousness and privately trying—reaching out for some aftertaste of life, dregs of the banquet; the testimony of pain or the old recreation of remorse. On the other hand perhaps she was afraid; if she should begin to know remorse at all it might take her too far. Isabel could perceive, however, how it had come over her dimly that she had failed of something, that she saw herself in the future as an old woman without memories. Her little sharp face looked tragical.

Mrs. Touchett's habitual moralistic denial of feeling as an aesthetic indulgence has left her deserted even by herself, even by her love of her son, even by memory, even by suffering. She is stranded in a morality that is tragically without meaning.

In Madame Merle and Osmond the ironies intrinsic to James's theme receive another turn. Madame Merle first appeals to Isabel's admiration by her capacity for "feeling"—for that kind of feeling to which the term "aesthetic" has been specially adapted in common modern use: feeling for the arts, the sensuous perceptivity underlying the arts, and, by extension, feeling for the finer conventions of manners as "arts of living." (Madame Merle "knew how to feel . . . This was indeed Madame Merle's great talent, her most perfect gift.") At Gardencourt, when she is not engaged in writing letters, she paints (she "made no more of brushing in a sketch than of pulling off her gloves") or she plays the piano (she "was a brave musician") or she is "employed upon wonderful tasks of rich embroidery." (The presentation is just a bit insidious, not only because of Madame Merle's so very great plasticity in going from one art to another, but also in the style of the phrases: the suggestion of conventional fluidity in the comparison of her ease in painting with the ease of "pulling off her gloves," the word "brave"—an honorific word in certain places, but carrying here the faintest note of bravado—and the word "employed," suggesting, as it reverberates, Madame Merle's not disinterested professional aestheticism.) Her senses are active and acute: walking in the English rain, she says,

> "It never wets you and it always smells good." She declared that in England the pleasures of smell were great . . . and she used to lift the sleeve of her British overcoat and bury her nose in it, inhaling the clear, fine scent of the wool.

Just how acute her perceptions are is shown never more clearly than in that scene in which she learns of the distribution of property after Mr. Touchett's death, occurring in Chapter 20 of Volume I. Mrs. Touchett has just told her that Ralph, because of the state of his health, had hurried away from England before the reading of the will, in which Isabel had been left half of the fortune accruing to him. With this news, Madame Merle "remained thoughtful a moment, her eyes bent on the floor," and when Isabel enters the room, Madame Merle kisses her—this being "the only allusion the visitor, in her great good taste, made . . . to her young friend's inheritance." There are no other signs than these (and the episode is typical of James's minor "recognition scenes") of just how quickly and acutely Madame Merle's senses—her perception, her intuition—have functioned in apprising her of the possibilities of exploitation now opened, and in apprising her also of the fact that Ralph is the real donor of Isabel's fortune, a fact of which Isabel herself remains ignorant until Madame Merle viciously informs her. Madame Merle's feeling for situation is so subtly educated that she needs but the slightest of tokens in order to respond. And yet, with a sensitivity educated so exquisitely and working at such high tension she is morally insensible —or almost so; not quite—for, unlike Osmond, whose damnation is in ice where the moral faculty is quite frozen, she still has the spiritual capacity of those whose damnation is in fire, the capacity to know that she is damned.

Madame Merle and Osmond use their cultivated aestheticism for utility purposes—Madame Merle, to further her ambition for place and power; Osmond, to make himself separate and envied. Their debasement of the meaning of the aesthetic becomes symbolically vicious when it shows itself in their relationships with people—with Isabel, for instance, who is for them an object of virtu that differs from other objects of virtu in that it bestows money rather than costs it. This is the evil referred to by Kant in his second Categorical Imperative: the use of persons as means —an evil to which perhaps all evil in human relationships reduces. In the case of Madame Merle and Osmond, it has a peculiar and blasphemous ugliness, inasmuch as the atmosphere of beauty in which they live —beauty of surroundings and of manners—represents the finest, freest product of civilization and is such, ideally, as to induce the most reverential feeling for people as well as for things. Isabel first appeals to Osmond as being "as smooth to his general need of her as handled ivory to the palm": it is an "aesthetic" image suggesting his fastidiousness but, ironically, suggesting at the same time his coarseness—for while ivory, like pearls, may be the more beautiful for handling, "handled ivory" might also be the head of a walking stick, and it is in some sort as a walking stick that he uses Isabel. An extension of the same figure, without the aesthetic and with only the utilitarian connotation, indicates Osmond's real degeneracy: Isabel finally realizes that she has been for him "an applied handled hung-up tool, as senseless and convenient as mere wood and iron." But the evil is not one that can be isolated or confined; it is automatically proliferative. Morally dead himself, incapable of reverence for the human quality in others, Osmond necessarily tries to duplicate his death in them, for it is by killing their volition that he can make them useful; dead, they are alone "beautiful." He urges upon Isabel the obscene suggestion that she, in turn, "use" Lord Warburton by exploiting Warburton's old love for herself in order to get him to marry Pansy; and Osmond can find no excuse for her refusal except that she has her private designs for "using" the Englishman. But it is in Osmond's use of Pansy, his daughter, that he is most subtly and horribly effective. He has made her into a work of art, the modeling materials being the least artful of childish qualities—her innocence and gentleness; and he has almost succeeded in reducing her will to an echo of his own. The quaint figure of Pansy, always only on the edge of scenes, is of great structural importance in the latter half of the book; for she shows the full measure of the abuse that Isabel resists, and it is to nourish in her whatever small germ of creative volition may remain—to salvage, really, a life—that Isabel returns to Rome and to Osmond's paralyzing ambiance.

The moral question that is raised by every character in the book is a question of the "amount of felt life" that each is able to experience, a question of how many and how various are the relationships each can, with integrity, enter into. Or, to put the matter in its basic metaphor, it is a question of how much each person is able to "see," and not only to see but to compose into creative order. The moral question, since it involves vision, feeling, and composition, is an aesthetic one as well. Madame Merle and Osmond are blind to certain relations: "I don't pretend to know what people are meant for," Madame Merle says, ". . . I only know what I can do with them." Mrs. Touchett is blind to certain others. Let us stop for a moment with Henrietta Stackpole's comic crudity of vision, for the "eye" is all-important, and the ranges of vision really begin with an eye like that of Henrietta. It is "a peculiarly open, surprised-looking eye." "The most striking point in her appearance was the remarkable fixedness of this organ."

> She fixed her eyes on [Ralph], and there was something in their character that reminded him of large polished buttons—buttons that might have fixed the elastic loops of some tense receptacle: he seemed to see the reflection of surrounding objects on the pupil. The expres-

sion of a button is not usually deemed human, but there was something in Miss Stackpole's gaze that made him, a very modest man, feel vaguely embarrassed—less inviolate, more dishonoured, than he liked.

Henrietta, with her gregariously refractive button-sight, has also "clear-cut views on most subjects . . . she knew perfectly in advance what her opinions would be." Henrietta's is the made-up consciousness, the pseudo consciousness, that is not a process but a content hopelessly once and for all given, able to refract light but not to take it in. (We can understand Henrietta's importance, caricatural as she is, by the fact that she is the primitive form of the pseudo consciousness which Madame Merle and Osmond, in their so much more sophisticated ways, exhibit: theirs too is the made-up consciousness, a rigidified content, impervious and uncreative.) The Misses Molyneux, Lord Warburton's sisters, have "eyes like the balanced basins, the circles of 'ornamental water,' set, in parterres, among the geraniums." Let us note that the figure is drawn from an "aesthetic" arrangement, that of formal gardens—and in this sense has directly opposite associations to those of Henrietta's buttons (presumably very American, very *useful* buttons). The Misses Molyneux's eyes, like Henrietta's, also merely reflect surrounding objects, and reflect more limitedly, far less mobilely; but the image is significant of certain kinds of feeling, of "seeing," that Henrietta is incapable of, and that have derived from ancient disciplines in human relationships—contemplative feeling, reverence, feeling for privacy and for grace. Extremely minor figures such as these, of the buttons and the basins, are pregnant with the extraordinarily rich, extraordinarily subtle potentialities of the theme of "seeing" as an infinitely graduated cognizance of relations between self and world.

In this book, the great range of structural significance through figurative language is due to the fact that whatever image vehicle a figure may have—even when the image is not itself a visual one—the general context is so deeply and consistently characterized by acts of "seeing" that every metaphor has this other implied extension of meaning. For example, a very intricate and extensive symbolic construct is built on a metaphor of opening doors. Henrietta, Ralph says, "walks in without knocking at the door." "She's too personal," he adds. As her eyes indiscriminately take in everything that is literally to be seen, so she walks in without knocking at the door of personality: "she thinks one's door should stand ajar." The correspondence of eyes and doors lies in the publicity Henrietta assumes (she is a journalist): her eye is public like a button, and responds as if everything else were public, as if there were no doors, as if there were nothing to be seen but what the public (the American newspaper public) might see without effort and without discomfort. In James's thematic system of surfaces and depths, "sight" is something achieved and not given, achieved in the loneliness of the individual soul and in the lucidity of darkness suffered; privacy is its necessary stamp, and it cannot be loaned or broadcast any more than can the loneliness or the suffering. "I keep a band of music in my ante-room," Ralph tells Isabel.

> "It has orders to play without stopping; it renders me two excellent services. It keeps the sounds of the world from reaching the private apartments, and it makes the world think that dancing's going on within."

The notation has its pathos through Ralph's illness. Isabel "would have liked to pass through the ante-room . . . and enter the private apartments." It is only at the end, through her own revelations of remorse and loss, that those doors open to her.

The ironic force of the metaphor of doors, as it combines with the metaphor of "seeing," has a different direction in the crucial scene in Chapter 51 of the second volume—one of the major "recognition scenes" in the book, where Isabel sees Osmond's full malignancy, a malignancy the more blighting as it takes, and sincerely takes, the form of honor, and where Osmond sees unequivocally the vivid, mysterious resistance of a life that he has not been able to convert into a tool. Isabel comes to tell him that Ralph is dying and that she must go to England. She opens the door of her husband's study without knocking.

> "Excuse me for disturbing you," she said.
> "When I come to your room I always knock," he answered, going on with his work.
> "I forgot; I had something else to think of. My cousin's dying."
> "Ah, I don't believe that," said Osmond, looking at his drawing through a magnifying glass. "He was dying when we married; he'll outlive us all."

Osmond is here engaged in an activity representative of a man of taste and a "collector"—he is making traced copies of ancient coins (the fact that it is an act of tracing, of copying, has its own significance, as has the object of his attention: coins). What he "sees" in the situation that Isabel describes to him is quite exactly what he sees in the fact that she has opened the door without knocking: a transgression of convention; and what he does not see is the right of another human being to feel, to love, to will individually. Further, what he appallingly does not see is his dependence, for the fortune Isabel has brought him, on the selfless imagination of the dying man, Ralph; or, even more appallingly (for one can scarcely suppose that Madame Merle had left him ignorant of the source of Isabel's wealth), what he does not see is any reason for the moral responsibility implied by "gratitude," a defect of vision that gives a special and hideous bleakness to his use of the word "grateful," when he tells Isabel that she has not been "grateful" for his tolerance of her esteem for Ralph. The metaphor of the "doors" thus goes through its changes, each associated with a depth or shallowness, a straightness or obliquity of vision, from Henrietta's aggressive myopia, to Ralph's reticence and insight, to Osmond's refined conventionalism and moral astigmatism.

Let us consider in certain other examples this reciprocity between theme and metaphor, insight and sight, image and eye. Isabel's native choice is creativity, a "free exploration of life," but exploration is conducted constantly—vision is amplified constantly—at the cost of renunciations. It is in the "grey depths" of the eyes of the elder Miss Molyneux, those eyes like the balanced basins of water set in parterres, that Isabel recognizes what she has had to reject in rejecting Lord Warburton: "the peace, the kindness, the honour, the possessions, a deep security and a great exclusion." Caspar Goodwood has eyes that "seemed to shine through the vizard of a helmet." He appears always as an armor-man: "she saw the different fitted parts of him as she had seen, in museums and portraits, the different fitted parts of armoured warriors—in plates of steel handsomely inlaid with gold." "He might have ridden, on a plunging steed, the whirlwind of a great war." The image is one of virility, but of passion without relation, aggressive energy without responsibility. The exclusions implied by Casper's steel-plated embrace are as great as those implied by the honor and the peace that Lord Warburton offers; and yet Isabel's final refusal of Caspar and of sexual possession is tragic, for it is to a sterile marriage that she returns.

Architectural images, and metaphors whose vehicle (like doors and windows) is associated with architecture, subtend the most various and complex of the book's meanings; and the reason for their particular richness of significance seems to be that, of all forms that are offered to sight and interpretation, buildings are the most natural symbols of civilized life, the most diverse also as to what their fronts and interiors can imply of man's relations with himself and with the outer world. Osmond's house in Florence has an "imposing front" of a "somewhat incommunicative character."

> It was the mask, not the face of the house. It had heavy lids, but no eyes; the house in reality looked another way—looked off behind . . . The windows of the ground-floor, as you saw them from the piazza, were, in their noble proportions, extremely architectural; but their function seemed less to offer communication with the world than to defy the world to look in . . .

(One notes again here the characteristic insistence on *eyes* and *looking*.) The description, perfectly fitting an old and noble Florentine villa, exactly equates with Osmond himself, and not only Isabel's first illusional impression of him—when it is his renunciatory reserve that attracts her, an appearance suggesting those "deeper rhythms of life" that she seeks—but also her later painful knowledge of the face behind the mask, which, like the house, is affected with an obliquity of vision, "looked another way—looked off behind." The interior is full of artful images; the group of people gathered there "might have been described by a painter as composing well"; even the footboy "might, tarnished as to livery and quaint as to type, have issued from some stray sketch of old-time manners, been 'put in' by the brush of a Longhi or a Goya"; the face of little Pansy is "painted" with a "fixed and intensely sweet smile." Osmond's world, contained within his eyeless house, is "sorted, sifted, arranged" for the eye; even his daughter is one of his arrangements. It is a world bred of ancient disciplines modulating through time, selection and composition, to the purest aesthetic form.

> [Isabel] carried away an image from her visit to his hill-top . . . which put on for her a particular harmony with other supposed and divined things, histories within histories . . . It spoke of the kind of personal issue that touched her most nearly; of the choice between objects,

ON *The Portrait of a Lady*

> subjects, contacts—what might she call them?—of a thin and those of
> a rich association . . . of a care for beauty and perfection so natural
> and so cultivated together that the career appeared to stretch beneath
> it in the disposed vistas and with the ranges of steps and terraces and
> fountains of a formal Italian garden . . .

The illusion is one of a depth and spaciousness and delicacy of relationships, an illusion of the civilized consciousness.

But while Osmond's world suggests depth, it is, ironically, a world of
surfaces only, for Osmond has merely borrowed it. The architectural
metaphor shifts significantly in the passage (Chapter 42 of Volume II) in
which Isabel takes the full measure of her dwelling. "It was the house of
darkness, the house of dumbness, the house of suffocation."

> She had taken all the first steps in the purest confidence, and then she
> had suddenly found the infinite vista of a multiplied life to be a dark,
> narrow alley with a dead wall at the end. Instead of leading to the high
> places of happiness . . . it led rather downward and earthward, into
> realms of restriction and depression where the sound of other lives,
> easier and freer, was heard as from above . . .

"When she saw this rigid system close about her, draped though it was
in pictured tapestries . . . she seemed shut up with an odour of mould
and decay." Again the architectural image changes its shape in that passage (quoted earlier in this essay) where Isabel takes her knowledge and
her sorrow into Rome, a Rome of architectural ruins. Here also are
depth of human time, "histories within histories," aesthetic form, but
not "arranged," not borrowable, not to be "collected"—only to be *lived*
in the creative recognitions brought to them by a soul itself alive. The
image that accompanies Ralph through the book—"his serenity was but
the array of wild flowers niched in his ruin"—gains meaning from the
architectural images so frequent in the Roman scenes (as, for instance,
from this:

> [Isabel] had often ascended to those desolate ledges from which the
> Roman crowd used to bellow applause and where now the wild
> flowers . . . bloom in the deep crevices . . .)

Whereas Osmond's forced "arrangements" of history and art and people
are without racination, blighting and lifeless, Ralph's "array of wild

227

flowers" is rooted, even if precariously rooted in a ruin; it is a life *grown*, grown in history, fertilized in the crevices of a difficult experience. The metaphor is another version of St. John's "Except a corn of wheat fall into the ground and die, it abideth alone; but if it die, it bringeth forth much fruit." Isabel, still seeking that freedom which is growth, goes back to Osmond's claustral house, for it is there, in the ruin where Pansy has been left, that she has placed roots, found a crevice in which to grow straightly and freshly, found a fertilizing, civilizing relationship between consciousness and circumstances.

ON *Lord Jim*

Marlow's last view of Jim, on the coast of Patusan, is of a white figure "at the heart of a vast enigma." Jim himself is not enigmatic. The wonder and doubt that he stirs, both in Marlow and in us, are not wonder and doubt as to what *he* is: he is as recognizable as we are to ourselves; he is "one of us." Furthermore, he is not a very complex character, and he is examined by his creator with the most exhaustive conscientiousness; he is placed in every possible perspective that might help to define him. The enigma, then, is not what Jim is but what we are, and not only what we are, but "how to be" what we are.

Jim's shocking encounter with himself at the moment of his jump from the *Patna* is a model of those moments when the destiny each person carries within him, the destiny fully molded in the unconscious will, lifts its blind head from the dark, drinks blood, and speaks. There is no unclarity in the shape that Jim saw at that moment: he had jumped —it is as simple as that. But because the event is a paradigm of the encounters of the conscious personality with the stranger within, the stranger who is the very self of the self, the significance of Jim's story is *our own* significance, contained in the enigmatic relationship between the conscious will and the fatality of our acts. Jim's discovery of himself was a frightful one, and his solution of the problem of "how to be" was to exorcise the stranger in a fierce, long, concentrated effort to be his opposite. The oracle spoke early to Oedipus, too, in his youth in Corinth, telling him who he was—the man destined to transgress most horribly the saving code of kinship relations—and Oedipus's solution of the problem of "how to be" was the same as Jim's: he fled in the opposite direction from his destiny and ran straight into it.

Jim is one of the most living characters in fiction, although his presentation is by indirection, through Marlow's narrative; that indirection is itself uniquely humanizing, for we see him only as people can see each other, ambivalently and speculatively. He is nevertheless an extraordinarily simplified *type*, obsessed with a single idea, divested of all psychological attributes but the very few that concretize his relationship with his idea. The simplification is classical; it is a simplification like that of Aeschylus' Orestes, possessed by the divine command, and like that of Sophocles' Oedipus, possessed by his responsibility for finding out the truth. Conrad is able thus to imply a clear-cut formal distinction between the man and his destiny (his acts), even though he conceives destiny as immanent in the man's nature and in this sense identical with him. Here is Jim, "clean-limbed, clean-faced, firm on his feet, as promising a boy as the sun ever shone on," and there are his acts—the destruction of his best friend, the destruction of himself, the abandonment of the Patusan village to leaderlessness and depredation. Similarly Orestes and Oedipus, human agents simplified to a commanding ethical idea, are analytically separable from their destinies, the *anankē* or compelling principle fatally inherent in their acts. This subtle but tangible distinction between the human agent and his destiny allows the classical dramatists to orient clearly what we may call the metaphysical significance of the hero's career, the universal problem and the law of life which that career illustrates. We see the hero as an ideal human type (literally "idealized" through his devotion to an idea of ethical action); but his fate is pitiful and terrible—a fate that, if a man's deserts were to be suited to his conscious intentions, should fall only on malicious, unjust, and treasonable men; and the problem, the "enigma," thus raised is the religious problem of the awful incongruity between human intention and its consequences in action, between ethical effort and the guilt acquired through such effort; and the law—if a law appears—will be the law that justifies, to man's reason and and feeling, that appearance of awful incongruity. Conrad's treatment of Jim's story is classical in this sense, in that he sees in it the same problem and orients the problem in the same manner.

"In the destructive element immerse," Stein says, voicing his own solution of the problem of "how to be." There is no way "to be," according to Stein, but through the ideal, the truth as it appears, what he calls "the dream," although it is itself "the destructive element." "Very funny this terrible thing is," Stein says,

> "A man that is born falls into a dream like a man who falls into the
> sea. If he tries to climb out into the air as inexperienced people

endeavour to do, he drowns—*nicht wahr?* . . . No! I tell you! The
way is to the destructive element submit yourself, and with the exer-
tions of your hands and feet in the water make the deep, deep sea keep
you up. So if you ask me—how to be? . . . I will tell you! . . . In the
destructive element immerse."

Stein's words are but one outlook on the universal problem that is Jim's,
but it is the outlook dramatized in Jim's own actions. It is that dramatized
by Sophocles also. Oedipus "submitted" himself to his ideal of the responsible king and citizen, self-sworn to the discovery of the truth. It was
the "destructive element," bringing about the terrible revelation of his
guilt. So also Jim submits himself to his dream of heroic responsibility and
truth to men, fleeing from port to port, and finally to Patusan, to realize
it. And, again, the ideal is the "destructive element," bringing about the
compact with Brown (a compact made in the profoundest spirit of the
dream) and inevitably, along with the compact, destruction. The irony
is that Jim, in his destructiveness, was "true." This is the classical tragic
irony: the incongruity and yet the effective identity between the constructive will and the destructive act.

Whether Conrad goes beyond that particular tragic incongruity to
the other ancient tragic perception, of ennoblement through suffering,
is doubtful. The "enigma" that Marlow finds in Jim's career has this
other dark and doubtful aspect. When, at the end, after receiving
Doramin's bullet, "the white man sent right and left at all those faces a
proud and unflinching glance," is he really fulfilled in nobility in our
sight? Has his suffering, entailed in his long and strenuous exile and his
guilt and his final great loss, given him the knowledge, and with the
knowledge the nobility, which is the mysterious and sublime gift of suffering? The answer is doubtful. We need to bring to bear on it the fairly
inescapable impression that the only character in the book in whom we
can read the stamp of the author's own practical "approval" is the French
lieutenant who remained on board the *Patna* while it was being towed
into port. The French lieutenant would not have acted as Jim did in the
last events on Patusan—indeed is inconceivable in the Patusan circumstances. If, in Conrad's implicit evaluation of his material, the French
lieutenant represents the ethically "approved" manner of action and the
only one, Jim can scarcely support the complete role of the tragic hero of
the classical type, the hero who achieves unique greatness through suf-

fering. (The French lieutenant suffers only for lack of wine.) For our notion of what constitutes a "hero" is thus surely divided: if the French
lieutenant's heroism is the true heroism, Jim's is not, and conversely. No
doubt the division—and it seems to be real in our response to the book—
is associated with a division of allegiance on Conrad's part,[1] between emotional allegiance to Jim's suffering and struggling humanity, in all its
hybristic aspiration, and intellectual allegiance to the code represented
by the lieutenant, in all its severe limitation and calm obscurity. With
this division in mind, it is impossible to identify the "view of life" in
the book as a whole with Stein's view of life, impressive as Stein is in his
broad and enlightened sensitivity: for the French lieutenant knows nothing of a "destructive element," and if he did—which he could not—
would doubtless think that to talk of "submitting" oneself to it was sheer
twaddle.

What intervenes between Conrad's ambivalent attitude toward Jim's
story and the attitudes of Aeschylus and Sophocles toward their subjects
is modern man's spiritual isolation from his fellows. Jim's isolation is profound, most profound and complete at that last moment when he "sent
right and left at all those faces a proud and unflinching glance": here his
aloneness in his dream—his illusion—of faith to men is unqualified, for
the material fact is that he has allowed a brigand to slaughter Dain Waris
and his party, and that he has left the village open to ravage. Moral isolation provides a new inflection of tragedy. Orestes freed Argos from a tyr-
anny, and Oedipus freed Thebes from a plague. Their guilt and suffering
had a constructive social meaning; they had acted for the positive welfare of
the citizens; and that social version of their heroism, internal to the dramas
in which they appear, is the immediate, literal basis of our (because it is
the citizen-chorus's) appraisal of their heroism. But Jim—to use parallel
terms—destroys his city. Thus there is nothing structurally internal to
Jim's story that matches the positive moral relationship, in the ancient
dramas, between the social destiny and the hero's destiny, the relationship
that is presented concretely in the fact that the hero's agony is a saving
social measure. There is nothing to mediate, practically and concretely,
between Jim's "truth" and real social life, as a benefit to and confirma-
tion of the social context. Jim is alone.

And yet one asks, is his last act, when he "takes upon his head" the

---

[1] Albert Guerard discusses this division of allegiance in his *Joseph Conrad* (New
York: New Directions, 1947).

blood-guilt, an atonement? If it were so, it would be atonement not in quite the same sense that the madness and exile of Orestes and the blinding and banishment of Oedipus were atonements, for these involved the restoration of community health, whereas Jim's final act brings about (projectively) the destruction of the community—but in the necessary modern sense, necessitated by the fact of the disintegration of moral bonds between men: an atonement for that social sterility, a sacrifice offered in the name of moral community. If it were so, Jim would still be, metaphorically speaking, the savior of the city. No doubt Sophocles, civic-minded gentleman, did not "approve" of Oedipus: when parricide and incest occur in the leading families, what are the rest of us to do? how is the world's business to be kept up decently? what model shall we look to? But the Greek cities were said to have carried on quarrels over the burial place of Oedipus, for his presence brought fertility to the land. So also the story of Lord Jim is a spiritually fertilizing experience, enlightening the soul as to its own meaning in a time of disorganization and drought; and Conrad's imagination of Jim's story has the seminal virtue of the ancient classic.

In James's *The Portrait of a Lady* we watched the creation of a self. In Conrad's austerely pessimistic work, the self stands already created, the possibilities are closed. Again and again, and finally on Patusan, a "clean slate" is what Jim thinks he has found, a chance to "climb out," to begin over, to perform the deed which will be congruent with his ideal of himself. "A clean slate, did he say?" Marlow comments; "as if the initial word of each our destiny were not graven in imperishable characters upon the face of a rock." The tension, the spiritual drama in Conrad, lie in a person's relation with his destiny. The captain in "The Secret Sharer" acknowledges his profound kinship with a man who has violently transgressed the captain's professional code (the man has murdered another seaman during a voyage, and murder at sea is, in Conrad, something worse than murder; whatever its excuses, it is an inexcusable breach of faith with a community bound together by common hazard); but by the acknowledgment he masters his own identity, integrates, as it were, his unconscious impulses within consciousness, and thereby realizes self-command and command of his ship. In contrast with the captain of "The Secret Sharer," Jim repudiates the other-self that has been revealed to him; at no time does he consciously acknowledge that it *was* himself who jumped from the *Patna*—it was only his body that had jumped; and his career thenceforth is an attempt to prove before men that the gross fact of the jump belied his identity.

James works through recognitions; the self-creating character in James develops by taking into consciousness more and more subtle relations—"seeing" more in a world of virtually infinite possibilities for recognition, and thus molding consciousness, molding himself. Conrad works through epiphanies, that is, through dramatic manifestations of elements hidden or implicit in the already constructed character. The difference of method is suggestive of the difference of world view: in James, the world ("reality" as a whole) being, as it were, an open and fluid system, essentially creative; in Conrad, a closed and static system, incapable of origination though intensely dramatic in its revelations. (Paradoxically, the environments in James's open world are the closed environments of city and house, while those in Conrad's closed world are those of the open, the mobile sea.) The word "epiphany" implies manifestation of divinity, and this meaning of the term can serve us also in analyzing Conrad's method and his vision, if we think of the "dark powers" of the psyche as having the mysterious absoluteness that we associate with the daemonic, and if we think mythologically of a man's destiny both as being carried within him, and, *in effect*—since his acts externalize his destiny—as confronting him from without.

The sunken wreck that strikes the *Patna* is one such epiphany in *Lord Jim,* and this manifestation of "dark power" is coincident with and symbolically identifiable with the impulse that makes Jim jump, an impulse submerged like the wreck, riding in wait, striking from under. Outer nature seems, here, to act in collusion with the hidden portion of the soul. But Conrad's supreme mastery is his ability to make the circumstance of "plot" the inevitable point of discharge of the potentiality of "character." [2] The accident that happens to the *Patna* is not merely a parallel and a metaphor of what happens to Jim at that time, but it is the objective circumstance that discovers Jim to himself. The apparent "collusion" between external nature and the soul, that gives to Conrad's work its quality of the marvelous and its religious temper, is thus, really, only the inevitable working out of character through circumstance.

Another major epiphany is the appearance of Brown on Patusan. The appearance of Brown is, in effect, an externalization of the complex

---

[2] Morton Dauwen Zabel points this out in his Introduction to *The Portable Conrad* (New York: The Viking Press, Inc., 1947).

of Jim's guilt and his excuses for his guilt, for he judges Brown as he judged himself, as a *victim of circumstances* (the distinction is radical) rather than as a character exposed by circumstances, at least to be given that benefit of doubt which would discriminate intention from deed, ethos from the objective ethical traits to be seen in a man's actions. Therefore he gives Brown a "clean slate," a chance to "climb out"—from himself! But Jim's compact with Brown is more than a compact with his own unacknowledged guilt; it is at the same time, and paradoxically, a lonely act of faith with the white men "out there," the men of Jim's race and traditions, the men upon the sea whose code he had once betrayed, the "home" from which a single impulse of nerves had forever exiled him. Brown is the only white man who has appeared on Patusan to put to test Jim's ethical community with his race and his profession, and in "taking upon his head" responsibility for Brown's honor, he is superbly "true" to that community. But his truth is, effectively, betrayal; it is "the destructive element." Since only a chance in thousands brings Brown to Patusan, again outer nature seems to have acted in collusion with the "dark power" within Jim's own psyche, in order to face him once more with his unacknowledged identity when he is in the full hybris of his truth and his courage. But again the apparent collusion is only the working out of character through circumstance.

The impossibility of escape from the dark companion within leaves a man more perfectly alone in this world because he has that companion —who is always and only himself. The physical settings of Jim's career concretize his isolation. In constant flight from the self that he reads on men's lips but that he refuses to acknowledge except as a freakish injustice of circumstances, and, as he flees, pursuing the heroic ideal which would reconstitute him in the ranks of men where his salvation lies (for, as Conrad says, "in our own hearts we trust for our salvation in the men that surround us"), he comes finally to Patusan, ascends the river to the heart of the island, unarmed (why carry a loaded revolver when it is only oneself that one must face?)—ascends, that is, the dark paths of his own being back to its source: [3] "thirty miles of forest shut it off."

The first description that Marlow gives of the interior of the island is of a conical hill that is "split in two, and with the two halves leaning slightly apart," and in his reminiscences he returns frequently to the image of the hill (it is, indeed, the hill up which Jim hauled the cannon,

[3] The observation is made by Mr. Guerard in *Joseph Conrad,* cited above.

in his first great exploit when he won the faith of the natives and became their protector), particularly to a scene of moonlight when the moon is rising behind the fissured mass.

> On the third day after the full, the moon, as seen from the open space in front of Jim's house . . . rose exactly behind these hills, its diffused light at first throwing the two masses into intensely black relief, and then the nearly perfect disc, glowing ruddily, appeared, gliding upwards between the sides of the chasm, till it floated away above the summits, as if escaping from a yawning grave in gentle triumph. "Wonderful effect," said Jim by my side. "Worth seeing. Is it not?"
>
> And this question was put with a note of personal pride that made me smile, as though he had had a hand in regulating that unique spectacle. He had regulated so many things in Patusan! Things that would have appeared as much beyond his control as the motions of the moon and the stars.

On Marlow's last night on the island he sees the same spectacle again, but the mood is different, oppressive.

> I saw part of the moon glittering through the bushes at the bottom of the chasm. For a moment it looked as though the smooth disc, falling from its place in the sky upon the earth, had rolled to the bottom of that precipice: its ascending movement was like a leisurely rebound; it disengaged itself from the tangle of twigs; the bare contorted limb of some tree, growing on the slope, made a black crack right across its face. It threw its level rays afar as if from a cavern, and in this mournful eclipse-like light the stumps of felled trees uprose very dark, the heavy shadows fell at my feet on all sides . . .

Together Jim and Marlow watch "the moon float away above the chasm between the hills like an ascending spirit out of a grave; its sheen descended, cold and pale, like the ghost of dead sunlight." Carried to the mind by the image of the fissured hill, with the suspiciously ghostlike moon floating out of the chasm, is the relentless solitude of Jim's fate. He is not only an outcast from his kind but he is also an outcast from himself, cloven spiritually, unable to recognize his own identity, separated from himself as the two halves of the hill are separated. And the rebounding moon, in which he has so much pride, "as though he had had a hand in regulating that unique spectacle," remains in the mind as a figure of the ego-ideal, even that ideal of truth by which, Marlow says, Jim approached "greatness as genuine as any man ever achieved": its illusionariness, and the solitude implied by illusion. At the end, after all —when the silver ring that is the token of moral community falls to the floor, and through Jim's "truth" his best friend has been killed and the village under his protection betrayed—Jim is only what he has been; he is of the measure of his acts. To be only what one has been is the sentence of solitary confinement that is passed on everyman. It is in this sense, finally, that Jim is "one of us."

Since Jim is "one of us," the truth about Jim will be—within the scope of the expressiveness of Jim's story—a truth about life; and in view of this responsibility, Conrad's task of evaluation demands that *all* the accessible evidence be presented and that it be submitted to mutually corrective hypotheses of its meaning. There are Jim's actions, which are concrete enough and simple as the concrete is simple. But the significance of action is significance in the judgments of men, which are various; and as soon as judgment is brought to the act, the act becomes not simple but protean. *What,* then, *is* the act? The question defines Conrad's method in this book, his use of reflector within reflector, point of view within point of view, cross-chronological juxtapositions of events and impressions. Conrad's technical "devices," in this case, represent much more than the word "device" suggests: they represent extreme ethical scrupulosity, even anxiety; for the truth about a man is at once too immense and too delicate to sustain any failure of carefulness in the examiner.

The omniscient early chapters give briefly the conditions of Jim's upbringing, his heroic dreams, two incidents in his sea training, the *Patna* voyage up to the moment when the submerged wreck strikes, and the courtroom scene with Jim in the dock: that is, the first chapters take us up to the point where the accused is placed before us and the processes of judgment have to begin. From here, Marlow takes over. Marlow is unofficial attorney both for the defense and the prosecution. He selects, objectifies, and humanizes the evidence on both sides, but he lets it— intensified and set in perspective through his intelligent, freely roaming curiosity—speak for itself. Marlow is the most familiar narrative mechanism in Conrad's work; and in this particular book *Marlow has to exist.* For Jim's "case" is not an absolute but a relative; it has a being only in relation to what men's minds can make of it. And Marlow provides the necessary medium of an intelligent consciousness, at once a symbol of that relativity, a concretization of the processes by which just judgment may be evoked, and—through his doubt and reverence—an acknowledgment of the irony of judgment of the relative.

The few particulars that are given of Jim's home environment are all we need to give the word "home" potency for this chronicle: there is the parsonage, its decency, its naïveté, its faith, its sterling morality, its representativeness of "the sheltering conception of light and order which is our refuge." In the thirty-fifth chapter, where Marlow takes final farewell of Jim, and Jim says,

> "I must stick to their belief in me to feel safe and to—to" . . . He cast about for a word, seemed to look for it on the sea . . . "to keep in touch with" . . . His voice sank suddenly to a murmur . . . "with those whom, perhaps, I shall never see any more. With—with—you, for instance."

the parsonage home, as well as the community of men upon the sea, contains the "those" with whom Jim must keep in touch through faithfulness in word and act. "Home" is the ethical code which enables men to live together through trust of each other, and which, in so binding them, gives them self-respect. The exclusiveness and naïveté of the parsonage background interpret the symbol of "home" in all its own relativity, its merely provisional status in the jungle of the universe. When we close the book, the symbol of "home" is as ghostlike as the moon over Patusan. But it is the only provision for salvation, in the sense in which Conrad uses the word salvation when he says, "In our own hearts we trust for our salvation in the men that surround us."

The two incidents in Jim's early sea training, the storm in Chapter 1, when he was "too late," and, in Chapter 2, his disablement at the beginning of a hurricane week, when he "felt secretly glad he had not to go on deck," counterpoint his belief in himself with actualities of frustration. A certain distinct polarity is already established, between his dreams and the "facts"; and when, in Chapter 2, Jim suddenly decides to ship as mate on the *Patna,* it is as if we saw a bar magnet curved into a horseshoe and bent until its poles closed, sealing personal will and the fatality of circumstances in a mysterious identity that is the man himself; for his unexplained choice of the *Patna* is in more than one sense a choice of exile. He could have gone back to the home service, after his convalescence;

but he throws in his lot with the men he has seen in that Eastern port (and disdained) who "appeared to live in a crazy maze of plans, hopes, dangers, enterprises . . . in the dark places of the sea," and with those others who had been seduced by "the eternal peace of Eastern sky and sea," who talked "everlastingly of turns of luck . . . and in all they said —in their actions, in their looks, in their persons—could be detected the soft spot, the place of decay . . ." Moreover, on the *Patna* he is in a special sense a man alone, alone with a dream that is unsharable because he is among inferiors: the third chapter presents "the *Patna* gang" from Jim's point of view—"those men did not belong to the world of heroic adventure . . . he rubbed shoulders with them, but they could not touch him; he shared the air they breathed, but he was different . . ." Is his choice of the *Patna* a measure taken to protect his dream from reality? Is it thus significant of his "soft spot"? There is no choice but reality, and actually none but the single, circumscribed, only possible choice that is one's own reality—witnessed by Jim's jump from the *Patna,* as by his shipping on the *Patna* in the first place.

When Sophocles, in his old age, wrote of Oedipus again, he had Oedipus assert his innocence and curse those who had banished him; for Oedipus had acted in ignorance of the circumstances, and therefore could not be held guilty for them. Jim puts up a fight as Oedipus did, and the causes involved are the same: is the self deducible from circumstances? is one guilty for circumstances? is one guilty for oneself when one has no choice but to be oneself? is one guilty for oneself when one is in ignorance of what oneself is? if, with lifelong strife, one refuses to acquiesce in the self, is one guilty for the self? who has a right to pronounce this judgment?

Obviously from this point another device of presentation must be used, other than either objective presentation by the author or subjective presentation through Jim, for Jim is too youthful, idealistic, and ingenuous to throw light on himself, and "objectivity"—the objectivity of the camera and the sound recorder—is hopelessly inadequate to the solution of these questions. Marlow has to take up the case, and Marlow—intelligent professional man of the sea, and insatiably curious psychological observer— brings to bear on it not only Jim's own evidence (and his friendship with Jim draws from Jim much more than he could ever say for himself— brings out gestures and tones, situations and impulses, that only sympathy could bring out), and not only the reactions of the judges (and the judges are more in number than those in the courtroom), but also a marvelously sensitive registration of the concrete detail of life, bits of color and form and movement, a chin, a hand, a shuffle, a vase of dry flowers, a striped pajama suit, that could not be admitted as "evidence" in a formal inquiry, but that are nevertheless essential psychological evidence to the sensitive investigator.

The *Patna* gang has to be presented over again, not now from Jim's point of view but from Marlow's. So far as the *Patna* gang is concerned, the question is, is Jim one of them or "one of us"? Marlowe has only to see the group on a street corner to know that Jim is not one of them; but he pushes further—he is around when the fat captain, in his night-suit, squeezes into the ramshackle gharry and disappears, "departed, disappeared, vanished, absconded; and absurdly enough it looked as though he had taken that gharry with him." It is Marlow's impression of the obscenely ridiculous captain that conveys to us the captain's sur-reality: he is, through Marlow's view, not simply stupid and inferior as he appeared to Jim, but a frightful manifestation of underground evil, as mysterious and unaccountable in its apparition as the captain's vanishing with the gharry is complete; that the captain wears a sleeping suit (like the murderer in "The Secret Sharer") emphasizes the psychological, that is to say spiritual, symbolism of his evil; he is another epiphany, a "showing" from the daemonic underground of the psyche—but he is only that, and the psyche, Jim's psyche, is more than the obscene man in the sleeping suit.

Then Marlow interviews the chief engineer in the hospital, the man with the noble head and the pink toads under his bed. The effort is an effort again to test his perception that Jim is not one of them, but "one of us"; for the initial perception alone is scarcely to be trusted, since Jim, whatever his excuses, had identified himself with the *Patna* gang by jumping from the ship. The pink toads under the chief engineer's bed are a fearful inversion of Jim's own dream: they too are a dream—and the dreamer has a noble head. The pink toads are a horrible degeneration of the dream. They serve as a commentary on the dream that cannot be evaded (no more than can the captain in the sleeping suit). But Jim had stayed for the trial, while the captain had disappeared, the chief engineer had cultivated the d.t.'s, and the second engineer wasn't around (the little man will reappear later, for the act is immortal). It is Jim's dream that makes him stay for the trial, and therefore Jim's dream cannot be identified with the chief engineer's, however identifiable they are in illusionary quality and spiritual potency. Marlow's visit with the chief engineer fixes this judgment of a difference, as well as of a similarity.

These two observations of Marlow's project the question of identity (the question "Who am I?" that is Oedipus' as well as Jim's), that can only be decided by comparison of like things and different things, discrimination of congruences and incongruences. Two identifications of Jim with other persons have been rejected—although even the impulse to distinguish suggests subtle similarities between the objects compared, and we can never forget that Jim was in the lifeboat with the *Patna* gang, though at the other end. The rest of the narrative moves through a devious course of identifications and distinctions. Brierly, the unimpeachable professional seaman, in some astounding way identifies himself with the accused man, Jim, and commits suicide. Is this another version of Jim's "jump"? If so, in avoiding by suicide the possibility of being Jim, Brierly succeeds merely in being what he was trying to avoid; this is Jim's "case" all over again. The loathsome Chester also identifies himself with Jim; Chester instantly spots him as the man for his job—fantastic exile on a guano island; "He is no earthly good for anything," Chester says,—"he would just have done for me"; the man has a "soft spot," and for men with a soft spot, as Jim himself had observed, "death was the only event of their fantastic existence that seemed to have a reasonable certitude of achievement"; for Chester, Jim is "one of us" in a sense that disgusts Marlow, and Marlow's disgust with Chester and therefore with Chester's appraisal of the man helps us to measure Jim: but the fact that Marlow, during those grueling hours in the hotel room when he is writing factitious letters in order to give Jim a chance for privacy with his ordeal, can hesitate between recommending Jim for a decent job and turning him over to Chester still suggests a doubt as to what "one of us" means, whether it has Chester's meaning or Marlow's.

The French lieutenant whom Marlow encounters, though he is a sympathetic man, does *not* identify himself with Jim; and curiously, while the French lieutenant represents the approved ethos of the profession (and not only of the profession of the sea, but of the profession of being human, as the author evaluates his material; for, in that evaluation, being human, as humans ought to be, *is* a profession, with an austere Spartan-like discipline [4]), he is the only person in the book who does not, in some way, identify himself with Jim except for Cornelius and Brown, who hate him

[4] In his *Joseph Conrad,* Mr. Guerard thoroughly clarifies this issue.

as an opposite and as an indictment of their evil (perhaps the captain of the *Patna* and the chief engineer could be included here, but their presentation is more objective and their attitudes less determinable; although the same point would hold): that is to say that the only cases in which subjective identification with Jim does not take place are those of a man —the French lieutenant—who is above Jim's failings by virtue of his mediocrity, and of men who are below Jim's problem by virtue of their psychotic maliciousness. The portrait of the French lieutenant is extremely careful, as all the portraits in the book are done with extreme care, for on the nature of the man who judges depends the validity of the judgment.

> He clasped his hands on his stomach again. "I remained on board that—that—my memory is going (*s'en va*). Ah! *Patt-nà. C'est bien ça. Patt-nà. Merci.* It is droll how one forgets. I stayed on that ship thirty hours . . ."

And just a moment before, we have learned that "all the time of towing we had two quartermasters stationed with axes by the hawsers, to cut us clear of our tow in case she . . ." The French lieutenant's failure to remember even the name of the ship, on which he had stayed for thirty hours *after* Jim had jumped, and the laconic tone of the information about the quartermasters' assignment, are a judgment of Jim in terms of Jim's own dream. The French lieutenant's unconscious heroism is the heroism that Jim had made a conscious ideal; and his witness measures Jim's failure by the painful difference of fact. And yet this damning commentary appears as inconclusive as that of the pink toads under the chief engineer's bed; it is as far from and as near to "the case."

The distinguished naturalist Stein offers another approach. Stein has been a hero of action like the French lieutenant, but he is also a hero of the intellect, and, in his way, a psychologist, a philosopher, and an artist. Stein is able to identify himself with Jim through his own profound idealism (as Marlow does through doubt). But Stein's idealism, so far as we know, has never differentiated itself from his actions; he has the gift of nature which is itself ideal; he had known, Marlow says, how "to follow his destiny with unfaltering footsteps." Stein "diagnoses the case" of Jim, making it quite simple "and altogether hopeless" by framing it in the question: "how to be." "I tell you, my friend," he says, "it is not good for you to find you cannot make your dream come true, for the reason that you not strong enough are, or not clever enough. *Ja!* . . . And all the time you are such a fine fellow, too! *Wie?* . . . How can that be? . . ."

The shadow prowling amongst the graves of butterflies laughed boisterously.

Stein gives Jim his great chance to make his dream come true, by sending him to Patusan. This journey is ambiguous: "once before Patusan had been used as a grave," Marlow reflects; while Stein prowls "amongst the graves of butterflies," Brierly's remark about Jim recurs to Marlow's mind: "Let him creep twenty feet underground and stay there"; and there is the fissured hill at the heart of Patusan, whose chasm is like a "yawning grave," from which the moon (the dream) rises "like an ascending spirit out of a grave . . . like the ghost of dead sunlight." The ancient mythical heroes, Odysseus and Aeneas, made the "journey underground" to Hades in search of wisdom, and brought it back to daylight —the wisdom which was knowledge of their own destinies. And shadowily behind them is the barbarous ritual that made a king by burying him and disinterring him, a surrogate perhaps, or a "story" (mythos), to stand for the killing of an old king and his "resurrection" in a new one. In the grave of Patusan—"the secular gloom and the old mankind"—Jim's dream does come true. But the doubt remains as to whether, like the ancient heroes, he brought back to daylight the wisdom of his destiny—or, in other terms, whether in that grave an old self was really buried and from it a new one congruent with his dream was resurrected.

The test of daylight, of the bright sea beyond the dark island, offers itself only through Brown. Jim identifies himself with Brown in two ways, through his guilt, and through his honor: Brown is at once the "dark power" in Jim's psyche and his only effective bond with the brightness outside himself, the community of tradition to which "we trust for our salvation." Brown's ambivalence for Jim is Jim's own ambivalence, and it is, in its most extensive sense, the ambivalence that exists in all historical and personal stages of experience where law (the "code") and the self question each other—as well in the Athens of Thucydides and Euripides as in our own time, and as well, we must surmise, in Conrad as in Jim. The tale Conrad prepared to narrate was a tale in the manner of the older classical dramatists, wherein law—whether divine, as with

Aeschylus, or natural, as with Sophocles—is justified to the self, whatever its agonies of discovery. But he managed to do a tale that put both the law and the self to question, and left them there. At the end (dated July 1900), Stein does not help:

> Stein has aged greatly of late. He feels it himself, and says often that he is "preparing to leave all this; preparing to leave . . ." while he waves his hand sadly at his butterflies.

ON *Sons and Lovers*

Novels, like other dramatic art, deal with conflicts of one kind or another—conflicts that are, in the work of the major novelists, drawn from life in the sense that they are representative of real problems in life; and the usual urgency in the novelist is to find the technical means which will afford an ideal resolution of the conflict and solution of the living problem—still "ideal" even if tragic. Technique is his art itself, in its procedural aspect; and the validity of his solution of a problem is dependent upon the adequacy of his technique. The more complex and intransigent the problem, the more subtle his technical strategies will evidently need to be, if they are to be effective. The decade of World War I brought into full and terrible view the collapse of values that had prophetically haunted the minds of novelists as far back as Dostoevski and Flaubert and Dickens, or even farther back, to Balzac and Stendhal. With that decade, and increasingly since, the problems of modern life have appeared intransigent indeed; and, in general, the growth of that intransigence has been reflected in an increasing concern with technique on the part of the artist. D. H. Lawrence's sensitivity to twentieth-century chaos was peculiarly intense, and his passion for order was similarly intense; but this sensitivity and this passion did not lead him to concentrate on refinements and subtleties of novelistic technique in the direction laid out, for instance, by James and Conrad. Hence, as readers first approaching his work, almost inevitably we feel disappointment and even perhaps shock, that writing so often "loose" and repetitious and such unrestrained emotionalism over glandular matters should appear in the work of a novelist who is assumed to have an important place in the literary canon. "There is no use," Francis Fergusson says, "trying to appreciate [Lawrence] solely as an artist; he was himself too often impatient of the demands of art, which seemed to him trivial compared with the quest he followed." [1] And Stephen Spender phrases the problem of Lawrence in this way: what interested him "was the tension between art and life, not the complete resolution of the problems of life within the illusion of art . . . For him literature is a kind of pointer to what is outside literature . . . This outsideness of reality is for Lawrence the waters of baptism in which man can be reborn." [2] We need to approach Lawrence with a good deal of humility about "art" and a good deal of patience for the disappointments he frequently offers as an artist, for it is only thus that we shall be able to appreciate the innovations he actually made in the novel as well as the importance and profundity of his vision of modern life.

Sons and Lovers appears to have the most conventional chronological organization—the extreme reverse of Conrad's intricate cross-chronology; it is the kind of organization that a naïve autobiographical novelist would tend to use, with only the thinnest pretense at disguising the personally retrospective nature of the material. We start with the marriage of the parents and the birth of the children. We learn of the daily life of the family while the children are growing up, the work, the small joys, the parental strife. Certain well-defined emotional pressures become apparent: the children are alienated from their father, whose personality degenerates gradually as he feels his exclusion; the mother more and more completely dominates her sons' affections, aspirations, mental habits. Urged by her toward middle-class refinements, they enter white-collar jobs, thus making one more dissociation between themselves and their proletarian father. As they attempt to orient themselves toward biological adulthood, the old split in the family is manifested in a new form, as an internal schism in the characters of the sons; they cannot reconcile sexual choice with the idealism their mother has inculcated. This inner strain leads to the older son's death. The same motif is repeated in the case of Paul, the younger one. Paul's first girl, Miriam, is a cerebral type, and the mother senses in her an obvious rivalry for domination of Paul's sensibility. The mother is the stronger influence, and Paul withdraws from Miriam; but with her own victory Mrs. Morel begins to realize the discord she has produced in his character, and tries to release her hold on him by unconsciously seeking her own death. Paul finds another girl, Clara, but the damage is already

1 "D. H. Lawrence's Sensibility," in *Critiques and Essays in Modern Fiction*, edited by John W. Aldridge (New York: The Ronald Press Company, 1952), p. 328.
2 "The Life of Literature," in *Partisan Review*, December, 1948.

too deeply designed, and at the time of his mother's death, he voluntarily gives up Clara, knowing that there is but one direction he can take, and that is to go with his mother. At the end he is left emotionally derelict, with only the "drift toward death."

From this slight sketch, it is clear that the book is organized not merely on a chronological plan showing the habits and vicissitudes of a Nottinghamshire miner's family, but that it has a structure rigorously controlled by an idea: an idea of an organic disturbance in the relationships of men and women—a disturbance of sexual polarities that is first seen in the disaffection of mother and father, then in the mother's attempt to substitute her sons for her husband, finally in the sons' unsuccessful struggle to establish natural manhood. Lawrence's development of the idea has certain major implications: it implies that his characters have transgressed against the natural life-directed condition of the human animal—against the elementary biological rhythms he shares with the rest of biological nature; and it implies that this offense against life has been brought about by a failure to respect the complete and terminal individuality of persons —by a twisted desire to "possess" other persons, as the mother tries to "possess" her husband, then her sons, and as Miriam tries to "possess" Paul. Lawrence saw this offense as a disease of modern life in all its manifestations, from sexual relationships to those broad social and political relationships that have changed people from individuals to anonymous economic properties or to military units or to ideological automatons.

The controlling idea is expressed in the various episodes—the narrative logic of the book. It is also expressed in imagery—the book's poetic logic. In previous studies we have discussed, from a number of points of view, the function of imagery in novels, but nowhere else do we find the image so largely replacing episode and discursive analysis and taking over the expressive functions of these, as it does in Lawrence. The chief reason for the extraordinary predominance of the image, as an absolute expressive medium, in Lawrence, lies in the character of the idea which is his subject. He must make us aware—sensitively aware, not merely conceptually aware—of the profound life force whose rhythms the natural creature obeys; and he must make us aware of the terminal individuality—the absolute "otherness" or "outsideness"—that is the natural form of things and of the uncorrupted person. We must be made aware of these through the *feelings* of his people, for only in feeling have the biological life force and the sense of identity, either the identity of self or of others, any immediacy of reality. He seeks the objective equivalent of feeling in the image. As Francis Fergusson says, Lawrence's imagination was so concrete that he seems not "to distinguish between the reality and the metaphor or symbol which makes it plain to us." [3] But the most valid symbols are the most concrete realities. Lawrence's great gift for the symbolic image was a function of his sensitivity to and passion for the meaning of real things—for the individual expression that real forms have. In other words, his gift for the image arose directly from his vision of life as infinitely creative of individual identities, each whole and separate and to be reverenced as such.

Let us examine the passage with which the first chapter of *Sons and Lovers* ends—where Mrs. Morel, pregnant with Paul, wanders deliriously in the garden, shut out of the house by Morel in his drunkenness. Mrs. Morel is literally a vessel of the life force that seems to thrust itself at her in nature from all sides, but she is also in rebellion against it and the perfume of the pollen-filled lilies makes her gasp with fear.

> The moon was high and magnificent in the August night. Mrs. Morel, seared with passion, shivered to find herself out there in a great white light, that fell cold on her, and gave a shock to her inflamed soul. She stood for a few moments helplessly staring at the glistening great rhubarb leaves near the door. Then she got the air into her breast. She walked down the garden path, trembling in every limb, while the child boiled within her . . .
>
> She hurried out of the side garden to the front, where she could stand as if in an immense gulf of white light, the moon streaming high in face of her, the moonlight standing up from the hills in front, and filling the valley where the Bottoms crouched, almost blindingly. There, panting and half weeping in reaction from the stress, she murmured to herself over and over again: "The nuisance! the nuisance!"
>
> She became aware of something about her. With an effort she roused herself to see what it was that penetrated her consciousness. The tall white lilies were reeling in the moonlight, and the air was charged with their perfume, as with a presence. Mrs. Morel gasped slightly in fear. She touched the big, pallid flowers on their petals, then shivered. They seemed to be stretching in the moonlight. She put her hand into one white bin: the gold scarcely showed on her fingers by moonlight. She bent down to look at the binful of yellow

[3] Fergusson, *op. cit.*, p. 335.

pollen; but it only appeared dusky. Then she drank a deep draught of the scent. It almost made her dizzy.

Mrs. Morel leaned on the garden gate, looking out, and she lost herself awhile. She did not know what she thought. Except for a slight feeling of sickness, and her consciousness in the child, herself melted out like a scent into the shiny, pale air.

She finally arouses Morel from his drunken sleep and he lets her in. Unfastening her brooch at the bedroom mirror, she sees that her face is smeared with the yellow dust of the lilies.

The imagery of the streaming moonlight is that of a vast torrential force, "magnificent" and inhuman, and it equates not only with that phallic power of which Mrs. Morel is the rebellious vessel but with the greater and universal demiurge that was anciently called Eros—the power springing in plants and hurling the planets, giving the "glistening great rhubarb leaves" their fierce identity, fecundating and stretching the lilies. The smear of yellow pollen on Mrs. Morel's face is a grossly humorous irony. This passage is a typifying instance of the spontaneous identification Lawrence constantly found between image and meaning, between real things and what they symbolize.

Our particular culture has evolved deep prohibitions against the expression, or even the subjective acknowledgment of the kind of phallic reality with which Lawrence was concerned—and with which ancient religions were also concerned. Certainly one factor in the uneasiness that Lawrence frequently causes us is the factor of those cultural prohibitions. But these prohibitions themselves Lawrence saw as disease symptoms, though the disease was far more extensive and radical than a taboo on the phallus. It was a spiritual disease that broke down the sense of identity, of "separate selfhood," while at the same time it broke down the sense of rhythm with universal nature. Paul Morel, working his fairly unconscious, adolescent, sexual way toward Miriam, finds that rhythm and that selfhood in the spatial proportions of a wren's nest in a hedge.

He crouched down and carefully put his finger through the thorns into the round door of the nest.

"It's almost as if you were feeling inside the live body of the bird," he said, "it's so warm. They say a bird makes its nest round like a cup with pressing its breast on it. Then how did it make the ceiling round, I wonder?"

When Paul takes his first country walk with Clara and Miriam, the appearance of a red stallion in the woods vividly realizes in unforced symbolic dimension the power which will drive Paul from Miriam to Clara, while the image also realizes the great horse itself in its unique and mysterious identity.

> As they were going beside the brook, on the Willey Water side, looking through the brake at the edge of the wood, where pink campions glowed under a few sunbeams, they saw, beyond the tree-trunks and the thin hazel bushes, a man leading a great bay horse through the gullies. The big red beast seemed to dance romantically through that dimness of green hazel drift, away there where the air was shadowy, as if it were in the past, among the fading bluebells that might have bloomed for Deirdre . . .
>
> The great horse breathed heavily, shifting round its red flanks, and looking suspiciously with its wonderful big eyes upwards from under its lowered head and falling mane . . .

A simple descriptive passage like the following, showing a hen pecking at a girl's hand, conveys the animal dynamics that is the urgent phase of the phallic power working in the boy and the girl, but its spontaneous symbolism of a larger reality is due to its faithfulness to the way a hen does peck and the feeling of the pecking—due, that is, to the actuality or "identity" of the small, homely circumstance itself.

> As he went round the back, he saw Miriam kneeling in front of the hen-coop, some maize in her hand, biting her lip, and crouching in an intense attitude. The hen was eyeing her wickedly. Very gingerly she put forward her hand. The hen bobbed for her. She drew back quickly with a cry, half of fear, half of chagrin.
>
> "It won't hurt you," said Paul.
>
> She flushed crimson and started up.
>
> "I only wanted to try," she said in a low voice.
>
> "See, it doesn't hurt," he said, and, putting only two corns in his palm, he let the hen peck, peck, peck at his bare hand. "It only makes you laugh," he said.
>
> She put her hand forward, and dragged it away, tried again, and started back with a cry. He frowned.
>
> "Why, I'd let her take corn from my face," said Paul, "only she bumps a bit. She's ever so neat. If she wasn't, look how much ground she'd peck up every day."

He waited grimly, and watched. At last Miriam let the bird peck from her hand. She gave a little cry—fear, and pain because of fear—rather pathetic. But she had done it, and she did it again.

"There, you see," said the boy. "It doesn't hurt, does it?"

There is more terse and obvious symbolism, of the typical kind in Lawrence, in that sequence where Clara's red carnations splatter their petals over her clothes and on the ground where she and Paul first make love, but we acquire the best and the controlling sense of Lawrence's gift for the image, as dramatic and thematic expression, in those passages where his urgency is to see *things* and to see them clearly and completely in their most individualizing traits, for the character of his vision is such that, in truly seeing them as they are, he sees through them to what they mean.

We have fairly frequently noticed in these studies the differentiating significance of a writer's treatment of nature—that is, of that part of "nature" which is constituted by earth and air and water and the nonhuman creatures; and we have found that attitudes toward nature were deeply associated with attitudes toward human "good," human destiny, human happiness, human salvation, the characteristic problems of being human. One might cite, for instance, in *Tom Jones,* Fielding's highly stylized treatment of outdoor nature (as in the passage in which Tom dreams of Sophia beside the brook, and Mollie Seagrim approaches): here nature has only generalized attributes for whose description and understanding certain epithets in common educated currency are completely adequate—brooks murmur, breezes whisper, birds trill; nature is really a linguistic construction, and this rationalization of nature is appropriate in Fielding's universe since everything there exists ideally as an object of *ratio,* of reasoning intelligence. We have noticed in Jane Austen's *Pride and Prejudice* (in the description of Darcy's estate, for example) that outdoor nature again has importance only as it serves to express rational and social character—wherefore again the generalized epithet that represents nature as either the servant of intelligence or the space where intelligence operates. In George Eliot's *Adam Bede,* where there is relatively a great deal of "outdoors," nature is man's plowfield, the acre in which he finds social and ethical expression through work; this is only a different variety of the conception of nature as significant by virtue of what man's intelligential and social character makes of it for his ends.

With Emily Brontë, we come nearer to Lawrence, though not very near. In *Wuthering Heights,* nature's importance is due not to its yielding itself up to domestication in man's reason, or offering itself as an instrument by which he expresses his conscience before God or society, but to its fiercely unregenerate difference from all that civilized man is—a difference that it constantly forces on perception by animal-like attacks on and disruptions of human order. In Hardy, nature is also a daemonic entity in its own right, and not only unrationalizable but specifically hostile to the human reason. It is worth noting that, among all English novelists, Hardy and Lawrence have the most faithful touch for the things of nature and the greatest evocative genius in bringing them before the imagination. But there are certain definitive differences of attitude. Both Emily Brontë's and Hardy's worlds are dual, and there is no way of bringing the oppositions of the dualism together: on the one side of the cleavage are those attributes of man that we call "human," his reason, his ethical sensibility; and on the other side is "nature"—the elements and the creatures and man's own instinctive life that he shares with the nonhuman creatures. The opposition is resolved only by destruction of the "human": a destruction that is in Emily Brontë profoundly attractive, in Hardy tragic. But Lawrence's world is multiple rather than dual. Everything in it is a separate and individual "other," every person, every creature, every object (like the madonna lilies, the rhubarb plants, the wren's nest, the stallion); and there is a creative relationship between people and between people and things so long as this "otherness" is acknowledged. When it is denied—and it is denied when man tries to rationalize nature and society, or when he presumptuously assumes the things of nature to be merely instruments for the expression of himself, or when he attempts to exercise personal possessorship over people—then he destroys his own selfhood and exerts a destructive influence all about him.

In *Sons and Lovers,* only in Morel himself, brutalized and spiritually maimed as he is, does the germ of selfhood remain intact; and—this is the correlative proposition in Lawrence—in him only does the biological life force have simple, unequivocal assertion. Morel wants to live, by hook or crook, while his sons want to die. To live is to obey a rhythm involving more than conscious attitudes and involving more than human beings—involving all nature; a rhythm indifferent to the greediness of reason, indifferent to idiosyncrasies of culture and idealism. The image associated with Morel is that of the coalpits, where he descends daily and from which he ascends at night blackened and tired. It is a symbol of rhythmic descent and ascent, like a sexual rhythm, or like the rhythm of sleep and awaking or of death and life. True, the work in the coalpits reverses the natural use of the hours of light and dark and is an economic distortion of that rhythm in nature—and Morel and the other colliers bear the spiritual traumata of that distortion; for Lawrence is dealing with the real environment of modern men, in its complexity and injuriousness. Nevertheless, the work at the pits is still symbolic of the greater rhythm governing life and obedience to which is salvation. Throughout the book, the coalpits are always at the horizon.

> On the fallow land the young wheat shone silkily. Minton pit waved its plumes of white steam, coughed, and rattled hoarsely.
> "Now look at that!" said Mrs. Morel. Mother and son stood on the road to watch. Along the ridge of the great pit-hill crawled a little group in silhouette against the sky, a horse, a small truck, and a man. They climbed the incline against the heavens. At the end the man tipped the waggon. There was an undue rattle as the waste fell down the sheer slope of the enormous bank . . .
> "Look how it heaps together," [Paul says of the pit] "like something alive almost—a big creature that you don't know . . . And all the trucks standing waiting, like a string of beasts to be fed . . . I like the feel of *men* on things, while they're alive. There's a feel of men about trucks, because they've been handled with men's hands, all of them."

Paul associates the pits not only with virility but with being alive. The trucks themselves become alive because they have been handled by men. The symbolism of the pits is identical with that of Morel, the father, the irrational life principle that is unequally embattled against the death principle in the mother, the rational and idealizing principle working rhythmlessly, greedily, presumptuously, and possessively.

The sons' attitude toward the father is ambivalent, weighted toward hate because the superior cultural equipment of the mother shows his crudeness in relief; but again and again bits of homely characterization of Morel show that the children—and even the mother herself—sense, however uncomfortably, the attractiveness of his simple masculine integrity. He has, uninjurable, what the mother's possessiveness has injured in the sons.

"Shut that doo-er!" bawled Morel furiously.

Annie banged it behind her, and was gone.

"If tha oppens it again while I'm weshin' me, I'll ma'e thy jaw rattle," he threatened from the midst of his soapsuds. Paul and the mother frowned to hear him.

Presently he came running out of the scullery, with the soapy water dripping from him, dithering with cold.

"Oh, my sirs!" he said. "Wheer's my towel?"

It was hung on a chair to warm before the fire, otherwise he would have bullied and blustered. He squatted on his heels before the hot baking-fire to dry himself.

"F-ff-f!" he went, pretending to shudder with cold.

"Goodness, man, don't be such a kid!" said Mrs. Morel. "It's *not* cold."

"Thee strip thysen stark nak'd to wesh thy flesh i' that scullery," said the miner, as he rubbed his hair; "nowt b'r a ice-'ouse!"

"And I shouldn't make that fuss," replied his wife.

"No, tha'd drop down stiff, as dead as a door-knob, wi' thy nesh sides."

"Why is a door-knob deader than anything else?" asked Paul, curious.

"Eh, I dunno; that's what they say," replied his father. "But there's that much draught i' yon scullery, as it blows through your ribs like through a five-barred gate."

"It would have some difficulty in blowing through yours," said Mrs. Morel.

Morel looked down ruefully at his sides.

"Me!" he exclaimed. "I'm nowt b'r a skinned rabbit. My bones fair juts out on me."

"I should like to know where," retorted his wife.

"Iv'ry-wheer! I'm nobbut a sack o' faggots."

Mrs. Morel laughed. He had still a wonderfully young body, muscular, without any fat. His skin was smooth and clear. It might have been the body of a man of twenty-eight, except that there were, perhaps, too many blue scars, like tattoo-marks, where the coal-dust remained under the skin, and that his chest was too hairy. But he put his hands on his sides ruefully. It was his fixed belief that, because he did not get fat, he was as thin as a starved rat.

Paul looked at his father's thick, brownish hands all scarred, with broken nails, rubbing the fine smoothness of his sides, and the incongruity struck him. It seemed strange they were the same flesh.

Morel talks the dialect that is the speech of physical tenderness in Lawrence's books.[4] It is to the dialect of his father that Paul reverts when he is
tussling with Beatrice in adolescent erotic play (letting the mother's bread
burn, that he should have been watching), and that Arthur, the only one
of the sons whom the mother has not corrupted, uses in his love-making,
and that Paul uses again when he makes love to Clara, the uncomplex
woman who is able for a while to give him his sexual manhood and his
"separate selfhood." The sons never use the dialect with their mother, and
Paul never uses it with Miriam. It is the speech used by Mellors in *Lady
Chatterley's Lover;* and, significantly perhaps, Mellors' name is an anagram
on the name Morel.

Some of the best moments in the children's life are associated with the
father, when Morel has his "good" periods and enters again into the intimate activity of the family—and some of the best, most simply objective
writing in the book communicates these moments, as for instance the passage in Chapter 4 where Morel is engaged in making fuses.

Morel fetched a sheaf of long sound wheat-straws from the attic. These
he cleaned with his hand, till each one gleamed like a stalk of gold,
after which he cut the straws into lengths of about six inches, leaving,
if he could, a notch at the bottom of each piece. He always had a
beautifully sharp knife that could cut a straw clean without hurting it.
Then he set in the middle of the table a heap of gun-powder, a little
pile of black grains upon the white-scrubbed board. He made and
trimmed the straws while Paul and Annie filled and plugged them.
Paul loved to see the black grains trickle down a crack in his palm
into the mouth of the straw, peppering jollily downwards till the straw
was full. Then he bunged up the mouth with a bit of soap—which he
got on his thumb-nail from a pat in a saucer—and the straw was
finished.

There is a purity of realization in this very simple kind of exposition that,
on the face of it, resists associating itself with any *symbolic* function—if
we tend to think of a "symbol" as splitting itself apart into a thing and a
meaning, with a mental arrow connecting the two. The best in Lawrence
carries the authenticity of a faithfully observed, concrete actuality that refuses to be so split; its symbolism is a radiation that leaves it intact in itself.

[4] This observation is made by Diana Trilling in her Introduction to *The Portable
D. H. Lawrence* (New York: The Viking Press, Inc., 1947).

So, in the passage above, the scene is intact as homely realism, but it radiates Lawrence's controlling sense of the characterful integrity of objects —the clean wheat straws, the whitely scrubbed table, the black grains peppering down a crack in the child's palm, the bung of soap on a thumbnail —and that integrity is here associated with the man Morel and his own integrity of warm and absolute maleness. Thus it is another representation of the creative life force witnessed in the independent objectivity of things that are wholly concrete and wholly themselves.

The human attempt to distort and corrupt that selfhood is reflected in Miriam's attitude toward flowers.

> Round the wild, tussocky lawn at the back of the house was a thorn hedge, under which daffodils were craning forward from among their sheaves of grey-green blades. The cheeks of the flowers were greenish with cold. But still some had burst, and their gold ruffled and glowed. Miriam went on her knees before one cluster, took a wild-looking daffodil between her hands, turned up its face of gold to her, and bowed down, caressing it with her mouth and cheeks and brow. He stood aside, with his hands in his pockets, watching her. One after another she turned up to him the faces of the yellow, bursten flowers appealingly, fondling them lavishly all the while. . . .
> "Why must you always be fondling things!" he said irritably. . . . "Can you never like things without clutching them as if you wanted to pull the heart out of them? . . . You're always begging things to love you. . . . Even the flowers, you have to fawn on them—"
> Rhythmically, Miriam was swaying and stroking the flower with her mouth. . . .
> "You don't want to love—your eternal and abnormal craving is to be loved. You aren't positive, you're negative. You absorb, absorb, as if you must fill yourself up with love, because you've got a shortage somewhere."

The relationship of the girl to the flowers is that of a blasphemous possessorship which denies the separateness of living entities—the craving to break down boundaries between thing and thing, that is seen also in Miriam's relationship with Paul, whom she cannot love without trying to absorb him. In contrast, there is the flower imagery in the eleventh chapter, where Paul goes out into the night and the garden in a moment of emotional struggle.

256

It grew late. Through the open door, stealthily, came the scent of madonna lilies, almost as if it were prowling abroad. Suddenly he got up and went out of doors.

The beauty of the night made him want to shout. A half-moon, dusky gold, was sinking behind the black sycamore at the end of the garden, making the sky dull purple with its glow. Nearer, a dim white fence of lilies went across the garden, and the air all round seemed to stir with scent, as if it were alive. He went across the bed of pinks, whose keen perfume came sharply across the rocking, heavy scent of the lilies, and stood alongside the white barrier of flowers. They flagged all loose, as if they were panting. The scent made him drunk. He went down to the field to watch the moon sink under.

A corncrake in the hay-close called insistently. The moon slid quite quickly downwards, growing more flushed. Behind him the great flowers leaned as if they were calling. And then, like a shock, he caught another perfume, something raw and coarse. Hunting round, he found the purple iris, touched their fleshy throats and their dark, grasping hands. At any rate, he had found something. They stood stiff in the darkness. Their scent was brutal. The moon was melting down upon the crest of the hill. It was gone; all was dark. The corncrake called still.

The flowers here have a fierce "thereness" or "otherness" establishing them as existences in their own right, as separate, strange selves, and the demiurgic Eros is rudely insistent in their scent. Paul's perception of that independent life puts him into relation with himself, and the moment of catalytic action is marked by the brief sentence: "At any rate, he had found something." The "something" that he finds is simply the iris, dark, fleshy, mysterious, alien. He goes back into the house and tells his mother that he has decided to break off with Miriam.

Darkness—as the darkness of this night in the garden—has in Lawrence a special symbolic potency. It is a natural and universal symbol, but it offers itself with special richness to Lawrence because of the character of his governing vision. Darkness is half of the rhythm of the day, the darkness of unconsciousness is half of the rhythm of the mind, and the darkness of death is half of the rhythm of life. Denial of this phase of the universal tide is the great sin, the sin committed by modern economy and modern rationalism. In acceptance of the dark, man is renewed to himself—and to light, to consciousness, to reason, to brotherhood. But by refusal to accept that half of the rhythm, he becomes impotent, his reason becomes destructive, and he loses the sense of the independence of others which is essential to brotherhood. In the thirteenth chapter of *Sons and Lovers* there is a passage that realizes something of what we have been saying. It occurs just after Paul has made love to Clara in a field.

> All the while the peewits were screaming in the field. When he came to, he wondered what was near his eyes, curving and strong with life in the dark, and what voice it was speaking. Then he realized it was the grass, and the peewit was calling. The warmth was Clara's breathing heaving. He lifted his head, and looked into her eyes. They were dark and shining and strange, life wild at the source staring into his life, stranger to him, yet meeting him; and he put his face down on her throat, afraid. What was she? A strong, strange, wild life, that breathed with his in the darkness through this hour. It was all so much bigger than themselves that he was hushed. They had met, and included in their meeting the thrust of the manifold grass-stems, the cry of the peewit, the wheel of the stars . . .
>
> . . . after such an evening they both were very still. . . . They felt small, half afraid, childish, and wondering, like Adam and Eve when they lost their innocence and realized the magnificence of the power which drove them out of Paradise and across the great night and the great day of humanity. It was for each of them an initiation. . . . To know their own nothingness, to know the tremendous living flood which carried them always, gave them rest within themselves. If so great a magnificent power could overwhelm them, identify them altogether with itself, so that they knew they were only grains in the tremendous heave that lifted every grass-blade its little height, and every tree, and living thing, then why fret about themselves? They could let themselves be carried by life, and they felt a sort of peace each in the other. There was a verification which they had had together. Nothing could nullify it, nothing could take it away; it was almost their belief in life.

But then we are told that "Clara was not satisfied . . . She thought it was he whom she wanted . . . She had not got him; she was not satisfied." This is the impulse toward personal possessorship that constantly confuses and distorts human relationships in Lawrence's books; it is a denial of the otherness of people, and a denial, really, of the great inhuman life force, the primal Otherness through which people have their independent definition as well as their creative community. Paul had felt that "his experience had been impersonal, and not Clara"; and he had wanted the same impersonality in Clara, an impersonality consonant with that of the manifold grass stems and the peewits' calling and the wheel of the stars. André Malraux, in his preface to the French translation of *Lady Chatterley's Lover,* says that this "couple-advocate," Lawrence, is concerned not with his own individuality or that of his mate, but with "being": "Lawrence has no wish to be either happy or great," Malraux says; "he is only concerned with being." [5] The concern with being, with simple being-a-self (as distinguished from imposing the ego or abdicating selfhood in the mass), can be understood only in the context of twentieth-century man's resignation to herd ideologies, herd recreations, herd rationalizations. Lawrence's missionary and prophetic impulse, like Dostoevski's, was to combat the excesses of rationalism and individualism, excesses that have led—paradoxically enough—to the release of monstrously destructive irrationals and to the impotence of the individual. He wanted to bring man's self-definition and creativity back into existence through recognition of and vital relationship with the rhythms that men share with the nonhuman world; for he thought that thus men could find not only the selves that they had denied, but also the brotherhood they had lost.

The darkness of the phallic consciousness is the correlative of a passionate life assertion, strong as the thrust of the grass stems in the field where Paul and Clara make love, and as the dynamics of the wheeling stars. "In the lowest trough of the night" there is always "a flare of the pit." A pillar of cloud by day, the pit is a pillar of fire by night: and the Lord is at the pit top. As a descent of darkness and an ascent of flame is associated with the secret, essential, scatheless maleness of the father, so also the passionate self-forgetful play of the children is associated with a fiery light in the night—an isolated lamppost, a blood-red moon, and behind, "the great scoop of darkness, as if all the night were there." It is this understanding of the symbolism of darkness in Lawrence that gives tragic dignity to such a scene as that of the bringing home of William's coffin through the darkness of the night.

Morel and Paul went, with a candle, into the parlour. There was no gas there. The father unscrewed the top of the big mahogany oval table, and cleared the middle of the room; then he arranged six chairs opposite each other, so that the coffin could stand on their beds.

[5] In *Criterion*, XII:xlvii (1932–1933), 217.

"You niver seed such a length as he is!" said the miner, and watching anxiously as he worked.

Paul went to the bay window and looked out. The ash-tree stood monstrous and black in front of the wide darkness. It was a faintly luminous night. Paul went back to his mother.

At ten o'clock Morel called:

"He's here!"

Everyone started. There was a noise of unbarring and unlocking the front door, which opened straight from the night into the room.

"Bring another candle," called Morel. . . .

There was the noise of wheels. Outside in the darkness of the street below Paul could see horses and a black vehicle, one lamp, and a few pale faces; then some men, miners, all in their shirt-sleeves, seemed to struggle in the obscurity. Presently two men appeared, bowed beneath a great weight. It was Morel and his neighbour.

"Steady!" called Morel, out of breath.

He and his fellow mounted the steep garden step, heaved into the candle-light with their gleaming coffin-end. Limbs of other men were seen struggling behind. Morel and Burns, in front, staggered; the great dark weight swayed.

"Steady, steady!" cried Morel, as if in pain. . . .

The coffin swayed, the men began to mount the three steps with their load. Annie's candle flickered, and she whimpered as the first men appeared, and the limbs and bowed heads of six men struggled to climb into the room, bearing the coffin that rode like sorrow on their living flesh.

Here the darkness appears in another indivisible aspect of its mystery— as the darkness of death. Perhaps no other modern writer besides Rilke and Mann has tried so sincerely to bring death into relationship with life as Lawrence did, and each under the assumption that life, to know itself creatively, must know its relationship with death; a relationship which the ethos of some hundred and fifty years of rationalism and industrialism and "progress" have striven to exorcise, and by that perversion brought men to an abject worship of death and to holocausts such as that of Hiroshima. *Sons and Lovers* ends with Paul a derelict in the "drift toward death," which Lawrence thought of as the disease-syndrome of his time and of Europe. But the death drift, the death worship, is for Lawrence a hideous distortion of the relationship of death to life. In the scene in which William's coffin is brought home, the front door "opened straight from the night into the room." So, in their rhythmic proportions, life and death open straight into each other, as do the light of consciousness and the darkness of the unconscious, and the usurpation of either one is a perversion of the other. Stephen Spender calls Lawrence "the most hopeful modern writer." His "dark gods," Spender says,

> are symbols of an inescapable mystery: the point of comprehension where the senses are aware of an otherness in objects which extends beyond the senses, and the possibility of a relationship between the human individual and the forces outside himself, which is capable of creating in him a new state of mind. Lawrence is the most hopeful modern writer, because he looks beyond the human to the non-human, which can be discovered within the human.[6]

[6] "The Life of Literature," *op. cit.*

ON *A Portrait of the Artist as a Young Man*

It is not accidental that the two novels with which this series of studies ends, Lawrence's *Sons and Lovers* and Joyce's *Portrait,* are both autobiographical "portraits of the artist as a young man." In a stable culture, the artist inherits certain broad assumptions as to the nature of reality which, in some degree, correspond with empirical experience of the kind of relationships people maintain with themselves, with each other, and with their natural environment. The subjective, introspective impulse is then quiescent; there is no spiritual need, on the part of the individual, to go questing backward over his personal life in an attempt to find in it a meaningful form or unity or direction; for his social environment objectively manifests to him a form, a unity, a direction, that correspond with his feelings. But in a time of cultural crisis, when traditional values no longer seem to match at any point with the actualities of experience, and when all reality is therefore thrown into question, the mind turns inward on itself to seek the shape of reality there—for the thinking and feeling man cannot live without some coherent schematization of reality. Here at least—in one's own memory, emotion, and thought—is empirical ground for such an investigation. The great autobiographical artists, St. Augustine, Montaigne, Pascal, Rousseau, made their self-inventories under historical compulsions of this kind. The dates 1913 for *Sons and Lovers* and 1914 for *Joyce's Portrait* carry their own obvious implication: they mark a time of shocking disclosure of the failure of the social environment as a trustworthy carrier of values.

The autobiographic impulse appeared contemporaneously in the French novel, as in Proust's great work, *A la recherche du temps perdu,* and as in Gide's *L'Immoraliste*, his *Si le grain ne meurt*, direct rather than fictionized autobiography, and later in his *Les Faux-Monnayeurs*, a novel which used a number of autobiographical materials and whose protagonist is a novelist who is deeply engaged in a reformulation of novelistic aesthetics. In this book Gide has his novelist say,

> My novel hasn't got a subject . . . Let's say, if you prefer it, it hasn't got *one subject* . . . Please understand; I should like to put everything into my novel. I don't want any cut of the scissors to limit its substance at one point rather than at another. For more than a year now that I have been working at it, nothing happens to me that I don't put into it—everything I see, everything I know, everything that other people's lives and my own teach me . . .

The passage (though it has to be taken in the merely provisional sense that it has in the context of Gide's book) suggests rather forcibly the kind of motivation of which we have been speaking as the motivation of the "autobiographical" artist: the attempt of the artist, living in an environment that has failed to provide sanctions not only for art but even for life, to test out in the materials of his own experience the possibility of a new conceptual and aesthetic form which will give him imaginative grasp of his world. Proust, in *A la recherche*, and Gide, in *Les Faux-Monnayeurs*, and Joyce, in the *Portrait*, have as a central part of their concern the sanctions of art, a concern that can be formulated in the questions: what is art? what is the relationship between art and life? can one discover the nature of reality through art? The coupling of autobiography with this concern is natural enough; for the novelist is desperately committed to find a valid schematization of the "real," one which will place his own function as artist in organic relationship with the rest of life.

One of the oldest themes in the novel is that language is a creator of reality. There is this theme in *Don Quixote*, as there is there, in one form or another, most of the themes that we have traced in the other novels we have read. Quixote is supremely a man animated by "the word"; and as the words he has read in books send him into action—creating reality for him by determining what he sees and what he feels and what he does—so Quixote in turn has a similar effect upon other people, subtly changing their outlook, creating in them new forms of thought and activity. *Don Quixote* may be looked on as an extensive investigation of the creative effects of language upon life. Joyce's *Portrait* is also an investigation of this kind; appropriately so, for the "artist" whose youthful portrait the book is, is at the end to find his vocation in language; and the shape of reality that gradually defines itself for Stephen is a shape determined primarily by the associations of words. We follow in the circumstances of the boy's life the stages of breakdown and increasing confusion in his external environment, as his home goes to pieces, and the correlative stages of breakdown in his inherited values, as his church and his nation lose their authority over his emotions. Very early the child's mind begins to respond to that confusion by seeking in itself, in its own mental images, some unifying form or forms that will signify what the world *really* is, that will show him the *real* logic of things—a logic hopelessly obscure in external relations. His mental images are largely associations suggested by the words he hears, and in intense loneliness he struggles to make the associations fit into a coherent pattern.

To the very young child, adults seem to possess the secret of the whole, seem to know what everything means and how one thing is related to another. Apparently in command of that secret, they toss words together into esoteric compounds, some words whose referents the child knows and many whose referents are mysterious; and the context of the familiar words guides him in his speculation about the unfamiliar ones, the unfamiliar ones thus taking on their meaning for him in a wondrously accidental and chaotic fashion. These accidents of context, however bizarre, build up his notion of reality and determine his later responses and the bias of his soul. There is the story that Stephen's father tells him about a cow coming down along a road. There is the song about the wild rose blossoming on the green place. He, Stephen, is evidently the "nicens little boy" toward whom the cow designs its path, and he, Stephen, can make the wild rose into a green one by a transposition of adjectives. The world's form, then, is apparently shaped toward him and out from him as its center. But how to put the story and the song intelligibly together, in a superior meaningful pattern of reality, with his father's hairy face looking at him through a glass? or with the queer smell of the oil sheet? or with Dante's two brushes? or with Eileen, the neighbor girl, who has a different father and mother? or with some shadowily guilty thing he has done for which he must "apologize," else eagles will pull out his eyes? In this extremely short sequence at the beginning of the book, the child's sense of insecurity, in a world whose form he cannot grasp, is established—and with insecurity, guilt (he must apologize) and fear (the horrible eagles). With these unpromising emotional elements established in him, the maturing child will try again and again to grasp his world imaginatively as a shape within which he has a part that is essential to its completeness and harmoniousness and meaningfulness.

Immediately there is a transition to the children's playground at Clongowes Wood, the child's earliest experience of a community other than that of the home. Again the auditory impression is predominant—sounds heard, words spoken—and the life-directed attempt of the young mind is to understand their meaning in relation to each other and in relation to a governing design. There are the "strong cries" of the boys and the "thud" of their feet and bodies; then comes a quick succession of references to special oddnesses in the names of things. To the child's laboring apprehension, which assumes all names to have intimate and honest connections with reality, the name "dog-in-the-blanket" for the Friday pudding must represent something about the pudding which is real and which other people know but which is obscured from him; it may have more than one meaning, like the word "belt," which means a strap on a jacket and also "to give a fellow a belt"; or it may have complex, mysterious, and terribly serious associations with destiny, understood by others but dark and anxious to himself, like his own name, Stephen Dedalus, which Nasty Roche says is "queer" with a queerness that puts the social status of Stephen's father in doubt. Through words the world comes to Stephen; through the words he hears he gropes his way into other people's images of reality. Doubts and anxieties arise because the words and phrases are disassociated, their context frequently arbitrary, like that of the sentences in the spelling book:

> Wolsey died in Leicester Abbey
> Where the abbots buried him.
> Canker is a disease of plants,
> Cancer one of animals.

The sentences in the spelling book at least make a rhythm, and a rhythm is a kind of pattern, a "whole" of sorts; they are therefore "nice sentences" to think about. But the threatening, overwhelming problem is the integration of all the vast heap of disassociated impressions that the child's mind is subjected to and out of which his hopeful urgency toward intelligibility forces him, entirely lonely and without help, to try to make superior rhythms and superior unities.

ON *A Portrait of the Artist as a Young Man*

The technique of the "stream of consciousness," or "interior monologue," as Joyce uses it, is a formal aspect of the book which sensitively reflects the boy's extreme spiritual isolation. There is a logical suitability in the fact that this type of technique should arise at a time of cultural debacle, when society has failed to give objective validation to inherited structures of belief, and when therefore all meanings, values, and sanctions have to be built up from scratch in the loneliness of the individual mind. When an author assumes the right to enter his novel in his own voice and comment on his characters—as Fielding does or George Eliot does—we are able to infer a cultural situation in which there are objective points of reference for the making of a judgment; the author and reader enter into overt agreement, as it were, in criticizing and judging the character's actions; and where there is this assumption of agreement, we are in a relatively secure social world. The "gregarious point of view" used by the older novelists reflects a world, comparatively speaking, of shared standards. As the technical point of view adopted by the novelist more and more tends to exclude the novelist's own expression of opinion from his book, the world which he represents tends more and more to be one whose values are in question; and we have, for instance, in the later work of Henry James, a work such as *The Ambassadors,* where the subjective point of view of the main character is dominant, a concentration on a process of mind in which values are reshifted and rejudged from top to bottom, all in the loneliness of an individual's personal experience. The technique of the "interior monologue" is a modification of the subjective point of view. It is not a departure from traditional convention, for even Fielding used this point of view when he wanted to show "from the inside" how a character's mind worked; but it is an employment of the subjective point of view throughout the entire novel—instead of sporadically, as in the older English novel—and it follows more devious and various paths of consciousness than traditional novelists were concerned with. Joyce's concern, in the *Portrait,* is with the associative patterns arising in Stephen's mind from infancy into adolescence. What we need to emphasize, however, is that he is concerned with these only as they show the dialectical process by which a world-shape evolves in the mind. The process is conducted in the absolute solitude of the inside of the skull, for Stephen has no trustworthy help from the objective environment. The technique of the "interior monologue" is the sensitive formal representation of that mental solitude.

267

"By thinking of things you could understand them," Stephen says to himself when he arrives at the conclusion that the epithet "Tower of Ivory," in the litany of the Blessed Virgin, means what Eileen's hand felt like in his pocket—like ivory, only soft—and that "House of Gold" means what her hair had looked like, streaming out behind her like gold in the sun. Shortly before, he has been puzzling over the fact that Dante does not wish him to play with Eileen because Eileen is a Protestant, and the Protestants "make fun of the litany of the Blessed Virgin," saying, "How could a woman be a tower of ivory or a house of gold?" Who was right then, the Protestants or the Catholics? Stephen's analytical quandary is resolved by the perception of the identity between the feel of Eileen's prying hand and the meaning of "Tower of Ivory." In the same way, by the same dialectical process, his flooding impressions reach a stage of cohesion from moment to moment, a temporary synthesis in which he suddenly sees what they "mean." As Stephen matures, there is mounted on the early association between the Virgin and Eileen an identification between his dream-Mercedes (ideal girl in a rose-cottage) and a whore. By extension, this association holds in it much of Stephen's struggle between other-worldliness and this-worldliness, for it has identified in his imagination flesh and spirit, while his intellect, developing under education, rebels against the identification.[1] Thus "the word"—Tower of Ivory, House of Gold—creates by accident and at random the reality of suffering and act.

Those moments in the dialectical process when a synthesis is achieved, when certain phrases or sensations or complex experiences suddenly cohere in a larger whole and a meaning shines forth from the whole, Joyce—who introduced the word into literary currency—called "epiphanies." They are "showings-forth" of the nature of reality as the boy is prepared to grasp it. Minor epiphanies mark all the stages of Stephen's understanding, as when the feel of Eileen's hand shows him what Tower of Ivory means, or as when the word "Foetus," carved on a school desk, suddenly focuses for him in brute clarity his "monstrous way of life." Major epiphanies, occurring at the end of each chapter, mark the chief revelations of the nature of his environment and of his destiny in it. The epiphany is an image, sensuously apprehended and emotionally vibrant, which communicates instantaneously the meaning of experience. It may contain a revelation of a per-

[1] Irene Hendry points this out in her admirable essay "Joyce's Epiphanies," in *James Joyce: Two Decades of Criticism,* edited by Seon Givens (New York: Vanguard Press, Inc., 1948).

son's character, brief and fleeting, occurring by virtue of some physical trait in the person, as the way big Corrigan looked in the bath:

> He had skin the same colour as the turf-coloured bogwater in the shallow end of the bath and when he walked along the side his feet slapped loudly on the wet tiles and at every step his thighs shook a little because he was fat.

In this kind of use, as revelation through one or two physical traits of the whole mass-formation of a personality, the epiphany is almost precisely duplicable in Dickens, as in the spectacle of Miss Havisham leaning on her crutch beside the rotten bridecake, or of Jaggers flourishing his white handkerchief and biting his great forefinger. The minor personalities in the *Portrait* are reduced to something very like a Dickensian "signature" —as Heron with his bird-beaked face and bird-name, Davin with his peasant turns of speech, Lynch whose "long slender flattened skull beneath the long pointed cap brought before Stephen's mind the image of a hooded reptile." Or the epiphany may be a kind of "still life" with which are associated deep and complex layers of experience and emotion. In the following passage, for instance, the sordor of Stephen's home, the apprehensive and guilty image of the bath at Clongowes, and the bestiality he associates with the bogholes of Ireland, are illuminated simultaneously by a jar of drippings on the table.

> He drained his third cup of watery tea to the dregs and set to chewing the crusts of fried bread that were scattered near him, staring into the dark pool of the jar. The yellow dripping had been scooped out like a boghole, and the pool under it brought back to his memory the dark turfcoloured water of the bath at Clongowes.

Here the whole complex of home, school, and nation is epitomized in one object and shot through with the emotion of rejection. The epiphany is usually the result of a gradual development of the emotional content of associations, as they accrete with others. Among Stephen's childish impressions is that of "a woman standing at the halfdoor of a cottage with a child in her arms," and

> it would be lovely to sleep for one night in that cottage before the fire

269

> of smoking turf, in the dark lit by the fire, in the warm dark, breath-
> ing the smell of the peasants, air and rain and turf and corduroy . . .

The early impression enters into emotional context, later, with the story Davin tells him about stopping at night at the cottage of a peasant woman, and Stephen's image of the woman is for him an epiphany of the soul of Ireland: "a batlike soul waking to the consciousness of itself in darkness and secrecy and loneliness." The epiphany is dynamic, activated by the form-seeking urgency in experience, and itself feeding later revelations. At the point of exile, Stephen feels, "under the deepened dusk,"

> the thoughts and desires of the race to which he belonged flitting
> like bats, across the dark country lanes, under trees by the edges of
> streams and near the pool mottled bogs.

The major epiphanies in the book occur as the symbolic climaxes of the larger dialectical movements constituting each of the five chapters. As Hugh Kenner has pointed out, in his essay *"The Portrait* in Perspective," [2] each of the chapters begins with a multitude of warring impressions, and each develops toward an emotionally apprehended unity; each succeeding chapter liquidates the previous synthesis and subjects its elements to more adult scrutiny in a constantly enlarging field of perception, and develops toward its own synthesis and affirmation. In each chapter, out of the multi-tude of elements with which it opens, some one chief conflict slowly shapes itself. In the first, among all the bewildering impressions that the child's mind entertains, the deeper conflict is that between his implicit trust in the authority of his elders—his Jesuit teachers, the older boys in the school, his father and Mr. Casey and Dante—and his actual sense of insecurity. His elders, since they apparently know the meaning of things, must therefore incarnate perfect justice and moral and intellectual consistency. But the child's real experience is of mad quarrels at home over Parnell and the priests, and at school the frivolous cruelty of the boys, the moral chaos sug-gested by the smugging in the square and the talk about stealing the altar wine, and the sadism of Father Dolan with his pandybat. With Stephen's visit to the rector at the end of the chapter, the conflict is resolved. Justice is triumphant—even a small boy with weak eyes can find it; he is greeted like a hero on his emergence from the rector's office; his consolidation with his human environment is gloriously affirmed.

The second chapter moves straight from that achievement of emo-

[2] In *James Joyce: Two Decades of Criticism,* cited above.

tional unity into other baffling complexities, coincident with the family's removal to Dublin. The home life is increasingly squalid, the boy more lonely and restless. In Simon Dedalus' account of his conversation with the rector of Clongowes about the incident of the pandying, what had seemed, earlier, to be a triumph of justice and an affirmation of intelligent moral authority by Stephen's elders is revealed as cruel, stupid indifference. In the episode in which Stephen is beaten for "heresy," the immediate community of his schoolfellows shows itself as false, shot through with stupidity and sadism. More importantly, the image of the father is corroded. On the visit to Cork, Simon appears to the boy's despairing judgment as besotted, self-deluded, irresponsible—and with the corruption of the father-image his whole picture of society suffers the same ugly damage. On the same visit, Stephen's early dim apprehension of sin and guilt is raised into horrible prominence by the word "Foetus" which he sees inscribed on the desk at Queen's College and which symbolizes for him all his adolescent monstrosity (the more monstrous in that Simon looks with obscene sentimentality on the desk carvings, thus condemning the whole world for Stephen in his own sickened sense of guilt). Meanwhile, his idealistic longings for beauty and purity and gentleness and certitude have concentrated in a vaguely erotic fantasy of the dream-girl Mercedes in her rose-cottage. Again, at the end of the chapter, Stephen's inner conflict is resolved in an emotional unity, a new vision of the relationships between the elements of experience. The synthesis is constituted here by a triumphant integration of the dream of Mercedes with the encounter with the whore. It is "sin" that triumphs, but sublimated as an ideal unity, pure and gentle and beautiful and emotionally securing.

As Hugh Kenner has observed, in the essay cited above, the predominant physical activity in *The Portrait* that accompanies Stephen's mental dialectics, as he moves through analysis to new provisional syntheses, is the activity of walking; his ambulatory movements take him into new localities, among new impressions, as his mind moves correspondingly into new spiritual localities that subsume the older ones and readjust them as parts of a larger whole. Living in Dublin, his walks take him toward the river and the sea—toward the fluid thing that, like the "stream" of his thoughts, seems by its searching mobility to imply a more engrossing reality. At first, in Dublin, the boy

> contented himself with circling timidly round the neighbouring square or, at most, going half way down one of the side streets; but

when he had made a skeleton map of the city in his mind he followed boldly one of its central lines until he reached the Custom House . . . The vastness and strangeness of the life suggested to him by the bales of merchandise stocked along the walls or swung aloft out of the holds of steamers wakened again in him the unrest which had sent him wandering in the evening from garden to garden in search of Mercedes . . . A vague dissatisfaction grew up within him as he looked on the quays and on the river and on the lowering skies and yet he continued to wander up and down day after day as if he really sought someone that eluded him.

On his visit to Cork with his father, in his wanderings in the brothel section of Dublin, on his seaward walk at the end of the fourth chapter when his chief revelation of personal destiny comes to him, on his later walks between home and the university, on his walk with Lynch during which he recapitulates his aesthetics, and with Cranly when he formulates his decision not "to serve"—on each of these peripatetic excursions, his mind moves toward more valid organizations of experience, as his feet carry him among other voices and images and into more complex fields of perception.

In the third chapter of the book, the hortations to which he is exposed during the retreat pull him down from his exaltation in sin and analyze his spiritual state into a multitude of subjective horrors that threaten to engulf him entirely and jeopardize his immortal soul. The conflict is resolved during a long walk which he takes blindly and alone, and that carries him to a strange place where he feels able to make his confession. A new synthesis is achieved through his participation in the Mass. Chapter 4 shows him absorbed in a dream of a saintly career, but his previous emotional affirmation has been frittered and wasted away in the performance of pedantically formal acts of piety, and he is afflicted with doubts, insecurities, rebellions. Release from conflict comes with a clear refusal of a vocation in the church, objectified by his decision to enter the university. And again it is on a walk that he realizes the measure of the new reality and the new destiny.

He has abandoned his father to a public house and has set off toward the river and the sea.

The university! So he had passed beyond the challenge of the sentries who had stood as guardians of his boyhood and had sought to keep him among them that he might be subject to them and serve their ends. Pride after satisfaction uplifted him like long slow waves. The end he had been born to serve yet did not see had led him to escape by an unseen path: and now it beckoned to him once more and a new adventure was about to be opened to him. It seemed to him that he heard notes of fitful music leaping upwards a tone and downwards a diminishing fourth, upwards a tone and downwards a major third, like triple-branching flames leaping fitfully, flame after flame, out of a midnight wood. It was an elfin prelude, endless and formless; and, as it grew wilder and faster, the flames leaping out of time, he seemed to hear from under the boughs and grasses wild creatures racing, their feet pattering like rain upon the leaves. Their feet passed in pattering tumult over his mind, the feet of hares and rabbits, the feet of harts and hinds and antelopes, until he heard them no more and remembered only a proud cadence from Newman:—

—Whose feet are as the feet of harts and underneath the everlasting arms.

The imagery is that of mobile, going things, increasingly passionate and swift—first slow waves, then fitful music leaping, then flames, then racing creatures. A phrase of his own making comes to his lips: "A day of dappled seaborne clouds." The dappled color and the sea movement of the clouds are of the same emotional birth as the images of music and flames. All are of variety and mobility of perception, as against stasis and restriction. Physically Stephen is escaping from his father—and the public house where he has left Simon is the sordid core of that Dublin environment whose false claims on his allegiance he is trying to shake off; at the same time he is realizing a "first noiseless sundering" with his mother, a break that is related to his decision against accepting a vocation in the church. Dublin, the tangible and vocal essence of his nationality, and the Roman church, the mold of his adolescent intellect, have failed to provide him with a vision of reality corresponding with his experience, and he thinks in terms of a movement beyond these—toward another and mysterious possible synthesis. "And underneath the everlasting arms": the phrase from Newman implies an ultimate unity wherein all the real is held in wholeness. Toward this problematic divine embrace Stephen moves, but it is only problematic and he can approach it only by his own movement. The epiphany which confronts him in this moment on the beach is a manifestation of his destiny in terms of a winged movement. He hears his name, Dedalus, called out, and the name seems to be prophetic.

> . . . at the name of the fabulous artificer, he seemed to hear the noise
> of dim waves and to see a winged form flying above the waves and
> slowly climbing the air . . . a hawklike man flying sunward above
> the sea, a prophecy of the end he had been born to serve and had been
> following through the mists of childhood and boyhood, a symbol of
> the artist forging anew in his workshop out of the sluggish matter of
> the earth a new soaring impalpable imperishable being . . .

The ending of Chapter 4 presents this new consciousness in terms of
an ecstatic state of sensibility. It is marked by the radiant image of the girl
standing in a rivulet of tide, seeming "like one whom magic had changed
into the likeness of a strange and beautiful seabird . . . touched with
the wonder of mortal beauty," while his own life cries wildly to him, "To
live, to err, to fall, to triumph, to recreate life out of life!" The girl is a
"wild angel" that has appeared to him, to "throw open before him in an
instant of ecstasy the ways of error and glory." The batlike woman-soul of
his race, flitting in darkness and secrecy and loneliness, has given place to
this angelic emissary from "the fair courts of life," of strange seabird
beauty, inviting him to exile across waters and into other languages, as the
sun-assailing and perhaps doomed Icarus. And it is in the flights of birds
that Stephen, standing on the steps of the university library, in the last
chapter, reads like an ancient haruspex the sanction of his exile.

With Chapter 5, Stephen's new consciousness of destiny is subjected to
intellectual analysis. Here, during his long walks with Lynch and Cranly,
all the major elements that have exerted emotional claims upon him—his
family, church, nation, language—are scrutinized dryly, their claims torn
down and scattered in the youthfully pedantic and cruel light of the adolescent's proud commitment to art. Here also he formulates his aesthetics,
the synthesis which he has contrived out of a few scraps of medieval learning. In his aesthetic formulation, the names he borrows from Aquinas for
"the three things needed for beauty"—*integritas, consonantia, claritas*—
are names for those aspects of reality—wholeness, harmoniousness, significant character—that he has been seeking all his life, from earliest childhood. His aesthetic formulation is thus a synthesis of the motivations of
his psychological life from the beginning; and the vocation of artist which
he has chosen is the vocation of one who consciously sets himself the task
of apprehending and then representing in his art whatever wholeness, harmony, and meaning the world has.

In an earlier version of *The Portrait,* called *Stephen Hero,* it is said that the task of the artist is to

> disentangle the subtle soul of the image from its mesh of defining circumstances most exactly and "re-embody" it in artistic circumstances chosen as the most exact for it in its new office . . .

The "new office" of the image is to communicate to others the significant character of a complete and harmonious body of experience. The artist is a midwife of epiphanies. Joyce's doctrine of the epiphany assumes that reality does have wholeness and harmony—even as Stephen as a child premises these, and with the same trustfulness—and that it will radiantly show forth its character and its meaning to the prepared consciousness, for it is only in the body of reality that meaning can occur and only there that the artist can find it. This is essentially a religious interpretation of the nature of reality and of the artist's function. It insists on the objectivity of the wholeness, harmony, and meaning, and on the objectivity of the revelation—the divine showing-forth.

At Clongowes Wood, there had been a picture of the earth on the first page of Stephen's geography, "a big ball in the middle of clouds," and on the flyleaf of the book Stephen had written his name and "where he was."

Stephen Dedalus
Class of Elements
Clongowes Wood College
Sallins
County Kildare
Ireland
Europe
The World
The Universe

His ambulatory, dialectical journey is a quest to find the defining unity, the composing harmony, and the significant character of each of these broadening localities containing Stephen Dedalus, and the intelligible relationships making each functional in the next. It is an attempt, by progressive stages, at last to bring the term "Stephen Dedalus" into relationship with the term "The Universe." Through the book he moves from one geographical and spiritual orbit to another, "walking" in lengthening radius until he is ready to take up flight. As a child at Clongowes it had pained him that he did not know what came after the universe.

> What was after the universe? Nothing. But was there anything round the universe to show where it stopped before the nothing place began? It could not be a wall but there could be a thin thin line there all round everything. It was very big to think about everything and everywhere. Only God could do that. He tried to think what a big thought that must be but he could think only of God. God was God's name just as his name was Stephen. *Dieu* was the French for God and that was God's name too; and when anyone prayed to God and said Dieu then God knew at once that was a French person that was praying. But though there were different names for God in all the different languages in the world and God understood what all the people who prayed said in their different languages still God remained always the same God and God's real name was God.

At the end of the book Stephen is prepared at least to set forth on the "dappled, seaborne clouds" that float beyond Ireland and over Europe. His search is still to find out "what came after the universe." The ultimate epiphany is withheld, the epiphany of "everything and everywhere" as one and harmonious and meaningful. But it is prophesied in "God's real name," as Stephen's personal destiny is prophesied in his own name "Dedalus." It is to be found in the labyrinth of language that contains all human revelation vouchsafed by divine economy, and to be found by the artist in naming the names.